EMERGING DIGITAL MEDIA ECOLOGIES

Emerging Digital Media Ecologies: The Concept of Medialogy investigates the profound ways in which digital media reshapes our cultural, socio-technological, political, and natural landscapes. Through interdisciplinary empirical and creative case studies, the book defines and illuminates the nuances of medialogy, emphasising the often-underestimated impact of emerging technologies across interactive education, data gathering, visual-data representations, and creative practice. It explores the intersection of the natural and technological worlds, contextualising our use of natural resources against climate change and sustainable economies.

Divided into two parts, the book delves into the theoretical underpinnings of digital media ecologies and their practical applications. Part 1 traces the evolution of media technologies, examining their environmental impact and the foundational approaches to understanding media's complex interconnections. Part 2 focuses on contemporary issues such as hyper-personalised media, digital literacy, and the transformative power of Indigenous media narratives.

Additionally, the monograph explores the revolutionary role of Artificial Intelligence (AI) and large language models like ChatGPT-4o and those that follow in shaping our digital future. It investigates how AI transforms creative practices, data processing, and communication, contributing to the formation of new media ecologies. The ethical implications, commodification, identity formation, and the impact of AI-driven technologies on everyday life are critically examined, offering insights into the future of human–technology interactions.

This book is a crucial reference for scholars, practitioners, and students in digital humanities, media studies, environmental humanities, and anyone interested in the cultural implications of emerging digital technologies and their impact on our environment and society.

Toija Cinque is an associate professor in communications (digital media) whose research explores the challenges and opportunities of digital life. Their work examines the media developments of digitisation, datafication, and platformisation, focusing on the socio-cultural and environmental implications of data-driven and algorithmically steered infrastructures and interfaces. Cinque co-produced *Memories That Make Us: Stories of post World War 2 Italian Migration to Australia*, a feature documentary that won Best Ethnographic Film in the New York International Film Awards and was an official selection at the Asti International Film Festival, Italy; and Fiorenzo Serra Film Festival, Italy. Cinque's works include *Changing Media Landscapes: Visual Networking* (2015); *The Dark Social: Online Practices of Resistance, Motility and Power* (co-edited, 2023); *Materializing Digital Futures: Touch, Movement, Sound and Vision* (co-edited, 2022); *Communication, Digital Media and Everyday Life* (co-written, 2015); and *Communication, New Media and Everyday Life* (co-written, 2012).

EMERGING DIGITAL MEDIA ECOLOGIES

The Concept of Medialogy

Toija Cinque

LONDON AND NEW YORK

Designed cover image: Getty Images

First published 2025
by Routledge
4 Park Square, Milton Park, Abingdon, Oxon OX14 4RN

and by Routledge
605 Third Avenue, New York, NY 10158

Routledge is an imprint of the Taylor & Francis Group, an informa business

© 2025 Toija Cinque

The right of Toija Cinque to be identified as author of this work has been asserted in accordance with sections 77 and 78 of the Copyright, Designs and Patents Act 1988.

All rights reserved. No part of this book may be reprinted or reproduced or utilised in any form or by any electronic, mechanical, or other means, now known or hereafter invented, including photocopying and recording, or in any information storage or retrieval system, without permission in writing from the publishers.

Trademark notice: Product or corporate names may be trademarks or registered trademarks, and are used only for identification and explanation without intent to infringe.

British Library Cataloguing-in-Publication Data
A catalogue record for this book is available from the British Library

ISBN: 9781032013190 (hbk)
ISBN: 9781032013183 (pbk)
ISBN: 9781003178149 (ebk)

DOI: 10.4324/9781003178149

Typeset in Galliard
by Newgen Publishing UK

CONTENTS

List of Figures	*viii*
List of Tables	*ix*
Preface	*x*
A Study of Digital Connection and Materialising	
Data Cultures x	
Why 'Medialogy'? xv	
Design of the Book xxii	
Acknowledgements and Dedication	*xxxiii*

PART 1
History and Theoretical Underpinning   **1**

1 Locating Media Ecologies: Ecosophy and
   Anthropogenic Events   3
   Cyborgs, Nature, and the Formation of Media 'Ecologies' 3
   Addressing Anthropogenic Events through the Lenses
     of Media Environments, Ecosophy, and the Ripples of
     Human Behaviour 15
   Conclusion 18

2 Archaeological and Archival Media   19
   Unearthing Media's Depths and the Layered Histories of
     Communication 19

vi Contents

*Material Qualities and Media: An Exploration of
    Obsolescent Systems in a Digital Epoch 30*
*From Resurrected Past to Speculative Futures: Bridging
    Zombie and Imaginary Media 36*
Conclusion 40

3 Network Nature's Algorithmic Turn   41
   Next Nature and Techno-Media Ecologies 41
   An Exploration of 'Next Nature' 49
   *Quantum Computing: Networked Nature and
       Digital Futures 55*
   Conclusion 60

4 Biomedia and the Post-Digital Age   62
   *Understanding Embodied Information through the
       Convergence of Biology and Technology 62*
   *The Emergence of Life-Like Behaviour in Machines:
       Digital Intelligences 65*
   *Emergent Realities: Navigating the Nexus of Organic
       and Digital Paradigms 73*
   *Exploring the Fusion of Biomedia, Neural Nets to
       Machine Vision 82*
   Conclusion 85

PART 2
Technecologies   **87**

5 Exploring Hyper-Personalised Media Confluence:
   The New Era of Media Consumption and Interaction   89
   *A New Era in Information Consumption and
       Decentralised Interaction 89*
   Manufacturing Intelligence 90
   Delving into Hyper-Personalised Media Confluence 95
   Conclusion 105

6 Designing Digital Media Literacies for Social Cohesion   107
   Contextualising Enhanced Media and Communications 107
   Bad Actors and Online Harms 108
   *Filter Bubbles and Echo Chambers: Multivalent
       Consequences of API Integration 112*
   Towards a Framework for Digital Media Literacy 120

Contents **vii**

*Adversarial Design: 'De-Biasing' Data with Large
    Language Model-based Co-pilot Tools and Countering
    Online Extremism 121*
LLMs and Civic Engagement 131
Conclusion 133

7 Extended Reality's Critical Interfaces and Applications   135
Spheres as the Topology of Emerging Media 135
*Augmented Reality: Mediating between the Inside and the
    Outside 137*
Augmenting Education in Immersive Spheres 143
*Digital Realm: A Case Study of Teaching Threshold
    Concepts in 360 Degree 146*
Conclusion 152

8 Indigenous Narratives and the Dynamics of Medialogy   154
First Nations 154
*Indigenous Media: Agency, Narrative Sovereignty, and
    Cultural Identity in a Global Context 157*
*Media as a Platform for Defining Indigeneity: Asserting
    Sovereignty and Constructing Identity 162*
Conclusion 175

Conclusion: Media, Humanity, and Non-human Others in
a Post-Digital Future   178
Next Steps: Data Provenance and Protections 185
Medialogy in Global Context 186

References   *189*
Index   *211*

FIGURES

3.1	Socio-Technological Concept Map of the Metaverse	51
4.1	Number of AI-Related Bills Passed into Law Globally by Country, 2016–2022	69
7.1	Nyaal Theatre Immersive Learning Space	145
7.2	Nyaal Theatre Immersive Learning Space	148
7.3	Nyaal Theatre Console	150
7.4	Digital Realm 2024, an Exhibit for Melbourne Design Week	151

TABLES

6.1 A Structured Analysis of the Digital Landscape that can Facilitate Radicalisation through Different Pathways   111

6.2 Capabilities of LLM-based Co-pilot Tools for Countering Extremism Online   130

PREFACE

A Study of Digital Connection and Materialising Data Cultures

The analysis of the materialising data cultures paints a complex landscape in which data access and communication technologies play an increasingly significant role. The transformation is sweeping, from altering boundaries between the private and public spheres to redefining cultural phenomena such as TikTok and generative Artificial Intelligence (AI) such as OpenAI's ChatGPT-4o. Undoubtedly, the 'datafication' of contemporary society has hastened unprecedented upstream and downstream data access and mobilisation. With the emergence of 'big data' alongside smaller data systems and the ubiquity of social media, we observe an augmentation in societal connectedness. This heightened connectedness inevitably morphs the contours between private and public life. Through communication systems, contemporary societies find themselves awash with data. Virtually every facet of our professional and social existence undergoes some form of digital transformation. While there are evident immediate and long-term advantages to this shift, concerns regarding disruptions—particularly in the realm of cognitive capitalism—loom large. Challenges and risks surface as personal and social interactions become increasingly mediated by an intricate web of human and non-human infrastructures. Such connections, although networked and mobile, invariably bear exclusionary and political undertones.

The digital infrastructures and interfaces anchoring our current communication paradigms facilitate swift data collection, storage, and processing. As a result, subsequent interactions can oscillate unpredictably. It has become irrefutable that data, mediated through algorithms, with decentralised connectivity and rapid interchange harnesses an analogous transformative power to that of electricity in previous centuries. Platforms like Google, Apple, Meta, and TikTok encapsulate both cultural significance and surveillance excess, wielding influence over billions of users. Recent high-profile events such as the CrowdStrike outage to Optus and Medibank data breaches in Australia highlight to the world the public's exposure and vulnerability vis-à-vis corporate data-collection methodologies and the criticality of the digital infrastructures that enable and interface our shared lived experiences. The Covid-19 pandemic served as a touchstone for the indispensability of virtual connections, with platforms such as Zoom and Microsoft TEAMS becoming ubiquitous. The tangible ramifications of digital infrastructures and interfaces permeate diverse realms—from how we learn, work, and play to how we mitigate or prosecute personal and international conflict.

Very recently, Large Learning Models (LLMs) and new AI techniques and approaches—including machine learning, neural networks, natural language processing, computer vision, and robotics—have demonstrated the capacity to analyse large amounts of data, recognise patterns, make predictions, and interact with the environment, prompting concern among researchers and developers. Leaders in the field including Sam Altman, the CEO of OpenAI; Elon Musk, entrepreneur, owner, Chief Technology Officer (CTO), and Executive Chairman of 'X', Tesla, and SpaceX; and Geoffrey Hinton, Director of the program on Neural Computation and Adaptive Perception funded by the Canadian Institute for Advanced Research (until 2013) and then at Google until 2023, have expressed their respective concerns about the swift development and implications of applications for AI. Their apprehension stems from the potential harms (i.e., privacy invasion, autonomous weapons, deep fakes) and existential risks associated with its unchecked advancements, including ethical dilemmas, economic disruption, and the possibility of superintelligence surpassing human control. Existential angst might arise here over the fear that advanced AI, particularly Artificial General Intelligence (AGI), could pose a pragmatic risk to humanity if the system becomes significantly smarter than humans. That is, it could become impossible to control and could potentially reshape the world in ways that are not beneficial to humans. The implication of such a transformation has been referred to as the 'singularity', a 'point where our models must be discarded, and a new reality rules'—a transformative moment when artificial systems eclipse human intellectual capacities, precipitating an era of profound and unpredictable change (Vinge, 1993, p. 12; Kurzweil, 2005; Bostrom, 2014). Bostrom's interest was the prospect of machine intelligence and the possibility of an intelligence explosion (Bostrom, 2014, p. 2). For Vinge (1993, p. 12), various scientific methods could lead to this significant breakthrough, and now realised years later, further fuels confidence that the event is indeed likely to happen:

> (1) the development of computers that are 'awake' and superhumanly intelligent (to date, most controversy in the area of AI relates to whether we can create human equivalence in a machine. But if the answer is 'yes, we can' then there is little doubt that beings more intelligent can be constructed shortly thereafter); (2) large computer networks (and their associated users) may 'wake up' as a superhumanly intelligent entity; (3) computer/human interfaces may become so intimate that users may reasonably be considered superhumanly intelligent; and (4) biological science may find ways to improve upon the natural human intellect.

Former Google CEO (2001–2011), Executive Chairman of parent company Alphabet (2015–2017), then Technical Advisor at Alphabet (2017–2020), Eric Schmidt, recently outlined where he believes AI is headed arguing it will quickly and profoundly change the world. According to Schmidt with regard to enhanced agency (Schmidt & Gardels, 2024):

> An agent can be understood as a large language model that can learn something new. An example would be that an agent can read all of chemistry, learn something about it, have a bunch of hypotheses about the chemistry, run some tests in a lab and then add that knowledge to what it knows. These agents are going to be really powerful, and it's reasonable to expect that there will be millions of them out there. So, there will be lots and lots of agents running around and available to you … at some point, these systems will get powerful enough that the agents will start to work together. So your agent, my agent, her agent and his agent will all combine to solve a new problem. Some believe that these agents will develop their own language to communicate with each other. And that's the point when we won't understand what the models are doing.

If not appropriately managed, such advancement could result in actual risks, like an AI developing beyond human control or value misalignment, consequently reshaping society in ways currently unimaginable. This pivotal juncture will redefine the paradigms of communication and human–machine interaction. Critically addressing these risks requires testing for the possible implications, thoughtful design, robust regulation, and international cooperation.

A collaborative team from Tsinghua University, Alibaba Group, Zhejiang Lab, and the Beijing Academy of Artificial Intelligence, recently published an important paper proposing a new framework designed for training extensive AI models based on the Mixture-of-Experts (MoE) architecture—a machine learning model that uses multiple 'expert' sub-models, each specialising in different data regions, and a 'gating network' that determines the relevance of each expert for a given input, thereby improving overall performance and scalability. This innovative work blends state initiatives, academic research, and private sector inputs to develop remarkable AI models. The researchers refer to these as 'brain-scale' AI models, signifying models that house more than 100 trillion parameters. In the contemporary AI landscape, the most sizeable models include Nvidia's Megatron NGL with 530 billion parameters, Google's Switch Transformer at 1.6 trillion, and WuDao 2.0 with 1.75 trillion parameters (Ma et al., 2022). Their work demonstrates that such expansive multi-modal pre-training carries far-reaching implications across multiple domains. These include, but are not confined to, image/video captioning and generation, cross-modal retrieval, visual question answering, general visual reasoning, object referral, and multi-modal dialogue systems and translation. Importantly, the knowledge gleaned from these explorations holds the potential for transference into diverse fields like AI applications in biology and chemistry (Ma et al., 2022, p. 204).

In the context of AI and deep learning, Geoffrey Hinton refers to 'weights', and he is alluding to the parameters within artificial neural networks that determine the strength of connections between neurons. These weights adjust during training, optimising the network's output by minimising the discrepancy between the predicted and actual results. Analogous to synapses in the human brain, these weights encapsulate the network's knowledge. Over decades of research, the sophistication of these networks has increased, with modern models boasting trillions of such weights, allowing for intricate representations and understandings of vast datasets, akin to vast cognitive capacities in humans. Reflecting on the capacity of GPT-3 and then GPT-4, Hinton (in Abbeel & Obradovic, 2023, 4:29–5:52) has stated that

> they were very impressive in what they could do and in particular they had about a trillion weights, but they knew much, much more than any one person. We [humans] have got about a hundred trillion weights, but these things [general artificial intelligence systems] know about a thousand times more common sense facts than we do … so that made me change my mind about whether the brain has a better learning algorithm of digital systems and I started thinking that maybe these digital systems have something the brain does not have which is: you can have many copies of the same model running on different hardware and when one copy learns something it can communicate that to all the other copies by communicating the weight changes with a bandwidth of trillions of bits. Whereas, when you learn something, to communicate it to me I need to try and change my weights so that I would say the same thing as you and the bandwidth of sentences is only hundreds of bits per sentence so maybe these things [AI] are much,

much better at acquiring knowledge because they can work in parallel much, much better than people can.

With reference to the release of ChatGPT-4, researchers from the Center for Security and Emerging Technology (https://cset.georgetown.edu/), Imbrie, Daniels, and Toner (2023, p. 29), argue that:

> While the system card itself has been well received among researchers interested in understanding GPT-4's risk profile, it appears to have been less successful as a broader signal of OpenAI's commitment to safety. The reason for this unintended outcome is that the company took other actions that overshadowed the import of the system card: most notably, the blockbuster release of ChatGPT four months earlier. Intended as a relatively inconspicuous 'research preview', the original ChatGPT was built using a less advanced LLM called GPT-3.5, which was already in widespread use by other OpenAI customers. GPT-3.5's prior circulation is presumably why OpenAI did not feel the need to perform or publish such detailed safety testing in this instance. Nonetheless, one major effect of ChatGPT's release was to spark a sense of urgency inside major tech companies.

These critical perspectives are compelling and together with BaGuaLu mark an unparalleled stride in AI, showcasing the capability to train models, but also reveal the limitations of current high-performance computing (HPC) interconnection for the latest AI models, necessitating novel, complecting techniques for extensive AI workloads. The potential applications in image/video generation such as OpenAI's unreleased but upcoming generative AI (GenAI) model Sora for text-to-video, multi-modal translation, and more mirror the wide-ranging capacity for medialogy to absorb emerging aspects of human communication and understanding.

To underscore the point of concern, advanced GenAI models like DALL·E 2 and Midjourney (deep learning models able to generate digital images from natural language descriptions or 'prompts'), while impressive in their capabilities, raise questions about the responsible, moral, and ethical uses of AI because these models can generate highly realistic images or generate text that mimics human conversation, leading to the creation of misleading content, inaccuracies, and manipulation. While not necessarily new arguments, academic scholars such as Stuart Russell and Peter Norvig (1995), Nick Bostrom (2014), and Max Tegmark (2017) have long delved into these concerns, discussing the potential dangers of AI alignment, autonomous weapons, and the impact of AI on the job market. Other scholars such as Kate Crawford (2016, 2021) and Virginia Dignum (2018) have extensively researched the ethical challenges of AI, highlighting issues of bias in training data, algorithmic accountability, and the potential for social, economic, and political consequences. Their respective works emphasise the urgency of developing robust regulations, transparent practices, and responsible governance frameworks to address the ethical implications and potential harm posed by AI technologies. What is, however, different are the current speeds with which AI-driven technologies are moving for the public's capacity to discern what is real versus fake media and the implications that consequently arise. Our understanding of 'intelligence' is necessarily pivoting in the process (Bubeck et al., 2023).

Alongside growing social embeddedness, GenAI products are also deeply integrated into the cutting-edge progress of digital infrastructures and interfaces. The respective models' intensive computational requirements tie them closely to advanced digital systems. In the realm of medialogy studies, the digital infrastructures and interfaces are pivotal. They represent the very scaffolding and processes driving modern digital communication. Digital infrastructures combine both the tangible aspects, like servers and cables, and the intangible elements, such as cloud systems and algorithms, all of which facilitate information flow across digital networks (Star & Ruhleder, 1996). While they provide the essential framework of our digital age, interfaces serve as conduits, shaping our experiences with digital media and associated technologies. From website designs to app user experiences, interfaces not only direct user engagement but also shape content perception and interpretation (Manovich, 2002; Couldry & Hepp, 2017). Moreover, the foundational neural networks of these AIs demand significant storage for their datasets, robust computational power, and swift connectivity for updates. Their dependence on modern cloud systems and powerful GPUs (Graphics Processing Units designed to accelerate graphics rendering like NVIDIA's DGX) is evident (Bowles, 2017). These AI models, despite their backend complexity, are made intuitive via modern interfaces. Such interfaces guide the user experience and influence their comprehension and trust in AI capabilities (Bucher, 2012). As technology advances, the blend of generative AI and interfaces blurs the lines between AI-created and human-made content. This fusion is promising, but also poses ethical, authenticity, and accountability dilemmas in AI dealings (Brundage et al., 2020).

Why 'Medialogy'?

Medialogy addresses this great socio-technological acceleration of advanced user connection and mobility, faster computer processing, and miniaturisation. It underscores a paradigm shift in understanding how traditional legacy media forms have emerged digitally and continue to do so in new and unpredictable ways. The ubiquity of internet connectivity and exponential growth in mobile device usage have engendered an understanding of users being perpetually 'plugged in'. Our interactions with technology and media are incessantly mobile, on-demand, computational, and hyper-personalised, catalysing

xvi Preface

unprecedented and fundamental change. The rapid pace of miniaturisation and increased processing capabilities have transformed computing devices from bulky machines to sleek, pocket-friendly tools, without compromising power or functionality. This not only alters the way we consume media now but will do so in the future and impacts how we perceive and engage with the world around us. Furthermore, advances in AI and machine learning are reshaping the media landscape, introducing more autonomous, predictive, and interactive media experiences. This unprecedented rate of change challenges traditional understandings of communication, privacy, and security. As such, it necessitates ongoing critical analysis and exploration of the profound implications for society, culture, and the individual. This 'great acceleration' signifies more than just technological progression; it encapsulates a comprehensive transformation in connectivity and interaction.

I introduce 'medialogy' as a way to bring into one space a wide range of texts, theorists, and their theoretical frameworks to unpack the contemporary normative frameworks. As a discipline, Media Studies emerged out of various theoretical frameworks and methodologies, encompassing aspects of sociology, cultural studies, psychology, and political economy to become a significant discipline in its own right dedicated to the specific study of broadcast media including radio, television, film, music, and print newspapers in recognition of media's influence on society and culture. Scholars and researchers sought to understand the complex interplay between media, communication, and society, investigating topics such as media representation, media effects, and media industries. By examining media texts, institutions, and audiences, Media Studies came to offer valuable insights into the construction of meaning, power dynamics, and the role of media in shaping identities and social structures. For instance, scholars like Stuart Hall (1973) pioneered the study of media representation and cultural identity, while others such as James Curran (2005, 2010) focused on the political and economic dimensions of media ownership and control. The academic contributions of figures including Ien Ang towards media and audiences (see Ang, 1991, 1996) and Manuel Castells on networked society (see Castells, 2000a, 2000b) and many others further enriched the field by exploring globalisation, digital media, and the transformation of communication landscapes. The emergence of Media Studies as a distinct discipline underscores the critical importance of analysing and understanding the multifaceted nature of media in contemporary society.

Through recent processes of digitalisation, convergence, and globalisation, the legacy media forms became integrated with telecommunications infrastructures and information technology platforms to offer more by blurring the previously distinct boundaries and affording dynamic relationships between media technologies, industries, and audiences (Penley, 1997; Deuze, 2006; Jenkins, 2006; Jenkins, Ford, & Green, 2013). That is, legacy media relied on physical distribution channels and one-way communication models.

However, the advent of digital media has fostered interactive platforms that have enabled users to actively and immediately engage with content. This transition can be attributed to several factors. First, the proliferation of internet access and mobile devices has empowered individuals to access information on demand, transcending geographical barriers. Additionally, digital media platforms facilitate user-generated content, encouraging participatory culture and democratising the production of media (see the work of McChesney, 2004; Jenkins, 2006; Castells, 2010; Chadwick, 2017). For example, citizen journalism platforms like the South Korean *OhmyNews*, taking as its motto 'Every Citizen Is a Reporter', have empowered many ordinary individuals to report news and contribute to public discourse. Moreover, social media platforms such as Twitter-now X and Facebook have transformed the dissemination of news, amplified the reach of data and information, and allowed for real-time conversations. Building on my previous work in *Changing Media Landscapes: Visual Networking* (2015, p. 10), I use the term 'legacy media' (rather than 'mass media' because audiences are far more complex than this term implies) with reference to notions of 'scarcity' as the limited capacity for ownership and content distribution, based on the high cost of entry and technological scope, across media devices such as analogue television, radio, film, and the print industries. This definition is set to contrast with the digital (ever-new) media descendants of social networking and the rise of new and 'globally' connected vital spaces for micro-publics available instantly across multiple digital devices. I proposed 'Visual Networking' as the conceptual terminology to understand and encapsulate our visual motivation and consequent interaction with technologies and the carriage that lies behind them; it was done with consideration given to the active individual agency of users when engaging with interconnected digital technologies across a range of ever-changing platforms. The term encompasses both technology and society, acts as a descriptive model of social interactions, and is applied to the contemporary use of digital screens, interfaces, and communication technologies in society—as well as the effects and affects (see Cinque, 2015, p. 5). It seems appropriate and possible, however, to go further.

The neologism 'medialogy' emerges by necessity in response to contemporary developments in technology, culture, and society and is ontologically born from studies in information communication technology and media ecologies. For its part, the suffix '-ology' is derived from the Greek word logia which means 'the study of' and is contracted and added to the word 'media' which is in focus to refer to its specific study and a critical development of knowledge. This term refers explicitly to the study of media and technology, through history, and their combined impact on societies. It combines media with '-ology' to indicate a specialised area of study that is needed to be expressed now for focusing on various forms of emerging media and their roles in communication. By way of provenance, the only other use of the

xviii Preface

term 'medialogy' is via an interdisciplinary postgraduate course in the applied computer science and technology behind interactive digital media products with a Problem-Based Learning (PBL) pedagogical approach and project work at Aalborg University. The term 'medialogies' has been drawn on previously, but applied in a specific, narrower context to a sociological exploration of reality in media and journalism by Castillo and Egginton (2017) and akin to a 'Presentation of Self in Everyday Life' (see Goffman, 1956).

In *medialogy* here, however, we enter a new terrain to critically develop a sustained study of the impacts of digitally networked media and data in societies today for the ecosophical and socio-cultural implications now arising. The conceptual terminology has not to date been used in the way being proposed. This present work goes beyond the technology alone and does so by first engaging with the threshold concepts of 'media ecologies' (Fuller, 2005), 'mediation' (Hepp, 2013, p. 38), and respected theories advanced by scholars with the intention of capturing the essence of our wider engagement with media forms (see Altheide & Snow, 1979; Silverstone, 1994, 2005; Couldry, 2012, pp. 134–7). Nick Couldry introduced the term 'media manifold' (2016) to describe the expanding media environment. Like Ien Ang, who explored the notion of 'what it means, or what it is like, to live in a media-saturated world' (1996, p. 72), Couldry (2012, p. 16) outlined what he perceives as 'waves of media saturation' in society. Other theorists continue to grapple with finding an appropriate term. The most suitable for anthropologists such as Mirca Madianou and Daniel Miller is 'polymedia' (2012), used to define the ways that interpersonal relationships are experienced and managed through different digital media and through visual-cultural analysis, which Lev Manovich (2020) sees simply as 'more media'. In my earlier edited work *Materializing Digital Futures: Touch, Movement, Sound and Vision* (2022a), a collection of new essays offered a complex study of the sensorial ways that the body together with media and technology interact in contemporary socio-cultural contexts.

This book extends this work-to-date and earlier studies by Hepp (2013) who convincingly argued that, in spite of its apparent vagueness, 'mediation' has a multivalence that usefully supplements accounts of the 'mediatisation' of the social. Hepp's suasory position (2013, p. 38) is that the terms 'mediation' and 'mediatisation' do capture different aspects of media use in everyday life, but need to be used together for a greater, holistic understanding of attitudes and beliefs surrounding media reception and use. Taffel's (2013) theoretical articulation of 'scalar entanglement' within digital media ecologies finds resonance here. Taffel postulates that a 'multiscalar approach' is needed for a robust analysis of the connectivity and mutual reliance prevalent across disparate scales—content, software, and hardware—within media systems (Taffel, 2013, p. 237). By invoking 'scalar entanglement', Taffel (2013) rigorously contests the notion of isolated entities within media systems.

Rather, the approach advocates for a holistic interrogation of these dimensions in unison, thereby foregrounding the intricate nexus of interactions and dependencies that intertwine them. It necessitates a comprehensive synthesis that appreciates the interplay of these components within the greater media ecology, while concurrently attending to the implications that media practices exert on technological frameworks, cultural constructs, and environmental systems (Taffel, 2013, p. 250). Yet, one must be circumspect of the spectrum of variables and dynamics that might elude this trichotomy, for they too exert significant influence upon media practices.

Common to terms outlined above is the primary focus on media: new media, media manifold, media ecologies, mediation, and mediatisation, among others, clearly demarking 'media' as the focal point. For its part, the term *Medialogy* has the same provenance as 'mediation' and is situated in the context of ongoing vibrant mediation; however, as a term it also expresses both pleasurable and functional activities across social, cultural, technical, and natural environments from the micro up to macro levels (including our social networks and other interpersonal communication at the level of the individual, as well as more broadly in 'smart homes', the management of transport, 'smartgrids' for power, and the like). This conceptual background is foundationally important as a premise for subsequently speculating upon the future of emerging digital technologies in a book of this nature where visual and visually spectacular technology is being investigated. The respective conceptual understandings are drawn together epistemologically and are linked to vital perspectives of techno/human/geo/species studies through this definition of *medialogy*. In so doing, *Emerging Digital Media Ecologies: The Concept of Medialogy* draws together exemplars to provide a deep understanding of how contemporary media and information communication technologies are materialising in and impacting upon everyday life for the socio-technical, cultural, and environmental implications emerging therefrom.

In taking the above approach, *medialogy* also addresses the 'swinging pendulum' away from technologically deterministic assessments of media and technology to incorporate (among important other concerns) various social issues found within and between nations such as user access and affordability, the needs of specific cultural groups and marginalised communities, and diversity of user-generated content. For this, I will pull on a thread from the work of Baruch Spinoza (1632–1677), philosopher and maker of telescopic lenses, that we need to move away from thinking primarily about technological artefacts and their origins (a material totality of things or objects) because they are just a vector of forces whereas the better considerations are around what they can do, for whom, and how. My motivation for using 'medialogy' in this book is not to simply classify any group of technologies, but rather to engage meaningfully with what we are variously doing with them in contemporary settings. I use the word 'we', but this too needs unpacking because there is

xx Preface

plurality and difference here also. Certainly, 'we' are not one and the same. The capacity to build upon and systematically pursue the momentum of digital media studies among important others to further address the critical questions of the significance and value of sensorily based computer–human interactions in contemporary society from a wholistic perspective will allow for the development of robust conversations on ways forward.

From the broader perspective, the approach contributes to Media and Communications Studies, a dynamic academic field that has become central to the work conducted by scholars across a range of disciplines and modes of enquiry taking a contemporary socio-cultural pulse. Through an inversion of the usual teleological approach, *Emerging Digital Media Ecologies: The Concept of Medialogy* evaluates digital technology for its communicative, creative, and artistic influences and outputs and in doing so will introduce the reader to the key terms, theoretical frameworks and concepts, dilemmas, and issues that are central to the critical understanding of digital communications media. *Medialogy* certainly intersects with different disciplines within the *Media Studies* field and across the Arts and beyond. The term 'Interdisciplinary research' has multiple definitions. Demharter et al. (2017, p. 1) defined it as 'the synthesis of 2 or more disciplines, establishing a new level of discourse and integration of knowledge', while Lyall and Meagher (2008, p. 1) defined it from a perspective of a researcher who is 'an individual who spans a number of disciplinary domains in their own personal research'. Payne (1999, p. 176) understood it more broadly as 'bringing together and interweaving content, methods, and research strategies of various existing fields of study'. This monograph brings into conversation a variety of philosophical positions to examine the impacts of emerging connected media and technologies through different critical entry points, recognising and embracing the differences to foster an innovative approach as it traverses multiple areas of study, methods, and actions. In the rapidly evolving landscape of media and communications, several pressing issues warrant critical exploration in this book. These include the profound ethical implications of advancements like synthetic media, deep fakes and AI-driven content creation; the complex interplay between pervasive media and mental health; the environmental footprint of our digital acceleration; challenges and progress in media representation and inclusivity; the imperative of media literacy in a densely saturated information era; shifts in economic paradigms, including blockchain's influence on media transactions; the transformative potential of technologies like AR, VR, spatial computing, and quantum computing; the undeniable role of media in political discourse and potential propaganda; the dynamic tension between global media conglomerates and localised outlets; and the implications of user data collection for hyper-personalisation and its broader impact on individual autonomy. Augmented Reality (AR), by overlaying digital information onto our physical environment, has the potential to revolutionise how we consume information and media. Imagine a world where journalism is not simply just read or watched, but experienced. News events could be visually reconstructed in our living rooms, or historical documentaries could be explored by 'walking' through time; and, a doctor explains your illness with manipulatable, 3D imagery. Advertisements could transform into interactive experiences, with consumers instantly visualising products in their real-world environment before purchase. Education, too, could be revolutionised with AR textbooks making subjects 'leap' off the page, offering students immersive experiences for deeper engagement and understanding. VR promises even more profound shifts. By creating wholly immersive environments, it allows media to become experiential, providing users with a sense of 'presence' rather than mere observation. This immersion can transform entertainment, where films and series might be 'lived' for a moment in time. VR can also reshape social interactions, allowing for more genuine virtual face-to-face meetings, or enabling people to visit virtual destinations with friends or colleagues. Moreover, the field of empathetic journalism, where one can 'step into' someone else's shoes, could drive profound societal understandings and shifts by allowing us to experience the worldviews of others. Here VR, AR, and Mixed Reality represent different points on the immersion spectrum of virtualised environments for users. Spatial computing provides the underlying framework, making 'us' aware of and responsive to their spatial context. Together, these technologies promise to redefine the boundaries of human–computer interaction, creating dynamic experiences that seamlessly weave digital and physical realities. Turning to a communications future with quantum computing—with its promise of processing capabilities beyond anything we currently understand—might find these sorts of experiences underpinned and empowered by this sort of advanced technology. Advanced simulations for VR environments, real-time AR data processing, or even dynamically adapting media experiences based on user emotions or reactions could be made possible with quantum computing's power. Its potential to revolutionise data analysis means that media producers could gain much deeper insights into user behaviour and preferences, allowing for hyper-personalised media delivery. With any technological leap, however, these innovations come with challenges. Ethical concerns about how immersive experiences might affect our psyche, especially for younger audiences, will need to be addressed. Moreover, as media consumption becomes more personalised and immersive, questions about privacy, data security, and even societal polarisation will become even more pressing. It is our responsibility to not only harness the potential of these technologies but also to guide their integration into our media landscape with care, foresight, and an unwavering commitment to the betterment of society.

xxii Preface

Design of the Book

The sightlines for *Emerging Digital Media Ecologies: The Concept of Medialogy* are the media as formidable, compelling, and reshaping not only our cultural, socio-economic, and political lives but also the natural landscape of our planet now. This research monograph closely examines the shifting grounds of the relationship between the natural and the technological world, and the wider consequences of our current use of natural resources contextualised against climate change and future sustainable economies. Through the use of interdisciplinary empirical and creative case studies drawn from international exemplars, the nuances of *medialogy* are illuminated to emphasise the often underestimated impact of emerging technologies across interactive education, processes of data gathering, forming visual-data representations, and creative practice all in consideration of the issues around commodification, identity, identification, ageing, political economy, and the alchemy of living in communities for the affecting encounters and perceptions that are brought to bear. The book builds a story of digital media's transformation and transforming capacity in everyday life through the lens of multiple processes—emerging, affecting, materialising encounters, and perceptions— that take in image production, cutting-edge research in mixed augmented and virtual reality (AR, VR, MR), the political economy, commodification, post-digitalism, subject identity, identification across social media use, and the ethics of artificial intelligence.

The reflections on trends and issues are aimed at bringing the material alive for the reader. Through the development of a new theoretical frame, *medialogy*, this book becomes a key reference for readers interested in the nuances of emerging and evolving digital technology and the associated and varied cultural meanings for audiences and the environment. Data capture and social media have become popular topics in the digital humanities over the past few years, generating a number of titles in academic publishing. This monograph *Emerging Digital Media Ecologies: The Concept of Medialogy* takes a unique and holistic approach to understanding the deep interconnections between our environment with digital 'things', the rising area of human augmentation (a field still so young that there is no commonly agreed-upon definition), quantified media, and their co-affordances in everyday life. The study of digital communication, screen media, data capture, data mining (comprising its collection, curation, storage, and dissemination), and robotics are some of the fastest-growing areas for industry and scholarship. At the tertiary level of study, papers and courses can be increasingly found on data cultures, critical digital infrastructures, and interfaces to motion capture, animation, and performance in virtual production, while a vast number of degrees/disciplines consider digital media's significance within their overall programmes (including Communications, PR, Advertising, Marketing, Journalism, IT, and Creative

Arts), and a number connected to 'environmental humanities'. As we are now at the fore of rapid and all-encompassing climate change impacts, *Emerging Digital Media Ecologies: The Concept of Medialogy* comments on the important concerns for the public interest enmeshed in emerging digital technology/ social media use and subsequent environmental sustainability to speculate on ecosophical future scenarios.

In this context, *Emerging Digital Media Ecologies: The Concept of Medialogy* first introduces the underpinnings of materialising digital media ecologies, which are so pervasive that we take their emergence for granted. By way of concentrating research debate and critical analysis around the concept of *medialogy* through digital media artefacts, nature, and human identity, this book circumnavigates the significant implications of living in a contemporary information-based society. Toward this critical exploration of 'the human' in and outside the digital environment, this book gets beneath the critical questions of how media ecologies are related to the notional Anthropocene and what roles 'our' media apparatuses play in this context. Underscored in this monograph is that urban spaces are living networks that adapt our natural ecosystems to provide conditions for the human habits and technologies of today. In detail, the work questions firstly how we might find a balance between maintaining the biodiversity of urban areas while at the same time exploring our technological potentials and possibilities; and secondly, how media can help us achieve this balance. Further to this focus is an important consideration of diverse others, for example, whether the understandings of First Peoples and their uses of media are similar to 'ours' (in First World, western nations), what the differences are (if any), and how they relate to the concept of *medialogy*.

Emerging Digital Media Ecologies: The Concept of Medialogy comprises a total of eight chapters divided into two parts. Each part includes a brief introduction that outlines the parameters of the section, guiding the reader through the work to reveal a clear thematic narrative by its conclusion.

Part 1: History and Theoretical Underpinning

The affordances of interconnected technologies are emerging in spectacular ways when media systems interact. Part 1 traces the past of the media to contextualise the present and future. The chapters herein engage with the foundational approaches to understanding the complex relations between former models of mechanic and industrial media production and the continuous transformation and fragmentation of the ways in which contemporary media are produced, regulated, consumed, and interacted with. As Matthew Fuller (2005, p. 2) convincingly states:

> [i]t is one of the powers of art or of invention more generally to cross the planned relations of dimensionality—the modes or dynamics that properly

xxiv Preface

form or make sensible an object or a process. As it does so, other worlds gently slip into, swell across, or mutate those we are apparently content that we live in.

Of not little significance, however, is the environmental impact that media consumption habits and the expanding quantity and quality of media devices have upon the Earth. The chapters herein trace a trajectory and evolution of [im]materialised media forms with a view to understanding how they translate into the 'actor-networks', value-creation processes, and social exchanges which shape our culture/s today.

Chapter 1: Locating Media Ecologies: Ecosophy and Anthropogenic Events

As a metaphor, 'media ecologies' is used to liken the complex interrelationships between different media forms and technologies to an ecosystem. Just as in a biological ecosystem, where various organisms interact, compete, and rely on each other to create a balanced environment, different media forms also interact, influence each other, and create a balanced or imbalanced communication environment.

By way of theoretical underpinning, the first chapter will also explain and explore in depth the concept of 'ecosophy'. The theoretical link between 'media ecology' and the concept of 'ecosophy' lies in their shared focus on the interconnections between media, technology, and the environment. Media ecology examines the impact of media on human and social systems, while ecosophy explores the ethical and sustainable relationship between humans, nature, and technology. Both concepts highlight the need for a holistic understanding of our mediated existence within ecological frameworks. Understanding the significance of ecosophy to media practices and use involves exploring the different approaches to this concept. For example, from Arne Naess's definition of ecosophy delivered in his 1972 talk in Bucharest at the Third World Future Research Conference (cited in Drengson & Inoue, 1995, p.8):

By an ecosophy I mean a philosophy of ecological harmony or equilibrium. A philosophy as a kind of sofia (or) wisdom, is openly normative, it contains both norms, rules, postulates, value priority announcements and hypotheses concerning the state of affairs in our universe. Wisdom is policy wisdom, prescription, not only scientific description and prediction. The details of an ecosophy will show many variations due to significant differences concerning not only the 'facts' of pollution, resources, population, etc. but also value priorities.

Naess defined ecosophy as an ecological worldview that surpasses mere scientific understanding by emphasising a deep, holistic connection between humans and nature. He advocated for an ecologically balanced society that transcends anthropocentrism and embraces a harmonious coexistence with the natural world. His influential ideas have shaped ecological philosophy, sustainability discourse, and environmental activism, inspiring a transformative shift towards a more ecologically conscious and interconnected global society.

Another approach to ecosophy is found in the philosophy of Felix Guattari in the seminal work *The Three Ecologies* (2000, p. 27) writing that:

> Without modifications to the social and material environment, there can be no change in mentalities. Here, we are in the presence of a circle that leads me to postulate the necessity of founding an 'ecosophy' that would link environmental ecology to social ecology and to mental ecology.

In the context of this claim, 'ecology' should not be limited to the physical systems studied by environmental science alone, but arguably pull upon levers of the social ecology of social relations and the mental ecology surrounding the production of subjectivity.

Chapter 2: Archaeological and Archival Media

Death of media is mourned. The transformative evolution of media technology often engenders a sense of nostalgia for 'retired' devices and formats. The cessation of production for the Technics 1200 vinyl turntable (1972–2010) and the Sony Walkman (1978–2010), for instance, marked the end of significant chapters in media history. Lost formats from magnetic tapes to floppy disks of various sizes have their own preservation enthusiasts. The term 'abandonware' was coined to refer to software, such as early 1990s games, that are no longer supported by its developers but continue to circulate in the digital ether, much like a virtual apparition (Penge, 1996). Media consumption practices are also reflecting this nostalgic trend. Take, for example, the recently established vinyl listening clubs in London such as Classic Album Sundays (https://classica lbumsundays.com). These sorts of clubs offer an immersive, nearly meditative experience where an entire vinyl record is played without interruption, honouring the spirit of retro audiophile culture. As Walter Benjamin stated in the 1930s, new technological developments stir the cultural imagination. However, the unconscious production of these images is not detached from our past: together we dream of a future where the old is suspended in the new (Benjamin, 1983, p. 46f.).

Chapter 2 explores the field and techniques of Media Archaeology, an approach: 'that understands media cultures as sedimented and layered, a fold

xxvi Preface

of time and materiality where the past might be suddenly discovered anew, and the new technologies grow obsolete increasingly fast' (Parikka, 2012, p. 192). In Parikka's (2010) adroit argument, the media archaeology has succeeded in establishing itself as a heterogeneous set of theories and methods that investigate media history through its alternative roots, its forgotten paths, and neglected ideas and machines that still are useful when reflecting the supposed newness of digital culture. The definitions have ranged from emphasising the recurring nature of media cultural discourses (Huhtamo & Parika, 2011) to media archaeology as an-archaeology, or 'variantology' (Zielinski & Wagnermaier, 2005) which in its excavation of the deep time layers of the way we sense and use our media always tries to find an alternative route to dismantle the fallacy of linear development. It is easy to see how a media archaeological approach fits into a wider cultural situation if we consider Marvin's (1988, p. 8) premise that 'the history of media is never more or less than the history of their uses, which always leads us away from them to the social practices and contexts they illuminate'. In this understanding, vintage sits side by side with the new, for example, Super-8, and 8-bit sounds are objects of not only nostalgia but also revival and retro-cultures seem to be as natural a part of the digital-culture landscape as high-definition screen technology and super-fast broadband.

Chapter 3: Network Nature's Algorithmic Turn

Against the background of the changing mediasphere, many discussions have centred on our emerging algorithmic culture, focusing on changed behaviours and improving outcomes for people. The red thread woven throughout many assessments has been a binary interpretation commonly found in the language used, that is, Humans/Machines. This conception is in turn related to other binaries critically investigated in this book's context: Bodies/Machines, Nature/Culture, Living/Nonliving, Human/Nonhuman, and Materiality/ Immateriality. Chapter 3 offers a way to re-evaluate deeply evocative futures, moving away from binary understandings, to one in which humans, species, and intelligent systems increasingly engage together in symbiotically connected experiences via continuous flows of data and information exchanges. A conceptual understanding of users might now be that, for better or worse, we are increasingly one and the same as other non-human interconnected matter—another variable in the network of networks (Latour, 2005).

Moving this forward, Coyne (2018, p. 6) counters suggestions that nature should succumb to the sovereignty of data, the 'algorithmic turn' (Cinque, 2022a, p. 93), to affirmatively suggest that 'data is just a by-product of the transfer of signs between communicants, agents, elements and the things of nature'. While these arguments are agreeable and persuasive, data is moving in/across liminal spaces of brackish indistinguishability whereby some hidden/dark data is in our most freely accessible 'light' (open) spaces such as

Facebook and Tik Tok to refrigerators, home 'assistants' such as the Google Nest, Amazon Alexa, Apple's Siri to organisations' doorbells and our cars. The tasks to which data might be set are neither neutral nor non-partisan.

Chapter 4: Biomedia and the Post-Digital Age

The focus of Chapter 4 is on the notion and effects of 'Biomedia'. The nomenclature of biomedia comprises virtual bodies, cyberbodies, cyborgs, avatars, and hypertext bodies, and a host of other 'incurably informed' corporealities continue to populate the ongoing discourses surrounding cyberculture and 'new media'—which, as Friedrich Kittler (1996) reminds us, are not so new. At the core of these and other formulations is a concern for the ways in which a medium associated with immateriality and disembodiment will affect our views of having bodies and being bodies (and becoming bodies). Eugene Thacker (2004, p. 58) has convincingly written that

> The specific locale of biomedia is an interdisciplinary one, in which biological and medical approaches to understanding the body become increasingly indissociable from the engineering and design approaches inherent in computer science, software design, microelectrical and computer engineering, and other related fields. The 'body' in biomedia is thus always understood in two ways: first, as a biological body, a biomolecular body, a species body, a patient body; and second, as a body that is 'compiled' through modes of information processing, modeling, data extraction, and in silico simulation.

In this almost mythic encounter, an assumedly pre-informatic body confronts a set of techniques and technologies whose central aim is to render everything as information—not only can everything be understood as information, but as *Thacker (2004) has argued,* the information is everything, in that every *thing* has a 'source code'.

Part 2: Technecologies

In developed countries now (and more unevenly in developing economies), young people are growing up in what Ohler (2010, p. 170) adroitly describes as natural, human, and digital 'ecosystems', with important implications for everyday life. For many, our digitally enforced lifeworld is an existential and ambivalent terrain. Questions concerning digital technologies are thus questions about human existence (Lagerkvist, 2017). Arguably, all human cultures are made from and out of stories (Turner, 1992). These narratives are often used to make connections between people, young and old, and to foster community relationships, no more so than when it comes to identity

xxviii Preface

and subjectivity. Arguably, 'storying the self' raises self-esteem, develops and nurtures group or community belonging, and produces inclusive ripples from community to community. One unique way this can be navigated is through storying the lived experiences that people come into contact with. Through intangible forms, we are afforded the capacity to see and hear ourselves and to create new socially inclusive stories out of these activities. In scrutinising the multifaceted nexus of screen media engagement and the cultivation of digital competencies, it becomes imperative to consider the profound implications these factors have on fostering personal resilience amidst the turbulent tides of digital communication channels. The measure of screen time and the qualitative discernment of digital interactions necessitate a critical eye towards the dual-edged nature of digital media—both as a 'tool' for empowerment through connectivity and information and as a potential vector for cognitive overload and misinformation. Gaining digital literacies emerges as a cornerstone for individuals to not only withstand but also strategically manoeuvre through constantly changing digital landscapes, which is inextricably linked to socio-economic and educational disparities. This underscores a critical societal mandate: to equip individuals with a dynamic set of skills—ranging from adaptive learning to critical analysis—that are indispensable for traversing the shifting sands of digital ecosystems, ensuring they remain robust and resilient in the face of techno-media changes.

Chapter 5: Exploring Hyper-Personalised Media Confluence: The New Era of Media Consumption and Interaction

The proliferation of online content has reached an unparalleled level, with users, consumers, companies, and governments all contributing to a dense ecology of virtual interaction. Individual users are not passive recipients but active producers of content, carving out personal spaces in social networks and beyond, while consumers, with their heightened engagement, have transitioned from so called 'mere audiences' to powerful influencers and trendsetters. Companies, recognising the shift, are producing content at an industrial scale, aiming to capture attention and convert engagement into commerce, amidst an arena where the consumer's voice can directly amplify or dampen a brand's message. Governments, too, have stepped up their online presence, not only to disseminate essential information but to foster a two-way dialogue with citizens, necessitating a recalibration of public communication strategies. This vast increase in content and engagement heralds a dynamic, sometimes chaotic, digital milieu where attention is fragmented, influence is fluid, and the power dynamics between these entities are constantly being rewritten.

With the rise of new, richer content openly available online and across mobile devices (some intimately worn on the body such as 'watches' or 'glasses'), ever more sophisticated social and corporate insights can be created from the data that may be generated. Just as electricity transformed the way industries functioned in the past century, artificial intelligence—the science of programming cognitive abilities into machines—now has the power to substantially change society. Algorithms and big data are today shaping our sociocultural and technical relations and our everyday experiences. Digital culture and communication are inevitably changing as media infrastructures, media practices, and social environments become increasingly 'datafied' (Schäfer & van Es, 2017). By drawing on key infrastructures, one is able to engage with big and small data sources from leading social media platforms in hitherto unprecedented detail and respond immediately to emerging phenomena in social media usage. Data interpellates us. Yet data is obscure and enigmatic.

Chapter 6: Designing Digital Media Literacies for Social Cohesion

Globally networked, interactive digital media have provided new opportunities to communicate with those near and far; however, they have also increased the potential to coerce, manipulate, and misrepresent. Digital platforms and emerging social screen technologies with APIs (Application Programming Interface) linked across Facebook, Instagram, Twitter/'X' and the like contribute to the circulation of user-driven, conversational, and networked content that can define and represent communities. Such practices afford important roles in this *neo*-communicative process. Not only do the various media forms have the potential to bring heterogenous actors and events into an alliance (Bratton, 2015), but they are technically 'open' to allow manipulation by end users. Once particular connections and patterns of interaction are established, algorithms that personalise digital content can lead to filter bubbles (March 2012), which limits the platform's potential as a democratic public sphere (Habermas, 1989), leading to 'us and them' narratives that erode social cohesion. Thus, concerns about the role that digital and social media play in politics and society are increasing (see Tucker et al., 2017; Omidyar, 2018). This chapter reports on developing digital literacies and critical thinking in order to build social cohesion and address complex issues associated with social media use.

Chapter 7: Extended Reality's Critical Interfaces and Applications

Presently, we are witnessing technology trends where machines are beginning to realise people's emotions and thoughts (McStay, 2018), a rapid growth in communication infrastructure with increasing bandwidth and pervasiveness, and advances in hardware that can capture the hearts and minds of people and their environment. Mixed Reality (MR) as introduced by Milgram and Kishino (1994) blends real and virtual worlds along the reality–virtuality continuum,

xxx Preface

Both MR and Virtual Reality (VR) can provide an immersive experience in either real or virtual environments. Being in a 3D environment means that a person can make use of their natural ability for spatial interaction. Well-designed interfaces could potentially make interaction and collaboration inside such systems more natural, effective, and engaging. As a threshold concept, understanding media ecologies and environmental stewardship together sits at the heart of *medialogy* in this monograph. Félix Guattari has proposed the idea of ecology as expanded from its mooring within environmentalism to include the psychological, the social, and the environmental together, with the aim of developing a critique of capitalism that deconstructs its workings across multiple scales down to the molecular and pre-conscious. I want to take Guattari's call as a starting point to explore the connectivity and interdependence of 'every media-thing that exists'. In this approach, I showcase by way of exemplar a creative treatment for an immersive audio-visual experience using mixed augmented reality to explore the socio-cultural and environmental implications of contemporary techno-media use and the ways that data and information are vital. The mixed reality experience comprises surround sound audio and 360-degree video simultaneously displayed and distributed around a circular 'imaginarium' screen. The chapter includes empirical methods (qualitative and quantitative analysis) to report on key themes and outcomes as they link to the era of digital communications technologies as critical communication tools for socio-environmental impact.

Chapter 8: Indigenous Narratives and the Dynamics of Medialogy

This final chapter emphasises the transformative power of Indigenous media within the broader fabric of societal communication systems. This chapter critically explores how First People use media not just as tools for communication, but as strategic instruments to sculpt their identity, assert their sovereignty, and preserve their culture in the face of a globally immediate and networked world. It considers how the communities—through the use of 'legacy' media such as radio, television, and film and digital platforms like YouTube and TikTok—enact a form of digital self-determination. In synopsis, the Virtual Reality film *Collisions* demonstrates the merger of Indigenous knowledge with digital innovation, proposing a model for future media representations of First Nations that can be inclusive and revolutionary. It embodies the rethinking of our interaction with digital systems, positioning media technology as a conduit for socio-ecological harmony and a platform for political activism and cultural transmission by creating content that bridges the past with the present while confronting the ongoing colonisation of the narratives by mainstream media.

The analysis demonstrates how First Nations' use of media extends beyond conventional consumption and production to be a reclamation of agency within the information age, where power dynamics are restructured through the decentralised networks of digital communication. This reclamation is not without its paradoxes and challenges, as the same tools used for cultural dissemination can also imperil privacy and cultural integrity. Thus, the chapter calls for a critical reflection on how media technologies are employed and governed, advocating for approaches that are both ethically grounded and ecologically sustainable.

Moreover, this dialogue would underscore the urgency of integrating Indigenous wisdom into our collective media praxis. Recognising diverse Indigenous identities and the unique cultural narratives they bring to the table enriches the entire media landscape. This recognition allows for a more complex understanding of media's role in society—one that acknowledges the plurality of experiences and knowledge systems. Finally, the discussion would situate technology as a potential ally in the pursuit of socio-ecological equilibrium, suggesting that Indigenous methodologies, coupled with digital innovations, can inform the creation of more equitable and inclusive social structures. The chapter posits that our future media ecology must be one that not only facilitates communication but also embodies the principles of solidarity, respect for diversity, and environmental stewardship—principles that are often at the core of Indigenous cultures and that are critically vital in our journey towards sustainable interconnected societies.

Conclusion: Media, Humanity, and Non-human Others in a Post-Digital Future

Mediascapes and digital culture have gone through major changes throughout history and have been undergoing fundamental changes in recent years and will continue to do so in the near future. The changes have intensified in the last two decades starting with the digitalisation of broadcast signals and presently with the development of streaming platforms and the development of broadband infrastructures and cloud platforms that most likely will result in the end of dedicated (e.g., broadcast) infrastructures for media distributions. Time shifting, place shifting, video and audio on demand, and global networks for distribution of audio-visual content are just a few examples of these changes. The implications are, for example, the disruption of traditional media distribution and delivery forms, distribution of content markets, disruption of home video markets, disruption of the record and music industry, and the death of 'television' directly from 'the box'. Furthermore, there are major changes in the usage and consumption behaviour connected with terminal devices and the combination of audio-visual applications for work, education, and services with social networking applications. These changes are driven by the interplay between technological developments, market developments new business models, and the policy and regulatory environment. The aim

xxxii Preface

of this monograph has been to critically discuss the driving forces for such changes and to examine the implications for the market, industry, users, and the technological development. The work of Scolari (2012, p. 204) can be applied in examining the conceptual registers within *medialogy* and used as a diagnostic regarding the contemporary mediascape. They note that firstly, '[t]he concept of *evolution* (my emphasis) creates a theoretical framework for studying the history of media and suggests new concepts and questions about media extinction, survival, and coevolution'. Secondly, '[t]he concept of interface focuses on the media, subject, and social interactions'. Here we find a convergence between media, subject, and the socio-cultural so that thirdly, 'the analysis of media hybridizations is basic for understanding the appearance of new media that combine different devices, languages, and functions' (Scolari, 2012, p. 204). According to Postman (1985, p. 9), each medium provides a: 'new orientation for thought, for expression, for sensibility [...] (they) classify the world for us, sequence it, enlarge it, reduce it, color it, argue a case for what the world is like'. For now, media surrounds many of us, is increasingly attached to us via small screen devices, but may well be embedded as contact-lensed recording devices or even retinal implants in the individual. Along with other socialising agents such as school, peers, culture, and others, media reflects and models perception and cognition of the world around us. The concluding chapter summarises and contextually positions future scenarios for citizens communicating in the digital age through the ubiquity of computing hardware and software, satellite usage, and an advanced telecommunications infrastructure. It considers the futures of being a post-digital society among other core elements.

ACKNOWLEDGEMENTS AND DEDICATION

This book is dedicated to my family. Your unwavering love, patience, and encouragement have been the quiet force behind each page and every word written. To Marco, whose support knows no bounds; and to our children, Oliver and Surija, who inspire me with their curiosity and enthusiasm for life.

I extend my heartfelt gratitude to my esteemed colleagues Sally-Anne McIntyre, luke gaspard, and Eamon Sprod whose insights and camaraderie have enriched this endeavour beyond measure.

To the dedicated team at Routledge, thank you for your faith in this project and for providing a platform for the work.

PART 1

History and Theoretical Underpinning

1

LOCATING MEDIA ECOLOGIES

Ecosophy and Anthropogenic Events

Cyborgs, Nature, and the Formation of Media 'Ecologies'

This chapter serves as an initial step towards crafting an understanding of medialogy as a way to encapsulate the intricate connections between media, transformation, and holistic integration of such in everyday life. By employing a detailed and incisive lens, the aim is to explore diverse implications such as digital connection, community building, privacy, security, usage and the. like, while also scrutinising the entities these implications impact (users, industry, political institutions, civil society and so forth). To ensure a well-rounded understanding, the concept of 'media ecologies' is first situated within the larger research landscape, thereby establishing relevant context. Towards this, a starting point of critical elaboration is Marshall McLuhan's (1964) important assertion that 'the medium is the message', which underlines the profound influence mediums exert on the messages that they carry, impacting not only content interpretation but also societal structures. For McLuhan, the media we use shape our experience and understanding of reality. Not only does the content matter but so too does the medium itself profoundly influencing structures in society and thought processes—here we might consider the structure of education where traditional classrooms have evolved to include e-learning, digital textbooks, and virtual classrooms, affecting how students learn and interact with information. Another is the capacity for the media to play an indispensable role in shaping political landscapes. From print media to television to social media, the way political information is disseminated and consumed has drastically altered political engagement, campaigning, and voter behaviour. The phenomena of 'sound bites', 'viral texts', and 'data lakes' afford content that can significantly impact public opinion. Regarding its early contribution,

DOI: 10.4324/9781003178149-2

4 Emerging Digital Media Ecologies

the advent of television changed the way we consume information, fostering a more visual culture. Neil Postman's (1985) book, *Amusing Ourselves to Death*, underscores this by demonstrating how television as a medium influences the societal perception of political discourse and reinforces the importance of understanding medium attributes in the dissemination and influence of messages within society (see also Meyrowitz, 1986).

The conceptual understanding of 'media ecology' is the construct drawn upon in this present work for examining the intricate interplay between technology, symbols, and human behaviour within a media-saturated environment. In the context of media ecology, a view of evolution has been applied to study the history and development of media. Evolution in media ecology refers to the emergence, survival, and changes in media forms over time, much like biological evolution—and just as biological evolution involves natural selection, self-organisation, and symbiotic processes, media evolution is founded on the relationships between technologies, subjects, and institutions within the media ecology (Scolari, 2012, p. 213). By applying the concept of evolution to the study of media within media ecology, researchers can gain insights into the historical trajectories, patterns of change, and interdependencies that shape the mediasphere. This evolutionary perspective allows for a deeper understanding of how media forms adapt, compete, and coevolve within the dynamic ecosystem of media technologies, subjects, and institutions (Scolari, 2012, p. 213). With respect to understanding the role and effects of media and communications in everyday life via media ecology, we might hold that all communication is an ecology upon the premise that: 'every communication system and process is connected with every other communication system and process in a complex network; and that the study of communication processes is the study, not of elements, but of elements in relationships' (Postman, 1974, p. 4). With present-day media, data, and technology, the metaphor works to critically assess how social media (as one example) have become an integral part of our current-day media ecologies, shaping communication (e.g., Meltwater and Cision for social and consumer intelligence) and information sharing, and influencing our world view, behaviour, and even democracy. When we watch television, go to the cinema, or post content on social media, each environment signals that a certain set of behaviours, and not others, are in order. This is because each communication environment has boundaries that are 'more or less arbitrary dividing lines signifying the end of one system and the beginning of another', not necessarily fixed or universally agreed upon (Postman, 1974, p. 5). They are 'arbitrary' in the sense that they are determined by various factors such as technology, societal norms, regulatory policies, and so on.

Following Postman's (1985) approach—that our attention is focused not on who says what to whom through what medium and so forth, but on *how* the who, what, whom, and medium are inter-related—we might understand through this thinking that digital platforms such as Meta Platform's Facebook, WeChat, or Twitter (now X) are not mere transmitters of information; they embody a unique set of socio-cultural codes and dynamics that fundamentally alter the nature of human interaction. Indeed, they may help to shape our experience and understanding of reality. In addition, the rise in increased international interconnectivity and global communication is redefining not only 'community' but privacy, trust, and security. Social media platforms have resulted in new forms of cultural expression, discourse, and social dynamics, transforming how people relate to each other and to societal issues. McLuhan might argue that the medium of social media does not just enable these changes but actually creates them.

Charting a contextualised view of media ecologies builds the thesis for medialogy and encompasses the idea that media and communication systems constitute environments, which, in turn, influence and shape the complex interplay of societal structures, individual behaviours, and cultural norms. This theory is put to work in the examination of wider perspectives of media and their ecologies that encourage us to view media not as isolated entities—as legacy forms of radio or television, film, or print, for example—but as interconnected systems that are integral to culture and our natural environment (for the impacts and capacity for advocacy). With time, this thinking has invoked the term 'media archaeology' (and unpacked further in Chapter 2).

Media archaeology emphasises reading the ' "new" against the grain of the past' (Lovink, 2003, p. xii) and represents a novel approach to media studies that upends traditional linear histories of development and use by focusing on forgotten, repressed, or non-mainstream media technologies and practices. Its main tenet is to dig deep into the past to understand the present and future of media cultures (Parikka, 2012). One of the leading theorists of media archaeology, Siegfried Zielinski (2006), proposed the concept of 'variantology' or the study of variations, deviations, and anomalies in media history (Zielinski & Wagnermaier, 2005). Here, media history is not a linear progression, but a heterogeneous collection of singular events and alternative paths, some of which were taken and others left behind. This approach seeks to excavate neglected, marginalised, or alternative media artefacts, systems, and practices and brings them into a dialogue with contemporary media conditions. Similarly, Friedrich Kittler used media archaeology to critique the perceived neutrality of media technologies. Kittler argued that media technologies are not just passive carriers of information, but they actively shape the ways in which information is structured, disseminated, and perceived (Kittler, 1999).

This view reveals the materiality of communication and emphasises the implications of the technological apparatus on media production, consumption, and interpretation. Not at risk of obscuring broader social, cultural, and political contexts by focusing on the materiality of media technologies, Jussi

6 Emerging Digital Media Ecologies

Parikka (2010) has conceptualised media archaeology as an 'insect media'. Parikka offers the insect as a contemporary symbol representing the intricacy of non-human structures and patterns of organisation—like swarms, and instances of distributed intelligence—that have deeply permeated not only the crafting of digital technologies but also the cultural theorisation of such media systems. This understanding resonates with some of our most profound technological metaphors, such as the *world wide web* and 'the swarm'. That is, the insect in this context becomes a philosophical metaphor deployed for the cultural examination of the fundamental non-human elements of modern media technology. This understanding is not defined by the conscious singularity of human beings, but rather by the collectively intelligent, swarm-like behaviour of insects, combined agents, and the eerie potentialities of the so-called 'autonomy' of emotional responses. Moreover, Parikka (2010) challenges anthropocentric views of media by introducing a biological and distributed perspective whereby media systems are aligned with insect swarms and ecologies to emphasise the decentralised, non-human actors and systemic networks. In doing so, the intricate intersections of technology, biology, and media culture are usefully revealed.

With regard to intersections between technology, biology, and media culture, Donna Haraway's (1985) article 'A Manifesto for Cyborgs: Science, Technology, and Socialist Feminism in the 1980s' was one of the first to offer a critique of conventional understandings of gender, technology, and identity. It emerged from the scholarly interrogation of dualisms that are deeply embedded within the intellectual traditions of the sciences and humanities (e.g., human/animal, nature/culture). The pronounced boundaries and divisions produced within and between scholarly fields have also tended to dissociate humans and nature, sometimes to the point of exempting humans from basic physical properties and laws of nature. Haraway persuasively challenged the traditional dualistic categories of 'human' and 'machine' to posit that they were no longer relevant in our contemporary, technologically mediated world. Instead, Haraway introduced the concept of the cyborg as a representational figure blurring the boundaries between human and machine, nature and culture. At the heart of Haraway's argument was the idea that the cyborg is a powerful metaphor for understanding the fluidity and complexity of our identities. Her suasory and influential argument was that our bodies and identities are not fixed, but rather are constantly shaped and transformed through the interplay of biology, technology, and culture thus highlighting our hybridity and necessitating reconsideration of identity, agency, and societal structures within this complex techno-human entanglement. Parikka's insect media and Haraway's cyborg manifesto share a common thread then in exploring non-human entities' role in shaping technology and culture. Where Parikka proposes an 'insect theory of media', arguing that insects, like media technologies, are mediators of information and affect, Haraway's cyborg theory posits the blurring of boundaries between human–machine and physical–digital interfaces. Both authors explore the hybridity and interconnectedness of biological and technological forms, thereby challenging conventional anthropocentric views (a topic taken up in the final Chapter 8 that explores indigenous media of First peoples). These works particularly push the frontier of post-humanist thought, exploring how techno-culture is inseparable from the biological world.

Along the same vein, Philippe Descola and Gísli Pálsson offered an account of the diversity in cultural understandings of nature from perspectives drawing from social theory, biology, ethnobiology, epistemology, and sociology of science to ethnographic case studies from Amazonia, the Solomon Islands, Malaysia, the Mollucan Islands, and rural communities in Japan to north western Europe. Their edited volume, *Nature and Society: Anthropological Perspectives* (1996) offered an interdisciplinary, critical examination of the nature–culture divide emphasising the need for more nuanced understandings of human–nature relationships, highlighting the interplay of cultural, social, and ecological factors. What becomes apparent are the significant implications for our understanding of the relationship between humans and the natural world, as well as for our contemporary approach to environmentalism and technology. This shift has acted to redefine environmentalism, demanding more than preservation, in recognition of our inherent entanglement with nature. On the heels of this deep enquiry, the work of geographer, Sarah Whatmore, explores the intricate relationships between nature and culture in the context of environmental politics and resource management (2002). Whatmore also contests the conventional binaries separating nature and culture and introduces the concept of 'hybrid geographies' to emphasise the complex intertwining of human and non-human agencies in shaping spaces and experiences. This further insistence to crack open binaries to consider 'things' anew acts to move us away from conventional thinking and expectations and sheds further light on the entanglements between social and ecological processes, emphasising the need for interdisciplinary approaches. In subsequent work, Haraway introduced the concept of 'naturecultures' to underscore the complexity of entanglements between nature and culture (2008). Haraway rejected the traditional dichotomy between nature and culture in acknowledgement that human societies and non-human beings are inextricably intertwined; and, their interactions constitute the complex fabric of life on Earth. Haraway underscored that these interactions are not hierarchical, but rather involve reciprocal relationships, where both parties influence and transform one another. This paradigm challenges the notion of nature as a static and separate entity, urging us to recognise the interdependencies that shape the world around us.

In prior work that built on the early discussions of the cyborg and the intersection of humans and technology, we see the claim for the sorts of interdependencies that shape us in Haraway's (2003) exploration of the notion of companion species as a way of reconceptualising human–animal relationships, emphasising mutual shaping and co-evolution. Haraway's exploration of dogs offers a complex analysis of kinship, science, ethics, and culture in a multispecies world. As noted, dogs have evolved alongside humans, becoming integral to human societies while simultaneously being shaped by their human companions. She argues that the facultative mutualistic relationship between humans and dogs transcends a simple master-pet dynamic, reflecting a complex web of mutual influence and reliance. Haraway also integrates thinking on bio-engineering, genetic modification, and other forms of scientific intervention that manipulate the genetic makeup of organisms to draw our attention to scientific practices that blur the boundaries between nature and culture. By highlighting these examples of companion species and the need to reconceptualise the nature–culture divide, Haraway challenges the idea that nature is separate from human intervention and underscores the profound impacts our actions have on the natural world. These seminal works continue to inspire critical engagement and scholarly debates, contributing to our understanding of the complexities of technology, identity, and power in contemporary society.

Situated squarely in the techno-mediated age, Coyne's (2018) work *Network Nature* explores the evolving relationship between nature, humans, and digital technologies. Coyne's central argument posits that in the digital age, our understanding and experience of 'nature' is increasingly mediated and shaped by digital networks and technologies. He argues that these digital interfaces blur the boundaries between the natural and artificial, creating a 'networked nature' where the digital and physical realms are deeply intertwined. Coyne's work resonates strongly with the concept of media ecologies through his adroit framing of nature as part of our digital network, extending the idea of media ecologies as inclusive of the natural world, and suggesting that our interactions with nature are part of a broader media ecology that encompasses both the digital and physical realms. We might find this born out in the phenomenon of digital nature photography and videography. With advancements in drone technology, virtual reality, and high-definition digital cameras, we can now capture, share, and experience nature in unprecedented ways. We can view stunning aerial footage of remote landscapes, immerse ourselves in virtual nature walks, or engage with wildlife photography on platforms like Instagram. In this sense, our experience of nature is increasingly mediated by digital technologies. The images and videos that we consume shape our perceptions and understandings of nature, potentially affecting our attitudes towards conservation and environmental stewardship. However, they also distance us from direct, unmediated interactions with the natural world. This raises critical questions about the implications of this digitally mediated nature for our relationship with the environment. Moreover, the use of digital technologies in environmental monitoring and conservation draws on a myriad of digital tools, including satellite imagery, remote sensing technology, AI, and citizen science apps. Each is being harnessed to monitor biodiversity, track wildlife, and map deforestation. These technologies provide us with powerful ways to understand and protect nature. For instance, platforms like iNaturalist allow citizen scientists worldwide to contribute to biodiversity monitoring, fostering a sense of connection and stewardship towards nature (www.inaturalist.org). On the other hand, these technologies also create a 'networked nature' that is increasingly quantified, surveilled, and managed through digital interfaces. Again, this prompts reflection on what it means to experience and relate to a nature that is so deeply intertwined with digital networks. What *Coyne* calls our attention to, through the thoughtful exploration of 'networked nature', is that our media environments extend far beyond human-made artefacts to include the natural world. This perspective prompts us, again, to reconsider the binary of the natural and artificial, offering instead a vision of a world where digital networks and nature are inseparable. That is, Coyne's work calls attention to the complex implications of this networked nature, raising crucial questions about authenticity, representation, and power in our digitally mediated interactions with the environment.

The understanding of media ecologies for its part also finds an interconnection to a vast number of phenomena, drawing upon theoretical perspectives from various disciplines, most notably, those that resonate with the ecological sensibilities as found in Arne Naess's (1990) work on 'deep ecology' that presents a profound rethinking of our relationship with the natural world, offering a philosophical foundation for environmental ethics. The central tenet of 'deep ecology' is the recognition of intrinsic value in all living beings, irrespective of their utility to human purposes. Naess challenges the anthropocentric perspective that sees nature merely as a resource for human use. Instead, he proposes an eco-centric approach, positioning humans as an integral part of the wider ecological community. Deep ecology urges a shift from shallow, short-term environmental fixes to addressing deeper, systemic causes of environmental issues. It advocates for a profound transformation in our attitudes and lifestyles towards greater sustainability and respect for all forms of life. Naess underscores the importance of personal experiences with nature in fostering ecological consciousness (see Chawla, 1998; Sobel, 1996; and Louv, 2005). He emphasises that experiencing nature's beauty and interconnectedness can lead to a sense of ecological self, extending beyond our individual self to encompass other beings and the Earth itself. Naess also introduced the concept of 'ecosophy'—a personal philosophy derived from lived experiences with nature. He encourages each individual to develop their own ecosophy, guiding their interactions with the natural world and reflecting a commitment to the principles of deep ecology.

Félix Guattari (2000) drew on the concept of 'ecosophy' to propose a philosophical framework that intertwines three interconnected ecologies: the mind, society, and the environment. Guattari's ecosophy underscores the indivisibility of these realms, advocating for a holistic approach to ecological crises (see also the 1940 work of Bateson, 2000). Mental ecology calls for a transformation of our individual and collective consciousness, challenging consumerist lifestyles and promoting sustainable values. Social ecology looks at the restructuring of social and political systems to create more equitable, democratic, and sustainable societies. Lastly, environmental ecology examines our relationships with the natural world, emphasising respect for biodiversity and sustainable resource use. In the context of media ecologies, Guattari's ecosophy is particularly relevant. Where media ecology refers to the study of media as environments—a matrix of technologies, practices, and social relations that shape our cultural and intellectual life— the notion of ecosophy, with its emphasis on interconnection, offers a lens to critically examine these dynamics. For example, mental ecology calls for a transformation in how we perceive and interact with media. It encourages us to critique our information consumption habits and challenge the values propagated by dominant media forms. Social ecology urges us to scrutinise the societal structures that shape media production and distribution, advocating for more equitable, democratic media systems. Environmental ecology, meanwhile, highlights the physical aspects of our media systems— from resource extraction to e-waste generation—urging a recognition of the 'materiality' of our media practices. By situating media within the larger ecological systems, Guattari's ecosophy compels us to consider the deep entanglements between our media practices, social structures, and the health of our planet. This perspective aligns with current dialogues in media ecology that demand a more conscious, critical, and sustainable approach to our media engagements.

In essence, media ecologies encapsulate a wide-ranging exploration of interconnections, encompassing cultural, technological, and biological systems and their influences on social structures and individual behaviours. One prominent example is the recent rise of social media and online communities. Social media platforms such as Facebook, 'X'/Twitter, Instagram, and the like represent media ecologies to the extent that they create vast interconnected networks where information, data, trends, and ideas are exchanged rapidly at a global level. Social media can be seen to impact individual behaviour when users modify their online presentations to align with perceived social norms or expectations, leading to concepts like 'performative activism' (Thimsen, 2022). Technologically, the constant evolution of these platforms (like the introduction of new features or algorithms) shapes the behaviour of users. Culturally, these platforms facilitate the spread of global phenomena, transforming cultural expressions, and impacting societal norms—an example would be the influence of social media on the globalisation of popular culture. For instance, the worldwide proliferation of K-pop was driven by groups like BTS (the Bangtan Boys). Through key social media platforms such as YouTube, Instagram, and TikTok, K-pop has transcended its South Korean origins, influencing fashion, music, and dance worldwide. The idea of smart cities also encapsulates media ecologies through combinations of technological, cultural, and biological systems. Smart cities integrate digital technology (IoT, AI, big data analytics) into urban infrastructure with the aim to improve the quality of life, efficiency of urban services (such as smart waste management that leverages IoT to reduce unnecessary trips around streets, lower emissions, and prevent the accumulation of overflowing waste or Intelligent Traffic Systems that use sensors, AI, and data analytics to optimise traffic flow and reduce congestion), and citizen participation. This integration not only changes a city's technological landscape but also influences individual behaviour and social structures. For instance, the rise of smart transportation systems and virtual meetings might influence people's commuting habits, while e-governance initiatives can alter citizen engagement in political processes. Culturally, these shifts challenge traditional notions of urban space and foster new cultural practices. Finally, with regard to climate change communication, media ecologies play a significant role in environmental discourse and action. The proliferation of digital media has reshaped how (and what) information about climate change is disseminated and interpreted, impacting public perception and behaviour (Boykoff & Roberts, 2007). Platforms like YouTube and podcasts can amplify the voices of climate activists, scientists, and affected communities, broadening public engagement with environmental issues. These interconnected media ecologies also interact with biological systems—the representation of biodiversity loss, for instance, can mobilise societal action towards conservation efforts. Furthermore, the emergence of technologies like virtual and augmented reality and spatial computing for immersive environmental storytelling exemplifies this interconnection. In short, media ecologies transcend understanding media as mere communication conduits, instead emphasising the contextual, dynamic, and holistic nature of media systems.

The ties between media ecologies and Guattari's notion of 'ecosophy' are important here, tethered by an ecological sensibility that seeks to recognise and examine systems of interconnection and interdependence. Ecosophy, as proposed by Guattari, emphasises three interconnected ecologies: the environment, social relations, and human subjectivity. This holistic approach—an argument for the integration of nature, culture, and mind—reveals its kinship with media ecologies and ecosophy both sharing a common grounding in the understanding of systems as complex, dynamic, and interconnected. The media, in all its forms, can be said to influence and shape social relations, individual subjectivities, and our environmental interactions, reinforcing Guattari's conceptualisation. An example of this can be seen in the role of social media in mobilising global responses to environmental crises, such as climate change, as they shape individual awareness, affect social relationships, and prompt collective action. Social ecology then, as per Guattari, concerns the dynamics and arrangements of human interactions and societal structures. The rise of networked digital technologies, for example, has brought about new forms of sociality and communicative practices. From the co-creation of knowledge in Wikipedia to the decentralised communication in blockchain communities, these new social arrangements disrupt traditional hierarchies and thus transform our social ecology. Paradoxically, the pervasive influence of the same social media platforms, their algorithms and persuasive designs, can be viewed as forces shaping our mental landscapes, thereby creating a specific form of mental ecology. Further, media technologies are not exempt from the environmental ecology—the natural and built environments we inhabit—as they play an integral role in shaping our interaction with and understanding of the environment. For instance, satellite imaging technology and geographic information systems (GIS) have drastically changed our environmental perception and management, creating a unique environmental ecology in the process. In essence, Guattari's ecosophy necessitates us to view the environmental, social, and mental realms not in isolation but as intrinsically interwoven.

The association of media ecologies with anthropogenic events is another manifestation of the field's multi-dimensional approach. Anthropogenic events refer to occurrences and changes in the environment significantly influenced by human activities. The role of media in both the causation and mitigation of such events is considerable. The advent of digital technologies and the proliferation of electronic waste, as well as the minerals mined for their construction—for instance, Copper (Cu) is vital for its role in electrical wiring and connectors; Gold (Au) is used for electronic connectors and printed circuit boards; Rare Earth Elements such as neodymium, dysprosium, and yttrium are essential for magnets used in speakers, microphones, and headphones—present a clear anthropogenic concern (Bajaj et al., 2024; Sheoran & Das Gupta, 2024). These technologies, while essential components of our contemporary media ecology, contribute to environmental degradation and global warming, both being prominent anthropogenic events. In Canada, for one example, buying a claim or mineral exploration licence is easily done online and costs around seventy dollars (about fifty euros) to start the process of accessing the 'minerals of the future'. Waste from open-cut mining—which is tenfold compared to underground or in-situ leach mining—in proximity to urban areas becomes significant with impacts on the people and the environment. In western Quebec, for example, are multiple claims over bodies of water, lakes, rivers, as well as the land. Using the Mining Lands Administration System, introduced in 2018, anyone can go online, register, and stake an Ontario mineral claim with a few clicks of a mouse. To counter the onslaught of mining exploration, however, a number of citizens are now buying the exploration titles around their towns in an attempt to protect themselves and their land (France 24 International News, 2024).

Media can also serve as an effective tool for raising awareness about the environmental impacts of our actions, leading to more sustainable behaviours. The widespread dissemination of Greta Thunberg's speeches on climate change through various media platforms underscores the influential role of media in raising awareness and addressing anthropogenic issues. In the broader scope, media ecologies provide a comprehensive framework for examining the interactions and influences between media technologies, social structures, and the environment. It is by engaging with ideas such as 'ecosophy' and the Anthropocene that the study of media ecologies becomes truly multi-dimensional, connecting technological innovations, social phenomena, and ecological concerns. This approach enables a deeper understanding of how media shapes our world, opening up new avenues for research and offering fresh insights into the complex relationships between media, society, and the environment. It is critical as we navigate the complexities and challenges posed by our ever-evolving media ecologies which are themselves integral to the theoretical mosaic that informs the notion of medialogy.

Moreover, media ecologies comprise complex systems with multi-dimensional interactions among various elements within this system, which include, but are not limited to, technology, culture, society, and individuals (Fuller, 2005). Fuller's conceptualisation of media ecologies is notable for its grounding in materialism and its insistence on the dynamism and inherent activity of media and their associated technologies. For Fuller (2005, p. 2), the term ecology is used because: 'it is one of the most expressive language currently has to indicate the massive and dynamic interrelation of processes and objects, beings and things, patterns and matter'. By invoking Fuller's explanation, we understand that media ecologies are not just passive landscapes shaped by human activities; instead, they are dynamic, ever-changing systems in which the media technologies themselves are active participants. His perspective underscores the integral role that technology plays in shaping our societal structures, cultural practices, and individual behaviours. This concept is both ecological and materialist. The term ecology is used to refer to the dynamic, complex, and interconnected nature of media systems. For example, consider the evolution of Facebook from simply encouraging user engagement on its platform through 'Likes', 'shares', and 'posting images' to becoming something like 'the future of digital connection' (see <about.meta.com>). Promoting the company as a 'social metaverse', through its acquisition of Instagram and WhatsApp, Facebook (now Meta) is cultivating an environment whereby users are invited to consume content by watching, engaging, commenting, and actively participating through both casual and structured content creation. That is, the design of Instagram, WhatsApp, Messenger, TikTok and Facebook encourages more specific types of behaviour depending on which app people are using including immersive experiences using virtual and augmented reality. The 'materialist' aspect of Fuller's concept underscores the tangible, physical aspects of media technologies and the ways they interact with human and non-human entities. An example Fuller provides is the phenomenon of software studies. He argues that the software itself is an active agent that profoundly impacts our interaction with digital media. The design and structure of software guide users' behaviours, decisions, and perceptions, thus shaping the broader media ecology. In this way, Fuller suggests that it's not just how we use technology that matters, but the materiality and design of the technology itself are equally influential across social, cultural, technological, geographical, geological, and environmental variables.

We might look to radically inclusive perspectives of rhizomatic media ecologies to extend beyond traditional communication devices to consider them anew. John Durham Peters (2014) asks questions of that great metaphor of contemporary de-materialisation 'the cloud' to suggest the incorporation of elements into our understanding such that fire, water, earth, and sky are included as infrastructural media that facilitate the dissemination and transformation of matter, energy, and information. For example, the author claims that fire, one of humanity's earliest 'technologies', mediates our world such that fire's transformative properties—converting raw food into cooked meals—allowed early humans to expand their diets, affecting our physical evolution. The sky for its part in the thesis, particularly clouds, is seen as an elemental media because long before the science of meteorology was drawn upon, humans would 'read' the clouds to predict weather patterns, guiding farming and travel decisions. Today, as we know, 'cloud computing' continues to be used as the metaphor for the act of (seemingly) endless storage capacity, wireless functioning, and 'implication-free' dissemination of information across international digital networks. His central tenet challenges us to reconceptualise 'media' more broadly, embracing the myriad ways our environment mediates experiences and interactions. This perspective opens up new understandings of our symbiotic relationships with the world, suggesting that the media landscape is not just human-made but is a vital component of the natural world itself.

Following Peters, Melody Jue, in her work *Wild Blue Media: Thinking Through Seawater* (2020), presents a novel perspective on media theory by positing the ocean itself as a media environment. Jue draws from her experiences as a scuba diver and combines insights from media studies, oceanic studies, and philosophy to explore the unique materiality and phenomenology of the sea. She proposes the concept of 'wet media' challenging land-based media theories and emphasising the unique properties of seawater as a medium. For instance, seawater's conductive and corrosive characteristics impact how information can be transmitted or stored underwater, demanding distinct technological solutions like the design of undersea cables (Starosielski, 2015).

Jue also explores how the ocean influences our perceptions and cognitive processes. Immersed in seawater, human senses operate differently compared to terrestrial environments, leading to new forms of perception and embodied knowledge. This, she argues, invites us to reconsider our relationships with media technologies and the environments we inhabit. With a variation on the theme, Jue also introduces the concept of 'depth' in media theory. In contrast to the flat and surface-focused nature of many digital interfaces, the ocean's three-dimensionality challenges us to think beyond flatness in the design and understanding of media. In Jue's unique interdisciplinary approach, attention is brought to the ocean's critical role in our media ecologies, urging us to recognise and critically engage with its material, sensory, and spatial aspects.

Addressing Anthropogenic Events through the Lenses of Media Environments, Ecosophy, and the Ripples of Human Behaviour

We can neither escape the interconnectedness of our media ecologies nor the co-evolution of media technologies, society, and culture. Towards a holistic understanding of media ecologies and the myriad of impacts being grappled with under the umbrella term 'medialogy', we must consider the complex interplay of factors that shape our media-saturated world. Turning to explore media ecologies in the specific context of their impact on human behaviour and social interaction turns the spotlight on the extent of human-induced changes now affecting Earth's ecosystems. As a conceptual framework, media ecologies can help illuminate the intricate relationships and feedback loops between technology, culture, and nature as explored in the preceding section, providing a nuanced understanding of how our media practices intersect with the Anthropocene—a Western understanding of the current epoch defined by human activities significantly affecting the planet and life thereupon. One primary way media ecologies intersect with anthropogenic events is through the representation and communication of environmental issues. Traditional media outlets like television, newspapers, and now digital platforms such as social media, blogs, and podcasts have become crucial in raising awareness about climate change, biodiversity loss, and other environmental crises. These media entities shape the narrative—for good, and ill as we shall see in Chapter 6 on the role of biased content and 'filter bubbles'—around these issues, influencing public perception, discourse, and action.

Consider, for instance, how the coverage of extreme weather events in news media can draw public attention to the tangible impacts of climate change, or how viral images of plastic pollution in oceans circulated on social media platforms can ignite conversations and action around waste management. On the flip side, media technologies and their associated infrastructures also contribute to the anthropogenic changes they seek to highlight. The production, operation, and disposal of electronic devices entail significant resource extraction, energy consumption, and electronic waste, contributing to environmental degradation and pollution. Data centres supporting our digital activities demand substantial energy, with consequent carbon emissions. This dual role of media technologies, as both conveyors of environmental messages and contributors to environmental issues, encapsulates the complexities of media ecologies within the Anthropocene era. Moreover, media ecologies play a pivotal role in shaping our collective and individual environmental consciousness and ethics. The media we consume can significantly affect our understanding and attitudes towards nature, influencing our behaviours and lifestyle choices. For instance, documentaries like the 'Planet Earth' television series (BBC One) narrated by David Attenborough, or the film *An Inconvenient Truth* (2006, dir. Davis Guggenheim) on Al Gore's campaign to educate people about global warming, can provoke reflection on our environmental impact, nudging viewers towards more sustainable practices. Furthermore, digital media technologies are increasingly being harnessed to monitor and respond to environmental changes. Geospatial technologies like remote sensing and GIS, social media data mining, and citizen science platforms all offer powerful tools for environmental monitoring, disaster response, and conservation efforts. However, the utilisation of these technologies also raises important questions about access, equity, and power dynamics. Who has the means to generate, access, and interpret this data? How are decisions about environmental management made based on this data, and who benefits or loses from these decisions? Again, Guattari's ecosophy is relevant to contemporary discussions around the Anthropocene and confronts us with the intertwined crises of climate change, biodiversity loss, and social inequity, all of which resonate with Guattari's three ecologies. Guattari's ecosophy encourages us to deeply understand and address the Anthropocene's challenges at multiple levels, from personal attitudes to societal structures and our interactions with the natural world. His holistic approach calls for an integrated, systemic response to the Anthropocene, underlining the need for transformative change across our mental, social, and environmental ecologies. Media ecologies, thus, are deeply intertwined with the social and political aspects of anthropogenic events.

The movement in recent times to use terms such as 'dirty media' now and away from broadcast or legacy media, even dirty media alone, illustrates the complex interactions with/within media ecologies. This theoretical concept—dirty media—highlights the often-unseen ecological consequences and ethical implications of digital technologies. This central tenet, rooted in media materialism, challenges the prevailing notions of digital media as immaterial, clean, and detached from environmental impact (Maxwell & Miller, 2012). Digital media devices and infrastructures, while appearing clean and sleek to users, entail a 'dirty' lifecycle—resource extraction, manufacturing, energy consumption, e-waste generation, and disposal—all of which have significant environmental repercussions (Parikka, 2015). For instance, the extraction of rare earth minerals as noted above that are essential for manufacturing smartphones often leads to environmental degradation and human rights violations in regions like the Democratic Republic of Congo (Seay, 2020). Likewise, data centres, the backbone of our cloud-based services, consume vast amounts of energy, contributing to global carbon emissions (Shehabi et al., 2016). Further, e-waste—the discarded electronic devices—is a growing global problem. Often exported to developing countries, it exposes vulnerable populations to hazardous substances, exacerbating health and environmental crises (Oteng-Ababio, 2012). Through the concept, dirty media urges us to critically engage with these 'invisible' aspects of our digital technologies. By acknowledging these 'dirty' realities, we can begin to envision and advocate for more sustainable, ethical practices in the digital realm (Gabrys, 2011). From these representative examples, it becomes apparent that dirty media directly contributes to the framework of media ecologies, which considers media and technology not as isolated objects but as part of a complex network that intersects with social, cultural, and environmental systems (Fuller, 2005). This critical perspective allows us to view digital media as integral components of broader ecological systems contributing to environmental degradation, climate change, and social inequality. By acknowledging the 'dirtiness' of digital media, we realise that our seemingly 'clean' digital activities (e.g., streaming, social networking) are part of larger ecologies that contribute to the environmental crisis, thereby prompting a need for sustainable and responsible media consumption and production practices. Here, however, we might leverage the 'dirtiness' to create unexpected opportunities for creativity, innovation, and change within the media ecology, further emphasising the system's dynamism and non-linearity.

A view emerges here that acknowledgement of dirty media can spark innovation in the design and development of digital technologies. Understanding the environmental footprint of digital media can lead to the creation of more sustainable and efficient technologies, such as energy-efficient data centres, devices with longer life spans, or technology relying on less resource-intensive materials. This 'green' innovation can transform the media ecology, promoting a circular economy approach where waste is minimised and resources are reused. The notion of dirty media might instigate novel practices and discourses around digital technology use. We can observe this in movements such as 'digital minimalism' where individuals actively limit their digital consumption or 'right to repair' campaigns, which advocate for the ability to repair our devices, reducing e-waste and promoting technological sustainability. By extension, digital minimalism can foster interdisciplinary collaborations between environmental science, media studies, computer science, and policy-making producing novel insights and holistic strategies to address the ecological impact of digital media. All these opportunities

18 Emerging Digital Media Ecologies

underline the non-linearity and dynamism of media ecologies. Changes in one part of the system—whether in technology design, user behaviours, or policy—can have ripple effects throughout the entire ecology, reconfiguring relationships and influencing the trajectories of digital futures.

Conclusion

In conclusion, the concept of media ecologies provides us with a comprehensive lens through which we can speculate on the future of emerging digital technologies and consider their implications for society, individuals, and cultural norms. Proponents of a media ecologies framing view media and communication systems as interconnected environments that shape and influence societal structures, individual behaviours, and cultural norms. This perspective challenges the traditional linear histories of media development and encourages us to explore forgotten, marginalised, or non-mainstream media technologies and practices through the lens of media archaeology. Such an excavation of neglected media artefacts, systems, and practices brings them into dialogue with contemporary media conditions. Moreover, the biological and distributed perspective challenges anthropocentric views of media and highlights the decentralised, non-human actors and systemic networks. Haraway's cyborg serves as a metaphor for the complexity and hybridity of our identities, requiring us to reconsider traditional notions of identity, agency, and societal structures within the techno-human entanglement. In their respective ways, both Parikka's 'insect media' and Haraway's 'manifesto' challenge anthropocentric views and explore the interconnectedness of biological and technological forms. They push the boundaries of post-humanist thought, highlighting how technology and culture are inseparable from the biological world.

The approach being taken in this book is under the overarching paradigm of medialogy to grapple anew with a full and also emerging range of communication transactions that we want to know something about. What is offered is a framework for exploring the future of emerging digital technologies and their implication by pulling on existing understandings such as media archaeology through which we can excavate forgotten media technologies and practices, while the concepts of insect media and the cyborg challenge anthropocentric views and emphasise the interconnectedness of biological and technological forms. By expanding our understanding of media as complex systems shaped by biology, technology, and culture, we can navigate the ever-evolving landscape of media and communications in a more nuanced and informed manner.

2

ARCHAEOLOGICAL AND ARCHIVAL MEDIA

Unearthing Media's Depths and the Layered Histories of Communication

In the process of making a case for an overarching 'medialogy' that brings multiple perspectives into conversation with each other, echoes of the past are encountered that mingle with the noise of the present, generating an intricate understanding of media culture and history. Huhtamo and Parikka (2011, p. 2) use the term media archaeology with reference to an interdisciplinary approach, 'or a bundle of closely related approaches', that scrutinises the historical dimensions of media technologies and systems, examining their origin, development, and obsolescence. This concept of media archaeology, enriched by theories of 'zombie media' (Hertz & Parikka, 2011) and 'imaginary media' (Kluitenberg, 2006/2011), encourages us to excavate past media artefacts and technological systems not as relics to be isolated within a specific temporal framework, but as active components of our contemporary media landscape that shape our understanding of the past, present, and future. According to Parikka's (2010) proposition, media archaeology has successfully carved a niche for itself as a diverse amalgamation of theories and methodologies which delve into the history of media via its unconventional origins, overlooked trajectories, and disregarded concepts and technologies. These forgotten elements remain relevant as they challenge the perceived novelty of digital culture. The subsequent characterisations range from accentuating the repetitive nature of media cultural dialogues (Huhtamo & Parikka, 2011) to positioning media archaeology as 'an-archaeology' or variantology (Zielinski & Wagnermaier, 2005). Variantology, through its excavation of the profound temporal layers of our media usage and perception, consistently

DOI: 10.4324/9781003178149-3

20 Emerging Digital Media Ecologies

seeks an alternate path to debunk the myth of linear evolution. The media, for Leurs and Seuferling (2022), requires an understanding that: '[t]hey are not isolated devices or external change agents, but always embedded in longer temporalities and genealogical connections over time, that are not necessarily linear or progressing to a logical destination' (p. 291). The relevance of a media archaeological approach to the broader cultural context becomes apparent when considering Marvin's (1988, p. 8) assertion that: 'the history of media is never more or less than the history of their uses, which always leads us away from them to the social practices and contexts they illuminate'. In this view, antiquated technologies coexist with modern ones—for instance, Super-8 and 8-bit sounds become objects of both nostalgia and revival. This implies that retro-cultures are as inherent to the digital cultural landscape as cutting-edge screen technology and ultra-fast broadband connections. This chapter will delve into the realm of Media Archaeology—a field of study that interprets media cultures as layered and stratified, a fusion of time and matter where the past can resurface unexpectedly, and the lifespan of new technologies shortens rapidly—a 'coupling of degeneration and regeneration' (Parikka, 2012, p. 120). For Kluitenberg (2011, p. 51):

> Media archaeology can most productively be read as an alternative to the dominant writing of media history, whose implicit construction of a unitary narrative of progress—the idea that the course of technological development over time in and of itself equals progress, the predominant orientation regarding the realized and successful media forms and apparatuses—tends to marginalize the significance of failed projects, the shards of media history, and to exclude the role of the phantasmatic in media culture.

In setting up a normative framework for medialogy, Siegfried Zielinski's work on *Deep Time of the Media: Toward an Archaeology of Hearing and Seeing by Technical Means* (2006) presents an important critical exploration of non-linear, layered media histories. The concept of 'deep time' borrowed from the realms of geology posits a temporal continuum far surpassing our immediate historical contexts. When used with reference to media, it beckons us to delve beyond canonical chronicles and venture into the profound depths of forgotten, overlooked, and uncharted territories of media's past. Indeed, Zielinski's (2006) articulation of deep time does challenge conventional narratives that often endorse linear, teleological progressions of media evolution. Instead, he beckons us to acknowledge the complexities, ruptures, and recursions that permeate the media's historical landscape. Such an approach, while seemingly unconventional, shares academic thought with, for example, Michel Foucault, and his work on the archaeology of knowledge which also championed a layered, non-continuous understanding of historical discourses (Foucault, 1972). Zielinski's work can be perceived as an extension of this philosophy, albeit tailored to the intricacies of media histories. One of the fundamental tenets of Zielinski's study is the pursuit of variantology—seeking alternative, often marginalised narratives that challenge the dominion of mainstream media trajectories. This endeavour is reminiscent of Walter Benjamin's call for 'brushing history against the grain' (Benjamin, 1969, pp. 256–7). Benjamin, much like Zielinski, was sceptical of homogeneous, deterministic historical accounts and championed the retrieval of lost subjugated voices.

In excavating these deep temporal layers, Zielinski also reminds us of the cyclical nature of media innovations. Technologies and ideas that seem revolutionary today often have antecedents buried deep in history. For instance, the concept of virtual reality, perceived as a cutting-edge technological marvel, finds echoes in the panoramic paintings and stereoscopic viewers of the 19th century—a fact that aligns seamlessly with Zielinski's archaeological approach. Huhtamo and Parikka's (2011) work on media archaeology resonates with Zielinski's deep time proposition rejecting the seductive allure of novelty that often accompanies contemporary media forms. Each recognises that beneath the veneer of innovation lie age-old motifs, desires, and fascinations that have continually shaped humanity's engagement with media and the tools of communication. The strength of this position lies not just in its revisionist perspective but also in its potential for future-forward insights. By understanding the recursive patterns, historical continuities, and ruptures, we are better positioned to anticipate the trajectories of emerging media landscapes. But as Jonathan Sterne posits in his exploration of sound technologies, the past sets the conditions for the present, but: 'the origins do not guarantee the present or the future' (Sterne, 2003. p 349). As we stand at the cusp of unprecedented technological advancements, such an understanding is not just desirable, but imperative.

From Telegraph to Tweet: Tracing the Arc of Communication through Electricity, Telephony, and Media Archaeology

The intricate interplay between electricity and telephony serves as a historical bedrock for contemporary networked digital and social media landscapes. The transformative potential of electricity not only redefined energy consumption but also revolutionised communication channels, epitomised by the telegraph's capability to bridge vast distances in real time. Telephony further elevated this by introducing immediate bidirectional communication, setting the stage for the immediacy that we now associate with the internet and contemporary social media. Employing a media archaeological lens, this analysis delves into the layered histories of these technologies, highlighting their roles not merely as isolated innovations, but as deeply intertwined elements within a broader evolutionary media narrative. Through medialogy's lens, the emergence

22 Emerging Digital Media Ecologies

of electricity and plain old telephony stand as transformative periods, underpinning the fabric of our (post)modern networked social media age.

Electricity is often misconstrued as merely a utilitarian development. It did, however, radically alter the communicative terrains. Prior to its widespread deployment, human interactions were bound by the analogue constraints of time and space. The introduction of electricity signified more than mere illumination; it catalysed a departure from conventional communication methods—shifting from protracted handwritten correspondences to the immediacy of the telegraph's electrical pulses. This new paradigm heralded a reimagining of distances, making vast geographies feel proximate. Yet, this was merely the precursory ripple before significant socio-technical change. Marvin (1988) provides insight into the transformative power of electric communication technologies during a critical juncture in history during the late 19th century. This period witnessed a significant shift in the way information was transmitted and received, fundamentally transforming communication patterns and social dynamics. During this time, the telegraph emerged as a ground-breaking technology that allowed messages to be sent rapidly over long distances through electric signals. The development of telegraph networks, such as the transatlantic cable, enabled near-instantaneous communication across continents, connecting individuals and nations like never before. This marked a critical juncture as it challenged the limitations of physical distance and reshaped the concept of time and space, creating a sense of global interconnectivity without eliminating the essence of place, space, and time (see Tsatsou, 2009). Simultaneously, the invention of the telephone by Alexander Graham Bell in 1876 represented another pivotal moment in electric communication. The telephone enabled direct, real-time voice communication, further revolutionising interpersonal connections. This marked a transformative shift from written communication to oral interaction, significantly impacting social relationships and the way people conducted business, coordinated activities, and maintained personal connections—perfect for building nations.

The late 19th century also witnessed the rise of mass media through the introduction of technologies such as telegraph-based news services and the proliferation of newspapers. Electric communication technologies facilitated the rapid dissemination of information, enabling the news to travel across vast distances quickly. This gave rise to new forms of public discourse, shaping public opinion, and contributing to the formation of a shared cultural and informational landscape. Beyond its apparent novelty, telephony signified an inflection point in human communication, offering a level of intimacy and immediacy hitherto unparalleled. The very tenet of telephony was not confined to its technical capacity but in its ability to cultivate a culture of instantaneity for information and connection. This ethos, while nascent in the age of telephony, resonates profoundly in today's age of instantaneous tweets, globally accessible live streams, and real-time digital interactions. When electricity and telephony are juxtaposed in this way within an archaeological narrative, they cease to be mere technological milestones. Instead, they emerge as foundational pillars, bearing the weight of an interwoven media evolution. Their legacy, though perhaps intangible in our WiFi-laden landscapes, undergirds every post, status update, Like, and digital broadcast.

At the heart of Marvin's (1988) analysis lies a central tenet that the societal impact of technological innovations is not solely determined by their intrinsic features or functions but is fundamentally shaped by the cultural, social, and historical contexts in which they emerge. They astutely argue that electric communication technologies such as the telegraph and telephone were not neutral tools for transmitting information but rather complex systems that influenced and were influenced by the prevailing cultural dynamics. These technologies became powerful agents of social change, transforming the way people interacted, conceptualised time, place, and space, and understood themselves in relation to others. That is, prior to its introduction, time was predominantly perceived as a local, subjective experience tied to natural rhythms and local clocks. However, the telegraph's ability to instantaneously transmit messages across vast distances disrupted this temporal perception, introducing the concept of 'real-time' communication. Suddenly, individuals were connected to events happening in far-away locations, challenging traditional understandings of time and creating a new sense of simultaneity. Furthermore, Marvin illustrates how the telephone revolutionised interpersonal communication, reshaping social relationships and redefining the boundaries of private and public spheres. Through the telephone, individuals could engage in intimate conversations across great distances, collapsing the physical separation between people. This transformed social interactions, as people adapted to the novel experience of communicating without the constraints of physical presence. The telephone thus became a catalyst for new modes of social connectivity, at times intense and robust and at others stretched (where capitalist modernisation was sped-up and the pace of economic processes accelerated) and a symbol of the modern era for many (Harvey, 1993). That is, the impact of technological innovations extends beyond their technical capabilities and is deeply intertwined with the cultural, social, and historical contexts in which they emerge.

While electricity and telephony can be considered significant precursors to present-day social media, it is the convergence, however, of these foundational technologies with the rise of the internet, advancements in computing, and the proliferation of digital devices that truly shaped the emergence of social media (Barr, 2000). Recognising and understanding the pivotal milestones of computer history is underscored by key developments including the seminal Commodore 64 and Vectrex Gaming Console from 1982, and the innovative NeXT Cube of 1990, to computational machines like the Apple Lisa (1983),

Macintosh (1984), and Apple IIe (1985). The Commodore 64 democratised computing, introducing many households to personal computers. Vectrex brought vector graphics home, revolutionising gaming. NeXT Cube, though niche, pioneered crucial technologies (the object-oriented operating system) later ubiquitous in Apple products (macOS, iOS, watchOS, and tvOS), impacting global tech design. The Apple devices played a fundamental role in personal computing's trajectory and fostered the capacity for computer-aided art and writing and a fierce loyalty of Macintosh computer owners (Belk & Tumbat, 2005). The Apple II series not only heralded the era of affordable personal computers using a command-line interface but was also celebrated for its open and adaptable design, much like the pioneering IBM PC which transformed businesses worldwide. In parallel, the Apple Lisa took a revolutionary leap by being the first to commercialise a Graphical User Interface (GUI) accessible to a broader audience and setting a precedent for the intuitive user interfaces most are accustomed to. This trajectory can be likened to Microsoft's Windows platform, which further democratised GUI-based systems, cementing a paradigm shift in how users interacted with their devices. More recently, users navigated even more sophisticated devices like the iPad and Microsoft Surface to augmented reality interfaces like the Microsoft HoloLens. Arguably, users are experiencing the ripple effects of the early ground-breaking innovations. The internet for its part served as the backbone via computational devices affording the global connectivity that contemporary social media platforms rely on, enabling the seamless exchange of information for many (not all due to access, capacity, and cost) and the ability to foster virtual communities. Additionally, the proliferation of personal computers, smartphones, and other devices equipped with internet connectivity created the user base and accessibility necessary for the widespread adoption of social media platforms.

The subsequent advent of social media platforms, such as from Myspace to Facebook, Twitter-now 'X', Instagram, Mastodon, Bluesky, Snapchat, and others, introduced new modes of communication, self-expression, and social interaction. These platforms harnessed the power of the internet and digital technologies to facilitate user-generated content, real-time updates, and social networking on an unprecedented scale. This rise of social media was influenced by broader social and cultural trends, such as a desire for self-presentation, connectivity, and the democratisation of information sharing. It tapped into fundamental human needs for connection, expression, and community-building. Social media as we know it today is the product of a complex interplay of foundational technologies, internet infrastructure, digital devices, and socio-cultural factors. It represents a distinct evolution that builds upon and extends the capabilities of its predecessors to create new modes of communication, community engagement, and information sharing—for good, bad, and everything between—in the digital age.

Batch and Loop

Viewing the evolution of media as a terrain riddled with alternate paths and overlooked possibilities, media archaeologists question the mainstream trajectory, examining the unique instances that strayed from the well-trodden path. Media archaeologists also see the past of media technologies as layered. Each layer, representing a specific era, medium, or technology, adds to the complex narrative of media evolution. They peel away these layers, one by one, uncovering the intricate web of influences and interactions that shape the media landscape. Sometimes, they choose to traverse time in reverse. Starting from the bustling metropolis of modern technology ('loop'), they trace the roots of innovation backward (to 'batch' media), venturing into the past where the seeds of present-day marvels were first sown. This 'reverse chronology' disrupts the conventional flow of historical narrative, offering fresh perspectives on the stories we thought we knew. As if seen through a magnifying glass, media archaeologists undertake a microanalysis of specific media artefacts or technologies to illuminate larger cultural and historical trends, revealing how each minute detail contributes to the grand mosaic of media history. The evolution from 'batch' to 'loop' media is emblematic of the transformative shifts in media landscapes and communication paradigms. Batch media, grounded in classical theories of communication, delineate platforms wherein the content is conceived, curated, and then disseminated in finite sequences (McQuail, 2010). This model mirrors the rhythms of print journalism or scheduled radio broadcasts, which catered to a large receptive audience and reflected a sender–receiver dynamic (Shannon & Weaver, 1949). In stark contrast, 'loop' media, emerging from the fluidity and interactivity of digital realms, is shaped by continuous feedback loops. Platforms like X and Meta, in their iterative nature, are exemplars of this shift, facilitating a constant dialogue between content delivery and immediate audience feedback (Jenkins, 2006). Moving away from a linear communicative trajectory, 'loop' media embodies a participatory culture, where both producers and consumers collaboratively construct the media narrative (Bruns, 2008).

To encapsulate, the transition from batch to loop signifies a shift from structured, temporally bound modes of content delivery to malleable, real-time engagements that emphasise active participation (Benkler & Nissenbaum, 2006). While batch media maintains predictability, loop media capitalises on immediacy, adaptability, and the collective agency of its community. Navigating the contours of today's media demands contextual nuance for understanding these foundational shifts (Castells, 2010). This is for several reasons. Firstly, it informs the strategies of content creators and distributors, emphasising the need for adaptability and real-time analytics. Secondly, it signals a change in audience expectations as today's consumers expect a more participatory and responsive media experience.

Media archaeology has, as outlined above, thrived on the spirit of 'variantology' (Zielinski & Wagnermaier, 2005) under the assertion that the past of media technologies is not a homogenous, linear progression but a collection of alternative paths and neglected possibilities that could have, and at times did, taken a different direction. This perspective invites us to challenge the traditional notions of media history, prompting a focus on what Boris Groys (2009) calls 'moments in time'—singular, unique, and present instances that may diverge from the mainstream trajectory of media development. According to Groys, every work of art or media represents a specific moment in time—not simply a static snapshot, but a dynamic intersection of past, present, and potential future. A powerful example is a news photograph that captures not only the event it directly portrays but also anticipates future interpretations and reflects historical contexts. Groys invites us to appreciate these media artefacts as dynamic temporal markers, not merely static products of a singular period. Of course, some media do completely degenerate (others are resurrected as discussed in the sections below). In their *Dead Media Manifesto*, Bruce Sterling and Richard Kadrey (1995) emphasise the inevitable obsolescence of media forms and the importance of chronicling their life cycles. They argue that media, regardless of its prevalence, eventually becomes 'dead' or obsolete. For example, before vinyl records, phonograph cylinders (initially covered in tin foil, then made of wax by the mid-1880s) were the primary medium for recorded sound. They were eventually replaced by gramophone discs due to their longer playtime and easier storage (Gitelman, 2006). Another example is the precursor to the modern projector, the magic lantern, which used glass slides to project images. While revolutionary in its time, it was eventually overshadowed by film and later by digital projectors (Huhtamo, 2013). While Groys' work does not fall squarely within the field of media archaeology, his examination of media artefacts as temporal markers echoes the media archaeological practice of excavating past media artefacts to better understand the present and predict the future.

The Resonance of the Record Player: Societal, Industrial, and Environmental Reverberations

Consider, for instance, how the vinyl record player, a subject of fascination for media archaeologists, exists not in a vacuum but is part of a broader ecological system that includes its production, consumption, societal implications, and seeming redundancy. The introduction of the record player marked not merely a technological advancement but a profound shift in the music landscape. Its impact resonated beyond the hum of the vinyl, influencing cultural norms, industry practices, and environmental patterns. In societal spaces, the record player held a key role in fostering cultural integration. That is, before its inception, music was largely experienced in live settings or through rudimentary devices. However, through vinyl, a plethora of musical genres became accessible to many listeners—the sounds of classical symphonies, jazz tunes, soulful blues, and energetic rock 'n' roll began filling households globally. The world was suddenly interconnected through grooves on a disc, promoting a unique form of cultural appreciation and integration. Music from distant lands was not just a privilege for those who could afford to travel; it henceforth offered a shared experience.

Beyond merely listening, however, the record player reshaped social dynamics. The act of placing a needle onto a spinning vinyl, waiting for the initial crackle before the music commenced, became an intimate ritual. Whether in grand family gatherings, intimate parties, or solitary introspections, the record player was a consistent companion. Additionally, it marked the dawn of the album era. Instead of focusing on standalone tracks, artists now had the canvas of an entire album to craft intricate narratives, offering listeners a deeper, more immersive musical journey.

Additionally, from an industrial perspective, the record player's influence was also profound. As demand surged, so did the need for mass production. Factories dedicated to pressing vinyl emerged, and the entire music distribution mechanism underwent a revolution. But it was not simply about the records— the album covers, with their expansive size, became iconic symbols of artistic expression, and fans would spend hours pouring over cover images and reading song lyrics on inside sleeves. This intersection of visual art and music set the stage for some of the most iconic album artworks in (Western) history—exemplars are The Beatle's *Sgt. Pepper's Lonely Hearts Club Band* (1967) which depicts the band surrounded by a collage of celebrities and historical figures indicating the diverse influences and the era's zeitgeist; and the stark simplicity of Pink Floyd's *The Dark Side of the Moon* (1973) and its profound image of a prism refracting white light into its constituent colours, representing the spectrum and a metaphorical reflection on life's multifaceted experiences and emotions.

Furthermore, the record industry became a behemoth, establishing a plethora of professions. Recording engineers, cover artists, vinyl press operators, and record store owners became essential cogs in the music industry machine. With this industrial progress, however, came environmental challenges. The production of vinyl records relied heavily on raw materials, notably petroleum, used in the creation of PVC, the primary component of vinyl records. This resource-intensive production had marked environmental ramifications—the generation of waste when vinyl ends up in landfills where PVC can take hundreds of years to decompose; album covers, while culturally significant, use paper, inks, and sometimes additional plastic materials, all of which have environmental production and disposal impacts; given the weight and bulk of vinyl records compared to digital media, transportation impacts can be considerable. On the flip side, the tactile nature of vinyl also cultivated

28 Emerging Digital Media Ecologies

a culture of collectors and enthusiasts who preserved records for posterity, reducing potential wastage. Even in the digital age, vinyl has retained a dedicated market and fanbase, for example, Billie Eilish's *When We All Fall Asleep, Where Do We Go?* (2019) was released on vinyl affording fans an experience of the haunting melodies in analogue; and, websites are dedicated to tracking the many new releases on vinyl (such as https://upcomingvinyl. com/). Collectors and audiophiles appreciate the tangible and aesthetic appeal of vinyl, as well as the perceived warmth and richness of its sound. The legacy of vinyl is a powerful testament to how a single innovation can resonate with the various facets of human existence. Through a medialogy lens then, we can examine how the record player's 'sound' flows across social spaces, how its production impacted industrial processes, and even environmental aspects. As such, media archaeology complements medialogy, adding to the synergistic approach that deepens our understanding of media culture, technological progress, and socio-environmental implications.

Against this backdrop are distinctive initiatives designed as 'listening events' to reignite the passion for physical music formats and to champion the art of deep, intentional listening. At their core, the platforms serve as a gathering for aficionados and casual listeners alike, inviting them to step away from the distractions of today's digital world and delve into the rich spaces of recorded music as it was traditionally experienced (e.g., The Classic Album Sundays website, www.classicalbumsundays.com). By emphasising the tactile and immersive qualities of music, live, international events such as 'Classic Album Sundays' not only offer a nostalgic journey for seasoned music lovers but also introduce newer generations to the profound joys of engaging with music in its tangible, unfiltered essence. This club's approach is both a celebration of music's storied past and a gentle reminder of the profound connection that can be forged when one truly listens.

Along the spectrum of thinking here, drawing on the work of Friedrich Kittler (1995), Michael Goddard (2015) explores the non-linear nature of media evolution and the heterogeneous pathways that technologies might traverse. Goddard argued that archaeological methodologies challenge the simplistic linear correlation between technology and its effects. This perspective is beneficial as it dismisses the presupposition that certain communities are merely passive recipients of technological progress. Instead, this lucid claim reorients the focus towards recognising individuals as engaged participants within the co-evolutionary processes of technological innovation—this non-linear, disruptive approach to media history is a vital aspect of media archaeology. While Goddard (2015) and Groys (2009) have distinct perspectives, their work converges on the understanding of media as non-linear, complex systems where past, present, and future intermingle. Moreover, media archaeology, as a theoretical framework that delves into the intricate histories and non-linear trajectories of media technologies and practices, offers an insightful lens to understand the transition from batch to loop media. This approach, rather than simply chronicling a linear progression of technological advancements, critically examines the layers, residues, and re-emergences in media history as posited by Parikka (2012).

Interconnected Memories: Media Archaeology and the Socio-Technical Dynamics of Digital Archiving

Undeniably, media archaeology is closely intertwined with the concept of media ecologies, an umbrella concept drawn on by Matthew Fuller (2005) with reference to the interconnectedness of media technologies and their environments, their relationships, subsequent influences, and impacts within a complex, dynamic network. This approach to understanding media systems not only as individual entities but as parts of an interdependent whole aligns seamlessly with the archaeological approach, grounding the historical study of media in a comprehensive socio-technical landscape. The connection between the concept of media ecologies and Wolfgang Ernst's ideas found in *Digital Memory and the Archive* (2013) is subtle yet profound. Ernst presents an intricately detailed exploration of how memory operates within digital systems using the concept of media archaeology to delve into the mechanics of digital archiving, demonstrating that machines too 'remember' through their ability to store, recall, and interact with data. For instance, when a user deletes an email, it does not disappear, but persists within the system's memory, recoverable under certain conditions. Ernst's framework thus dismantles the boundary between human and machine memory. Furthermore, he posits that digital archives, as part of larger media ecosystems, are subject to influences from their socio-technical surroundings. For example, an online newspaper archive's content is shaped not just by its data but also by factors such as algorithmic sorting and user interface. This approach offers a comprehensive understanding of the operational reality of digital archives, reorienting our perception of memory in the digital age. A digital archive, from the media ecologies perspective, is not simply a solitary entity, but a part of a broader media ecosystem involving software, hardware, users, designers, societal norms, and legal frameworks. Consider the phenomenon of social media in this context. As platforms like Facebook and Twitter/'X' have become pervasive, they have essentially created digital archives of personal, public, and historical events. However, these archives exist within a larger media ecology, shaped by factors such as algorithmic bias (see also Chapter 6), platform policies, and user behaviours—what Kittler (1990) would describe as an intricate network of influence, where the machine and the human intertwine and co-evolve. Hence, Ernst's claim for memory as viewed through a media ecological lens fosters an understanding of how media technologies, especially digital archives, operate within interconnected networks of influence. It urges us to discern the dynamics of digital memory not merely as an isolated, mechanical process, but as a component of a broader, socio-technical media landscape. When we juxtapose the batch and loop dichotomy in this context, within a media archaeological framework, we are encouraged to unearth the deeper historical, cultural, and technological antecedents that have informed today's media practices. For instance, while loop media may seem quintessentially modern, its iterative and responsive nature can be traced back to older forms of oral storytelling, where tales evolved based on audience reactions. Similarly, while batch media may be associated with a more 'broadcast' era, its structures can be connected to even older print media dynamics, echoing the periodicity of pamphlets or serialised novels. By situating these models within media archaeology, we come to appreciate that media practices are never truly novel; they are reconfigurations and evolutions of past logics and affordances (Huhtamo & Parikka, 2011). Therefore, comprehending the shift from batch to loop is not just about understanding contemporary changes, but about situating them within a deeper historical continuum. By doing so, we can identify recurring motifs, understand the re-emergence of forgotten media practices, and, crucially, predict potential future trajectories informed by these cyclical patterns. In essence, media archaeology contributes to the proposition for an overarching medialogy by inviting us to see the batch to loop transition as part of an intricate weaving of media evolution, where the past continually informs and reshapes the present.

Material Qualities and Media: An Exploration of Obsolescent Systems in a Digital Epoch

The often overlooked material properties of media systems critically influence the perception and value attached to those systems. A prominent illustration of this is the skeuomorph, a design phenomenon that embeds vestigial features (attributes) from antecedent technologies into newer platforms (Basalla, 1988, p. 107), often for affective rather than utilitarian reasons (Heskett, 2002, 2005). The emblematic 'click' of the single-lens reflex (SLR) cameras offers a potent example. Originally, this sound emerged from the mechanical operation of an internal mirror, serving as acoustic feedback during film exposure (Flusser, 2002). In contemporary digital cameras, which lack such mechanisms, this sound is nonetheless reproduced artificially (Goggin, 2006). This acoustic vestige not only commemorates the technological lineage but also appeases a user's psychological need for familiar auditory markers, highlighting the confluence of function and nostalgia (Van Dijck, 2007).

Discourses on media decline and eventual death also underscore the importance of materiality in understanding media trajectories. Notably, media archaeology reveals the intriguing phenomenon of the tangible endurance of so-called 'dead' media, as outlined above. These persistent artefacts defy traditional conceptions of death, suggesting that media demise is less about functional cessation and more about socio-cultural relegation—systems become obsolete not due to technical breakdowns but from their diminished significance in the rapidly evolving mediascape (Gitelman, 2006; Manovich, 2002). As such, media devices inhabit a complex interstice, buffeted by their intrinsic materiality and the ever-shifting cultural narratives that surround them. Their trajectories underscore the need to consider media not merely as conduits but as entities deeply interwoven in intricate ways through history, technology, and culture (Kittler, 1999).

Where Do Media Go to Die? Archival and Archaeological Perspectives

The question of the ultimate destination or transformation of media can be deeply explored through the dual lenses of archival and archaeological perspectives. The central tension in the query is the metaphorical understanding of the life cycle of media, asking whether media genuinely 'die' or whether they simply transform, becoming part of an enmeshed continuum. To untangle this, we can turn to the concepts of archival and archaeological media, each of which offers a unique lens to understand the media's trajectory. The concept of archival media posits that media—in their varied expressions, from legacy forms such as print or film to the ephemeral bytes of the digital—do not completely fade away. Instead, they find refuge in archives. Archives, as Derrida suggests, are not just about storage but about 'the commencement and the commandment' (Derrida, 1995, p. 9). In this paradigm, media in archives is not dead but rather in stasis, poised for potential reanimation upon their retrieval. In this suspended state, the essence and memory of the media remain preserved, often extending beyond its original zeitgeist moment. In the age of digital proliferation, as Manovich (2002) suggests, media follows a trajectory not of vanishing but of accumulating, creating possibilities for even seemingly 'dead' media to resurface with renewed vitality. Moreover, Archaeological media can be understood as stratified imprints of history, leaving behind layers of residue that undergo continuous transformation over time.

The concept of practice offers a compelling avenue for redefining the life cycle of media, shifting focus from static existence to dynamic interaction. Practice, in this sense, becomes the vital determinant of a medium's life or death. Sterne (2006) argued that media technologies should be understood not just as objects but as practices, tracing the continuities and ruptures in their usage. Media's life or death is not an inherent quality but rather a result of collective human practices that either integrate or abandon specific mediums over time. This notion prompts us to reframe our definitions, urging us to pivot from the age-old binary of life and death to a more dynamic, process-oriented understanding. Here, 'practice' emerges as the linchpin. As Sterne emphasises, it is pivotal to grasp media technologies not merely as static entities

Emerging Digital Media Ecologies

but as evolving practices that delineate the ebbs and flows in their engagement over time. In this disparate realm, the vitality or decline of a medium is not an intrinsic attribute; it is a manifestation of the collective human engagements that either assimilate or phase out specific mediums over time.

Just as archival media prompts us to think of media in suspended animation and archaeological media nudges us to view them as sedimented residues in human history, imaginary media invites us to consider the speculative, the unrealised, and the theoretical aspects of media. These are media that have not experienced a traditional life cycle as they have never been fully born into the tangible world. Yet, their impact can be palpable.

Imaginary Media and Speculative Realms as Lenses for Understanding Media Evolution

Imaginary media is a term rooted in media theory that encompasses both existent and non-existent media forms, technologies, and systems which shape the collective imaginations of societies (Kluitenberg, 2006). Linking back to the cyclical nature of media practices and their transformation, imaginary media brings an added dimension. While media like vinyl records moves from mainstream to obsolescence and back to revival, imaginary media might oscillate between the imagined and the verge of realisation. The unfulfilled potential of these media can serve as inspirations for future innovations or, in some cases, cautionary tales. The notion of imaginary media might seem, at first glance, to challenge the conventional understanding of media as tangible, material, and functional devices. However, when delving into theoretical and philosophical explorations, imaginary media offers a critical lens to think beyond the material constraints, allowing us to envision alternative media possibilities. Within the media archaeological frameworks of Parikka (2012) and Kluitenberg (2006), 'imaginary' and 'speculative' media are both tools to dissect and analyse media history and culture, emphasising the non-linear, cyclical, and multifaceted nature of media evolution and imagination. The link between the imaginary and speculative is given a weighty register via Kluitenberg (2006, p. 49):

> The archaeology of imaginary media is an attempt to shift attention somewhat away from a history of the apparatus and to focus on the imaginaries around technological media—communication media in particular—of both realized and unrealized media machines. The archaeology of imaginary media also suggests a shift away from the utilitarian and toward the phantasmatic in 'excavating' these imaginaries from the histories of technology and the media and from the (media) practices of everyday life. The aim of this 'archaeology' is not to establish a history or a set of lineages of media and technological imaginaries. Rather, it is to study these imaginaries in

action across different historical and discursive settings and contexts. ... If media archaeology offers possibilities to venture into the realms of both the realized and the imaginary, with the obvious intention of showing how these two domains influence each other, then the archaeology of imaginary media is a suggestion to shift attention to the domain of the imaginary and the unrealizable for both realized and unrealized media machines.

Drawing upon the theoretical positions of Parikka's media archaeology and Kluitenberg's exploration of imaginary media (2006), Vannevar Bush's (1945) concept of the Memex serves as a prime example of 'imaginary' media. It encapsulates an unrealised vision that intricately connects with the historical aspirations and future potentials of media culture, emphasising the non-linear and cyclical evolution of media technologies. The Memex (*mem*ory and *ex*pansion) was a hypothetical machine as an electromechanical tool for interacting with microform documents designed to enhance human memory by creating associative trails between documents (Bush, 1945, p. 106):

> A memex is a device in which an individual stores all his[*sic*] books, records, and communications, and which is mechanized so that it may be consulted with exceeding speed and flexibility. It is an enlarged intimate supplement to his memory.

While the Memex was never built, its speculative nature parallels the conceptualisation and design of the World Wide Web. The Memex exemplifies how imaginary media can presage real technological developments. Speculation in media studies provides a gateway to imagine a continuum of alternatives, be they utopian, dystopian, or simply different from the current status quo. This speculative dimension is crucial in an era where technological determinism—a theory that posits that technology is the dominant determining factor in a process—might restrict the imaginative potential and the capacity of networked publics via digital media (Aouragh & Chakravartty, 2016). The long-standing dichotomy of hope and fear (hype and scandal)— often situated within certain utopian and dystopian contexts, respectively— has arguably dominated much of media discourse. However, the spectrum of imagined media, brimming with potentialities, extends beyond such binaries, gesturing towards territories that are potentially and distinctively different from our current understanding. Drawing an example from popular media is *Star Trek* (original American television series, 1966–1969) which introduced audiences to 'the Communicator'—a device that allowed instant voice communication across distances. This imaginary piece of equipment used for voice communication (seen in episodes 'Tomorrow Is Yesterday' (1967, dir., Michael O'Herlihy) and 'Day of the Dove' (1968, dir., Marvin Chomsky)) can also serve as an emergency signalling device/beacon similar to a transponder.

34 Emerging Digital Media Ecologies

The tool enthralled fans of the show and may have inspired scientists and technologists. Today's mobile phones, particularly the flip-phone design, bear a striking resemblance to the fictional Communicator, underscoring once again the power of speculative concepts (see Doyle, 1997).

Another noteworthy example of imaginary media is the 'augmented reality' glasses depicted in William Gibson's 1984 cyberpunk novel *Neuromancer* which predates the arrival of Google Glass. In the ever-evolving landscape of technological innovation, some products like Google Glass highlight the socio-economic cautionary tales of imaginary media, where the gap between envisioned potential and market reception can result in significant cultural and financial miscalculations. In the early 2010s, Google introduced the world to Google Glass, a wearable device that projected a small display in front of the wearer's eye, allowing them to access digital information readily without the need for a conventional screen. The initial promotional videos (see Google Glass, 2013) and discussions surrounding Google Glass hinted at a utopian digital future, anticipating advances in business and access to healthcare and medicine (Widerschein, 2016). These glasses were imagined to effortlessly integrate digital and physical realities whereby users could receive directions, translate languages in real-time, record moments instantly, and even engage in augmented reality games. The prediction was of a world in which the separation between digital and physical became indistinguishably blurred.

While Google Glass was heralded as a breakthrough in wearable technology, its real-world reception underscored a pronounced tension between technological innovation and societal comfort levels regarding privacy. The device's camera and recording features raised security and serious privacy concerns at the time (McGee, 2013). People were uncomfortable around Glass wearers, unsure if they were being recorded or photographed. Establishments like bars, cafes, and cinemas began banning Google Glass due to these concerns (Costill, 2013; and see Eveleth, 2018). This unexpected social friction highlighted a gap between the imagined seamless integration of technology and real-world social dynamics. While Google had imagined a world where digital information would be effortlessly integrated into our field of view—and indeed continued development with Google Glass Enterprise Edition 2 announced in 2019 but was then discontinued in 2023—some users found the device disorienting because of the constant stream of notifications was more distracting than useful, and using voice commands in public was awkward. Overall, the functional (utilitarian) aspect of the product was inadequate to guarantee the use of the product (Nunes & Filho, 2018).

Baudrillard (1981), in his exploration of 'simulacra and simulation', posits that in the postmodern age, media representations might not echo reality but instead replace or precede it. Of simulation: '[i]t is the generation by models of a real without origin or reality: a hyperreal … produced from a radiating

Archaeological and Archival Media **35**

synthesis of combinatory models in a hyperspace without atmosphere' (Baudrillard, 1981, pp. 1–2). This suggests a media landscape that neither amplifies utopian prospects nor echoes dystopian fears, but rather creates a space for alternative realities. The prevalence of synthetic media and 'deepfake' videos in today's digital age stands as a testament to this, where artificial representations can seem indistinguishably real, forcing us to renegotiate our relationship with 'truth' and what is real. It can be argued that the media, in its imaginative capacities, does not merely extend existing paradigms but substantially reconfigures the human experience itself.

Taking this further, contemporary virtual reality (VR) technologies, like the Oculus Rift and Apple's Vision Pro, provide not just a 'better' (or 'worse') experience of reality but a fundamentally different experiential paradigm. Here, Lash's (2010) concept of 'intensive culture' reflects a shift from structures to flows (of technology and media, for example), from clear narratives to muddled intensities. This challenges us to understand media beyond linear progressions or declines, and instead as complex ecosystems that mould and are moulded by socio-cultural forces. Platforms like TikTok, with its fragmented yet intense bursts of content, exemplify this departure from traditional narrative media forms. The interplay between technology, media, and the human form suggests that imagined media can even lead us to envision human–machine symbiosis in novel ways (Hayles, 1999a). To rephrase Hoskins (2009), our memory processes are deeply intertwined with digital networks. Towards an actualisation, neural interfaces, as explored by companies like Neuralink (an American neurotechnology company working to develop implantable brain–computer interfaces), do not simply offer an improved human condition but aim to create a future wherein the line between human cognition and machine computation is blurred. This paradigm does not place digital media as better or worse carriers of memory but shifts our understanding of how memory works in a digitised age. When we consider phenomena like Google's 'Year in Search' compilations, it becomes evident how collective memory is both curated and presented through digital media. Further, Chun's discussion on 'the enduring ephemeral' (2012) of the internet illustrates that while digital media might seem fleeting, it has lasting impacts on cultural fabrics. The viral nature of memes, which momentarily capture global attention and then fade, only to resurface years later in new contexts, embodies this notion. For example, the 'Mocking SpongeBob' (or 'SpongeMock') meme uses an image of SpongeBob SquarePants from an episode where he mimics a chicken whenever he sees plaid. It was used to represent a mocking tone, where repeated text uses alternating capital and lowercase letters. The image from the 2012 episode *Little Yellow Book* (Nickelodeon) went viral in 2017 and is used to mock a statement someone else has made (Herrera, 2017). Over the years, it has resurfaced in various contexts, especially during online debates or as a way to poke fun at perceived illogical statements.

36 Emerging Digital Media Ecologies

In the context of practice, identified in the preceding sections as pivotal in determining a medium's life or death, imaginary media are engaged in a different mode. They are interacted with in stories, theoretical constructs, and speculative designs. They may never 'live' in the traditional sense, but they exist vibrantly in the collective psyche, influencing practices in indirect ways. As such, when contemplating the life and 'death' of media, folding in the concept of imaginary media expands the landscape. It underscores that the media universe is not just about what has been or what is, but also about what could be. Just as archival and archaeological media make us reconsider the notions of media life cycles, imaginary media remind us that the unrealised or the envisioned has a potent space in this discourse, challenging the very contours of media existence.

From Resurrected Past to Speculative Futures: Bridging Zombie and Imaginary Media

The concept of 'zombie media' was put forward by Hertz and Parikka (2012) as an understanding of the affordances from the melding of media archaeology with the practice of art, particularly through the act of 'circuit bending'. Circuit bending, essentially, is the creative short-circuiting of electronic devices to yield unexpected sounds and visual outputs. Hertz and Parikka (2012, p. 429) argue that through circuit bending, obsolete technologies are resurrected, becoming what they term zombie media:

> In this context, bending media archaeology into an artistic methodology can be seen as a way to tap into the economic potential of such practices as circuit bending, hardware hacking and other ways of reusing and reintroducing dead media into a new cycle of life for such objects. Assembled into new constructions, such materials and ideas become zombies that carry with them histories but are also reminders of the non-human temporalities involved in technical media.

As Bolter and Grusin (2000) suggest in their theory of remediation, all new media are, in a sense, built upon the repurposing of older media. The 'zombie' paradigm takes this a step further, proposing that it is not only in the conceptual space but also the physical that old media find new relevance. While the concept of 'zombies', traditionally, is considered mindless and driven by base instincts, this is not to suggest that by likening repurposed old media to zombies there is a lack of conscious thought or deliberate intent behind their reuse—this analogy does not imply that the reuse lacks creativity or conscious effort, but rather emphasises the resurrection of past ideas into the present, sometimes in unexpected or novel ways. The example of vinyl records given above is one example of being at one point in time a primary medium—for listening to music during much of the 20th century that by the 1990s had largely been replaced by CDs and by the 2000s by digital streaming—to find a revival of interest and many contemporary artists consequently releasing their albums on vinyl with a corresponding boost in sales. This 'zombification' of vinyl can be attributed to several factors. There is a tactile and nostalgic quality to handling and playing a vinyl record that digital formats cannot replicate. Moreover, many claim the analogue nature of vinyl provides a warmer and more authentic sound. This resurgence of vinyl highlights how old media can find new life, not as a dominant medium, but as a cherished alternative that coexists with modern formats. Remastered classic video games are another example. From the 1980s and 1990s, platforms like the Nintendo Entertainment System (NES), Super NES (SNES), and PlayStation video games were beloved by many, but became technologically outdated as graphics and gameplay evolved. Many classic games have been remastered or remade for modern gaming systems. For example, games like *Final Fantasy VII* (from 1997 for PlayStation) and *The Legend of Zelda: Link's Awakening* (originally released in 1993 for the Game Boy) have been re-released as completely remastered versions with full remakes, where graphics, sound, and sometimes even gameplay mechanics are overhauled for current audiences. The concept pushes forward the idea that while technological evolution continually delivers new media forms, older ones do not simply fade away; instead, they live on as undead entities, repurposed and given a new lease of life. This resurrection is not just about nostalgia but highlights an active resistance against the planned obsolescence embedded in modern technological production systems.

For balance, circuit bending and similar practices such as 'modding' (or game modification) might be critiqued as technologically deterministic. Such an approach might inadvertently suggest that technology drives cultural change. Moreover, while Hertz and Parikka's (2012) conceptualisation presents circuit bending as a challenge to mainstream capitalist production, one might question how subversive it is in contemporary, everyday life where the 'retro' and 'vintage' have become commercial categories in their own right. In this frame, circuit bending stands at risk of being co-opted, becoming another marketable niche. This recalls Horkheimer and Adorno's (1944) critique in *Dialectic of Enlightenment*, where they argue that even counter-culture movements can be absorbed and neutralised by capitalism. Zombie media does, however, force one to confront the materiality of media and serves as a significant reminder that media devices are not just ephemeral or transient commodities but can be repurposed, reinterpreted, and reintegrated into contemporary culture.

Practices like circuit bending or modding may be considered through a technologically deterministic lens according to the argument that these practices, while innovative, still operate within the confines of existing

38 Emerging Digital Media Ecologies

technological paradigms. In other words, the creators are not truly free in their artistic expression but are rather 'determined' or limited by the constraints of the original technology. Winner (1980) for example argues that technological artefacts can have political qualities. Albeit that his primary examples focused on larger infrastructures (bridges or nuclear power plants), they nonetheless have theoretical application to practices like circuit bending or modding. From Winner's (1980) perspective, one could argue that modding or circuit bending, while appearing subversive, might still be inherently bound by the politics of the original artefact. For example, a modded video game might still perpetuate certain ideologies or worldviews present in the original game's design, narrative, or mechanics. Similarly, a circuit-bent instrument, while producing novel sounds, might still reflect the consumerist or mass-produced origins of the original toy or device. If one were to use McLuhan's (1964) perspective to examine circuit bending or modding, one might argue that the technologies being modified (video game consoles, electronic toys, and so forth) still exert a significant influence on the end product, despite the creative alterations made by the practitioner. The original medium would still be shaping the message in a determinative way.

For other media scholars, including Raymond Williams (1974), it is the societal context that shapes how technology is perceived and utilised. These practices are not simply products of available technology being simultaneously influenced by cultural desires, such as nostalgia, rebellion against mass-produced culture, or the wish for personal expression. Circuit bending and modding, in turn, might influence cultural narratives about technology. By repurposing and altering existing technologies, practitioners might instead challenge prevailing notions of obsolescence, consumerism, and technological progress. These practices highlight the social choices embedded within technologies such that a video game, for instance, is not at all a neutral piece of entertainment. Its design reflects decisions about narrative, user agency, representation, and so on. Modders, by altering these elements, can bring attention to these embedded choices and perhaps offer alternatives. While Williams would not deny that technology has a shaping effect on culture, he might emphasise the dialectical relationship between the two. Practices like modding and circuit bending would be seen as part of this ongoing negotiation between technology and cultural form.

A thematic resonance can be found here with that of 'imaginary media'. Both ideas explore media not solely from a traditional, evolutionary perspective but delve deeper into alternative narratives and potentialities of media's existence and influence. Imaginary media can be understood as media that, though not yet existing (or may never exist), plays a crucial role in shaping our understanding and conception of present and future media landscapes. The term was introduced by Eric Kluitenberg in *Book of Imaginary Media*

Archaeological and Archival Media **39**

which explores the idea that visions of future technologies, or even depictions of them in science fiction, mythology, and art, have an effect on the actual technological developments that follow. We might recall the case made in a US court that the 'Newspad' in Stanley Kubrick's (1968) film *2001: A Space Odyssey* was an example of 'prior art', featured in a film released over 40 years before the arrival of the first iPad in 2010 and other tablet devices. The allegation suggested that a *New York Times* app Kubrick envisioned for this slimline computer may have anticipated the rise of the modern tablet long before its actual invention (Wigley, 2014).

Drawing parallels, zombie media deals with past technologies, bringing them back to life in unforeseen ways, while imaginary media deals with the potential futures, sometimes influencing the very trajectory of technological development. Both approaches also work to challenge the linear and deterministic models of media evolution, stressing the interplay between past, present, and speculative futures in the development and understanding of media technologies. A nexus between the two can be established in the context of how these 'media'—whether resurrected obsolescences or conceptual futures—interact with the cultural psyche. As Zielinski (2006) posits, it is not the teleological progression of technology that is of prime interest, but the anomalies, the unexpected applications, and the potentialities that they birth. Both zombie and imaginary media can be seen as these anomalies, pushing against the grain of traditional media trajectories.

Moreover, by understanding media as a cyclical phenomenon (zombie media) or as a realm of vast potentialities (imaginary media), we can better grasp the socio-cultural impacts of media. Marshall McLuhan's iconic phrase 'the medium is the message' underscores the notion that the nature of a medium (its structure and form) is as influential, if not more so, than the content it delivers. This holds true for both the revived 'zombies' and the speculative 'imaginaries'. For instance, the very idea of an imaginary technological concept although we might be skating close to this with predicitve alorythms, say, a machine that reads thoughts as depicted in a dystopian novel, might lead to profound debates on privacy, ethics, and human rights long before any such device is even in its nascent stage although, we do now skate close to this by using AI to infer and predict human intentions and desires from vast digital data patterns. Similarly, repurposing an old device in the zombie media context could lead to unforeseen socio-cultural changes, such as those examples presented above in regard to how the resurgence of vinyl in recent times has spawned renewed debates about audio quality, nostalgia, and the tangibility of media. The thematic overlap between zombie and imaginary media then lies in their respective challenge to the mainstream narratives of media history and progress. For medialogy, both are entwined in strengthening a variform, multi-dimensional exploration of media, stressing its role as a dynamic interplay of past possibilities, present realities, and future potentialities.

Conclusion

In exploring the intertwined nature of 'zombie media', 'imaginary media', and the wider purview of media archaeology in this chapter, it becomes evident that our comprehension of media's temporal dynamics is a complex amalgam of intersections, recursions, and speculations. Media Archaeology, as Parikka delineates, offers a rigorous methodology for unearthing the multitudinous and often marginalised trajectories of media history. Within this framework, the resurrectionist ethos of zombie media and the forward-looking speculations of imaginary media operate as complementary modes. Both challenge and extend our conceptions of media's diachronic flow. The cyclical reintroduction of obsolete technologies, epitomised by zombie media, disrupts traditional linear narratives, echoing Zielinski's advocacy for recognising media's deep temporal recursions. Concurrently, the speculative dimension of imaginary media, as Kluitenberg suggests, underscores the forward momentum of media's evolution, shaped by dreams and potentialities of what could be. Ernst's notion of the 'time-critical' processes further enriches this discourse, emphasising the dynamic temporalities inherent in media. Collectively, these concepts underscore a vital argument that the history and future of media are far more intricate and multifaceted than some large, progressive narratives might suggest. Recognising and navigating these complexities is crucial for a holistic understanding of media's ever-evolving landscape. This emphasis in the context of medialogy suggests a broader philosophical stance that critically understanding media requires a balance of respect for its historical trajectories with an openness to its unforeseen futures. This perspective, in turn, can inform a wide array of scholarly and creative endeavours, encouraging challenges to accepted narratives to explore uncharted territories.

3

NETWORK NATURE'S ALGORITHMIC TURN

Next Nature and Techno-Media Ecologies

Within the current 'mediamorphosis', many discussions have centred upon our emerging algorithmic cultures (Lazzeretti, 2023; Galloway, 2006) and their impact on changed behaviour and beliefs more broadly, as well as on values and improving outcomes for people. Spanning the years from the Second World War 1939 to 1945 onwards, machines began to be understood 'not merely as useful things but as custodians of orderliness' (Striphas, 2015, p. 398). The processes of digitalisation, globalisation, and convergence have led to the transition from widespread user engagement with legacy (analogue/'batch') media to 'new media' technologies (or 'loop media') as unpacked in the preceding Chapter 2. Respectively, digitalisation is the process of transforming information into digital formats, facilitating easy access, sharing, and processing (Bounfour, 2016); globalisation encompasses worldwide integration, transcending national boundaries, and is amplified by technological advancements, enhancing global communication and interactions (Scholte, 2005); and, convergence is the merging of distinct technologies, industries, devices into a unified whole, altering media landscape and consumption practices (Jenkins, 2006). Here, convergence sees previously separate industries (telecommunications, information technology, and media) come together to create a synergistic digital ecosystem where the boundaries between these sectors blur, facilitating the seamless flow and accessibility of information and content across various platforms, thereby reshaping communication paradigms and consumer engagement (Dwyer, 2010). A prime example of this is the smartphone which incorporates various

DOI: 10.4324/9781003178149-4

42 Emerging Digital Media Ecologies

technologies into one device including telecommunication, internet browsing, camera functionality, global positioning system (GPS) technology typically for navigating maps, and media players for television, music/video streaming, among others. This has reshaped media consumption, making it more mobile and on-demand where ' "the users" main challenges were related to network traffic and download speeds' (Lotz, 2014, p.84; 2021). New media has generally come to refer to digital forms of communication or entertainment that emerged following the widespread adoption of the internet. These forms of media contrast with 'old' or 'traditional' media, such as print newspapers, film, terrestrial radio, and broadcast television. In many evaluations, there is also a recurring theme characterised by a dualistic interpretation evident in the terminology, specifically, 'old/new'. This approach is in turn related to other binaries critically investigated and challenged as discrete categories at either end of a conceptual continuum, specifically humans versus machines, nature versus culture, living versus non-living, human versus non-human, and materiality versus immateriality.

Central to this discourse is a departure from viewing data merely as a vessel of static knowledge, akin to a fixed star in the firmament of understanding. This traditional perspective reduces data to an inert object, devoid of interaction with its broader context. In contrast, medialogy advocates for a posthumanist and relational lens, where data is perceived as an active participant in a continuous dialogue with both human and non-human elements. This paradigm shift is vital in acknowledging the fluid and ever-evolving nature of knowledge and perception. This approach challenges us to consider data not just as something to be observed but as something to be experienced— the integration of concepts such as multi-species knowledge, Indigenous knowledge, and sentipensar (feel-think) (Escobar 2020) or a:

> non-hierarchical understanding of knowledge, respecting the plurality and diversity of forms of knowledge, empirical, scientific, Western, non-Western as well as love and emotion. This way of conceiving life reveals the multiplicity of social experience, recognising the differences and diversity of ways of understanding the world, promoting ecological balance among people and between people and the environment.
>
> *(Reaes Pinto & Pinto, 2022, p. 314)*

This combined notion further broadens the horizon, advocating for an inclusive, empathetic approach to knowledge that transcends anthropocentric limitations. This chapter represents a clarion call for a fundamental re-evaluation of the relationship between data, nature, and embodiment. It urges us to adopt a more fluid, interconnected approach to understanding the world, recognising the intricate interplay of relationships that define our existence. By embracing this paradigm, we can foster a more diverse, empathetic, and sustainable engagement with the world, one that truly reflects the complexity and dynamism of the data-embodied experience.

In this chapter, medialogy is further unpacked in re-evaluating deeply evocative futures, moving away from such binary understandings to an alternative in which humans, species, and intelligent systems increasingly engage together in symbiotically connected experiences via continuous flows of data and information exchanges. Through this paradigm, medialogy advocates for an integrative exploration of media and mediation processes, which encompasses not only the intricacies of language, symbols, and meaning-making but also delves deep into the aesthetic and poetic realms of art, music, and literature. This framework acknowledges the vast interplay between form, pattern, and method, as well as the intricate connections between materials, energy, and information technologies. At its core, it seeks to understand the nuances of human cognition, practice, emotion, identity, and social interactions—the mind–body connection within its diverse affiliations and communities, spanning sectors like art, politics, economics, environment, and education. By bridging histories with futures and embedding this within evolving socio-cultural systems, the paradigm also underscores the dynamic nature of contexts, systems, and environments, always factoring in evolutionary and ecological perspectives. Furthermore, this paradigm places an emphasis on corporeality, viewing the human body not as an isolated entity but as intricately interwoven with various technologies, techniques, and technics. This perspective enables examination of the lived experiences within any given context, paying close attention to the transformative impacts that technological and technical advancements have on our sense of self, embodiment, and social interactions.

The detailed insights of human–computer interactions (HCI) also intersect with the broader narratives of medialogy, particularly as our global community confronts the far-reaching cultural ramifications of pervasive computing and the ubiquity of digital media. HCI bridges the nexus between individual users and digital technologies. As medialogy affords an exploration of media environments and their effects on human perception and values, HCI's focus on usability and experience aligns with concerns about technology's influence. For example, the constant connectivity via smartphones alters behaviours and cognition; affects attention spans, communication patterns, and societal norms; and restructures social rituals (Turkle, 2011; Carr, 2010). The evolution of immersive technologies, such as augmented reality (AR), virtual reality (VR), and brain–computer interface (BCI) (see Agnihotri & Bhattacharya, 2023), continues to affect like osmosis the boundaries between users and digital media.

In essence, the medialogy paradigm champions a holistic approach, through multi-discipline conversations, to understanding the complex interrelationships between media, mediation processes, technologies, human experiences, and

44 Emerging Digital Media Ecologies

the broader socio-cultural and environmental landscape that hosts us. This chapter delves into the transformative effects of media on culture and societal structures. It is deeply invested in exploring the broader philosophical and societal shifts driven by media's omnipresence through the notion of next nature.

Navigating the Next Nature: Medialogy in the Age of Digital Interconnectedness

Employing the lens of 'next nature', this section delves into the expansive and complex landscapes of techno-media ecologies, unveiling the particularised interplay between technology, media, and the evolving digital mediascape. The fundamental premise postulates a dynamic where our technologically saturated environments morph into a new form of nature, an evolution driven by humanity. At a time designated as an Anthropocene epoch, a discernible surge in endeavours to intertwine natural processes with cultural practices emerges, forging a distinct narrative of hybridisation. Artist, technologist, and philosopher Koert van Mensvoort's (2012) conceptualisation of next nature serves as a linchpin in this narrative, heralding a period in which people, nature, and technology engage in a subtle choreography, each interplaying with and influencing the other. This symbiotic nexus not only reconfigures the contours of human interaction with the natural and digital realm but also unveils a rich terrain for investigating the transformative role of media and communications in narrating and navigating this hybrid landscape. In many respects, medialogy encapsulates this sentiment. For van Mensvoort (2012, p. 31):

> Many agree that nature is vanishing. Untouched nature is increasingly rare. But while the wilderness retreats, the hard boundaries between nature and culture are disappearing too. The stock market is controlled by an ecosystem of autonomous computer programs. A 'natural' tomato is a marvel of selective breeding and genetic engineering.

In exploring the diverse terrains of medialogy, it is necessary to be aware that information embodies essences of quantity and magnitude, each dimension intricately influencing the contours and the vibrancy of communicative landscapes that we navigate. As Neil Postman (1979) has articulated, information patterns (and by extension various media) are not a set of neutral tools—but actively shape our cognitive processes, social structures, and cultural narratives. It is obvious that 'where information is codified in electrical impulses and moved at the speed of light, there must be a knowledge explosion' (Postman, 1979, p. 243). We find this born out in the now familiar. Social media is an immediate example via platforms such as Facebook, Mastodon, Bluesky, Threads, X, Instagram, LinkedIn, and TikTok which facilitate communication, entertainment, and sharing of information among users. They have become (to varying degrees respectively) major sources of news, opinion, and discussion. Blogs on websites such as Medium, WordPress, and Blogger have allowed individuals and organisations to publish written content for immediate access to a potentially global audience. Podcasts spanning an incredibly wide range of topics as audio content can be distributed and consumed globally and have evolved into a popular means of storytelling, news, interviews, and more. Video Streaming Services on platforms such as YouTube, Vimeo, Twitch, and TikTok have transformed the creation and consumption of video content, from user-generated clips to full-length movies and series. Online News Outlets have also contributed additional sources of media content and forums for public discussion (many traditional news organisations have digital outlets with a number existing as solely online sources such as BuzzFeed, HuffPost, and The Daily Beast). E-books and Digital Publishing for their part contribute to the vast circulation of information across transnational borders (this includes not only traditional books in digital form but also self-published works, fan fiction, and more interactive, multimedia experiences) as does Online Gaming and e-Sports (online multiplayer games, game streaming services, and competitive e-Sports leagues represent another rapidly growing facet of new media). Immersive technology and associated virtual production techniques such as VR and AR are creating new ways to experience media, from games to interactive narratives to virtual tours and for immersive education. Moreover, artists can create, sell, and distribute their works digitally in ways that were previously impossible with the rise of blockchain technology and non-fungible tokens (NFTs).

For its part, Blockchain is a decentralised and secure digital ledger technology that records transactions across a distributed network of computers. It ensures transparency and immutability by storing data in 'blocks' that are cryptographically linked and validated through consensus mechanisms like 'proof of work' or 'proof of stake'. This distributed nature eliminates the need for central intermediaries, arguably enhancing the system's resilience to fraud and cyber-attacks. By enabling verifiable and tamper-resistant record-keeping, blockchain supports various applications beyond cryptocurrencies, including smart contracts, supply chain management, and digital identity verification. Blockchain technology is pivotal in securing NFT transactions, offering authenticity, provenance, and security (Davis, 2023). It embeds a unique identifier and digital fingerprint (hash) for each NFT, documenting its creation, history, and ownership changes on the digital ledger. This, coupled with advanced encryption, shields NFTs from tampering and counterfeiting. Furthermore, blockchain's decentralised nature diminishes fraud and manipulation risks, fostering transparency and trust within the NFT ecosystem. Smart contracts on the blockchain streamline processes like royalty payments and ownership transfers, mitigating the need for intermediaries. Platforms like

Ethereum have led the NFT domain, underpinning these transactions and functionalities (Davis, 2023).

Together Blockchain and NFTs can transform artists' abilities to monetise and distribute digital art. NFTs ensure provenance, granting unique ownership to digital pieces (Berg, Davidson, & Potts, 2019). As a paradigm shift, NFTs in digital art represent an opportunity in terms of diversification and investment highlighting a developing sector using new technology to protect digital ownership (Boido & Aliano, 2023). Beeple's US$69M artwork sale exemplifies unprecedented earning potential via platforms like SuperRare (Reyburn, 2021). Additionally, artists may bypass traditional intermediaries, sometimes seen as gatekeepers, like galleries or auction houses, to directly access global audiences through online platforms like OpenSea, Rarible, and SuperRare and retain more of the profit. Before NFTs, digital art struggled with the concept of 'originality' because of easy replication. NFTs, being unique digital tokens, validate the authenticity and ownership of a digital piece, allowing artists to sell 'original' digital works. NFT platforms often have mechanisms where artists can earn a percentage of sales every time the NFT is resold, ensuring they benefit from the appreciation of their work. Of course, while NFTs offer new opportunities, they are also subject to criticism. The environmental impact of blockchain, the speculative nature of the market, and concerns over plagiarism are among the challenges the NFT art world faces. Several artists and creators have benefitted from this new model, but like all disruptive technologies, the landscape is evolving, and long-term implications are still unfolding.

And again, technologies are not neutral. As underscored by Winston (1990):

> They embody ideas, needs, imagination, and possibilities from specific periods and places. They are particular solutions to certain problems, usually not the only possible solutions. The same problem identified in another cultural context might find a quite different solution; for example, different architectural styles based on a variety of building materials have developed in different climatic and geographic regions, but all satisfy the basic need for shelter. Yet technologies can often have such profound impacts that we even define historical epochs on the basis of technological distinctions, from the 'iron age' to the 'industrial age' and even 'postindustrial society'. Technologies also have histories, usually a number of histories.

It is well documented then that just as we transitioned from the 'iron age', to agrarian societies marked by the domestication of plants and animals, to industrialised societies with mechanised production at their core, many have experienced the rise of a communications revolution characterised by digital interconnectedness. The above-mentioned ubiquity of smartphones and high-speed internet has fostered this environment where individuals can communicate instantaneously across vast geographical distances. Social media have become normalised for personal and professional interactions. Moreover, the COVID-19 pandemic accelerated the transition to extended periods of remote working and learning, demonstrating the critical role of digital communication technologies in maintaining societal functions and expectations. This paradigmatic shift mirrors the iterative process of societal metamorphosis, where each epoch is delineated by distinctive technological advancements and corresponding socio-cultural adaptations. The communications revolution, much like its agricultural and industrial predecessors, signifies a profound shift in the ways societal structures function, marking a departure from industrialised tangibility to digital ubiquity, thereby reshaping the nexus of human interaction, economic modalities, and cultural discourse (Castells, 2010; Benkler & Nissenbaum, 2006), and more.

This dialogic evolution underscores the profound role of media and communication technologies in shaping, mediating, and reflecting our understanding and engagement with the natural world and the socio-technological milieu. The concept of hybridisation signifies not merely a blend but a complex interplay and mutual shaping among these domains, a narrative where technology morphs into an extension or a reflection of both human and natural processes. By extension, 'biomedia' (taken up in Chapter 4) is an instance in which biological components and processes are informatically recontextualised for purposes that may be either biological or nonbiological. In questioning 'what the body can do' where the disciplines of computer science and molecular biology intermingle, the link between biological processes and media is given an evanescent register by Thacker (2004):

> Biomedia are novel configurations of biologies and technologies that take us beyond the familiar tropes of technology-as-tool, the cyborg, or the human-computer interface. 'Biomedia' describes an ambivalence that is not reducible to either technophilia (the rhetoric of enabling technology) or technophobia (the ideologies of technological determinism). Biomedia are particular mediations of the body, optimizations of the biological in which 'technology' appears to disappear altogether. With biomedia, the biological body is not hybridized with the machine, as it is in the use of mechanical prosthetics or artificial organs. Nor is it supplanted by the machine, as it is in the many science-fictional fantasies of 'uploading' the mind into the disembodied space of the computer. In fact, we can say that biomedia has no body-anxiety, if by this we mean the will to transcend the base contingencies of 'the meat' in favor of virtual spaces.

The term animism, for its part, evokes a sense of vitality and agency amidst this triad of human, nature, and technology (see Chapter 8). This recalls debates in media and communications about the extent of technology's agency, its role as an active constituent in social relations, and its capacity to mediate our perceptions of, and interactions with, the natural world. The animistic experience here, however, invites a re-evaluation of conventional binaries often upheld in the field—subject/object, natural/artificial, human/machine, among others because each is (or may be) increasingly integrated. Furthermore, the narrative of next nature presents an opportunity to delve into the ways media and communication practices are situated within and contribute to broader socio-cultural and ecological dialogues.

For instance, the proliferation of digital media platforms has not only altered human interaction but has reshaped our engagement with nature, through phenomena like virtual ecotourism (see, for example, virtual island talks that cover reef walks, snorkelling, and bird watching, as well as nursery tours and tours about the island's history <https://ladyelliot.com.au/virtual-tours/>) or digital activism for climate change with the remit to expand climate change advocacy, perception change, and awareness about environmental conservation (see, for example, the initiative of the Africa Region Social and Behaviour Change Communication Consultation <https://devcomsnetwork.org/update/africa-region-sbcc-consultation-programme-overview-march-22-23-2022-webinar>) as well as advances in BCI. As mentioned above, BCI captures and translates brain signals into computer commands, enabling direct communication between the brain and external devices such that they can enable individuals with paralysis to control wheelchairs, computers, or other devices using only their thoughts. For example, BrainGate offers systems that allow those affected by neurologic disease, paralysis, or limb loss to move a cursor on a screen, control robotic arms, or have speech restored (www.braingate.org/). Emotiv BCI enables players to interact with video games using brainwave patterns and wireless EEG headsets and software (www.emotiv.com/).

In line with Baudrillard (1981), we navigate now the hyperreal terrains constructed by digital media and associated technologies, which blur the lines between the real and the simulated. In drawing parallels between media ecology and next nature, this book essentially argues that the media landscape is not a passive background, but an active ecology—dynamic, influential, and transformative. It becomes a kind of nature in itself, a nature birthed from silicon, code, and waves, but nature nonetheless (van Mensvoort & Grievink, 2011). Just as the biomes of our planet—from rainforests to deserts—have their unique characteristics and evolutionary pressures, so too do the digital realms we inhabit, from social media platforms to virtual realities. The stakes of understanding this new environment are high. As Innis (1951) observed, shifts in dominant media forms—from oral to written, from print to electronic—have profound ramifications for culture, power dynamics, and knowledge structures. If we accept the premise of next nature then the critical enquiry within medialogy is neither just about understanding tools nor the platforms, but about navigating and potentially stewarding a new kind of wilderness. From McLuhan's (1964) oft-cited axiom, 'The medium is the message' we are reminded that technologies and media do not merely transmit content but may sculpt our sensory balance, social relationships, and modes of perception. The environment they create arguably becomes as integral to our experience as natural landscapes. Thus, the conceptual analogy of next nature provides an evocative lens.

This synthesis of next nature and medialogy offers both a fresh perspective and a profound depth of understanding. It asks us to reconsider our place within the media-saturated environments, prompting reflection not just on how we use media but on how the various media forms—and the vast digital ecosystems they/we create—shape the contours of our existence (see Manovich, 2002). A conceptual understanding of users might now be that, for better or worse, we are increasingly one and the same as other non-human interconnected matter—another variable in the network of networks (Latour, 2005). Moving this forward, Coyne (2018, p. 6) counters suggestions that nature should succumb to the sovereignty of data in the algorithmic turn to affirmatively suggest that 'data is just a by-product of the transfer of signs between communicants, agents, elements and the things of nature'. What 'we' do with data—how it is collected, interpreted, curated, stored, and circulated—is, however, significant. While Coyne's arguments might be agreeable and persuasive, data is nevertheless moving in/across liminal spaces of brackish indistinguishability whereby some hidden/dark data is increasingly in our most freely accessible 'light' (open) spaces such as refrigerators, digital home 'assistants' such as the Google Nest, Amazon Alexa, Apple's Siri, or Amazon's Echo Dot to organisations' doorbells and our cars with implications for individual privacy, corporate cyber security, and information manipulation.

An Exploration of 'Next Nature'

The concept of 'Next Nature' articulates a vision where technology and culture become an emergent extension or a new layer of nature, morphing together in an evolutionary process that transcends traditional separations between the natural and the artificial. This perspective challenges the dichotomy of nature versus technology, advocating for a more nuanced, symbiotic understanding of their intertwined existence. An illustration of the next nature can be seen in the advent of Genetically Modified Organisms (GMOs). Through this lens, genetic modification, while controversial for the economic powers exerted over crop control and the like, is seen not as an alien force imposed on nature, but rather as an extension of human ingenuity that unfolds within the broader context of natural evolution. In this narrative, the technology of genetic engineering intertwines with biological processes to yield new strains of plants or animals, embodying a juncture where human technological prowess becomes a driver of natural evolution. In the realm of new media next nature also finds expression in the digital landscapes and virtual realities that are fast becoming extensions of our natural environment. Take, for instance, the evolving metaverse—using VR, AR, and digital 3D worlds. It is the collective virtual shared space created by the convergence of virtually enhanced physical reality and physically persistent VR being championed by companies such as Meta as well as Microsoft to Nvidia, Unity, Roblox, Snap, and smaller companies and start-ups (see Figure 3.1).

In recent years, the metaverse has emerged as a captivating manifestation of next nature—denoting the convergence of the born and the made—wherein technology becomes so intricately intertwined with our natural world that it becomes a part of it. The metaverse, embodying a network of interconnected, immersive digital domains, reveals a phase where digital and physical realities might be understood not as polarised, but rather exist along a continuum (World Economic Forum, 2022). This dynamic becomes crucial in the context of frictionless smart cities to smart farms, which aim to significantly elevate the quality of life through technological infrastructure and operational improvements. The discourse around metaverse and smart cities and farms is not merely an examination of advanced technological integration, but a step into a realm where technology emulates, supplements, and extends natural processes. The fusion of the metaverse exemplifies a stride towards a novel ecosystem where interactions, governance, and urban functionalities to agriculture each transcend traditional boundaries. It creates a techno-natural environment where urban living to smart farming and agriculture are augmented and enriched through virtual capabilities, essentially redefining the boundaries between the organic and the artificial.

At the intersection of the digital economy and traditional agriculture, smart farming powers traditional agriculture with data-centric methodologies and intelligent technologies through multiple facets of the agricultural process—from seeding to harvesting—and is optimised through the lens of digital analytics. This merger manifests a comprehensive transformation in digital agricultural practices, to boost productivity and improve safety, rendering farming more precise, communicative, and actionable through digital channels. Central is the integration of the Internet of Things (IoT) which facilitates perpetual connectivity and real-time data analysis. IoT, alongside Artificial Intelligence (AI), machine learning, and blockchain technologies, orchestrates a multifaceted communicative matrix that may accrue a diverse array of data from the agricultural environment. This data, when processed through advanced AI algorithms, engenders predictive insights that are crucial for informed decision-making, resource optimisation, and risk mitigation. Machine learning augments this analytic mechanism by iteratively refining the accuracy and predictive capacity of the system, embodying a progressive

Network Nature's Algorithmic Turn 51

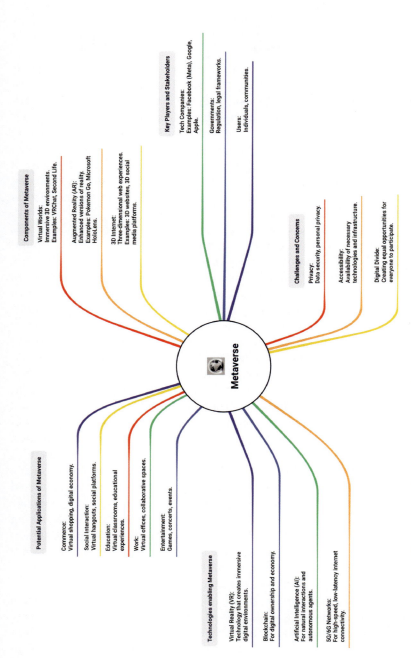

FIGURE 3.1 Socio-Technological Concept Map of the Metaverse.
Source: Created by the author.

learning curve in agricultural practices. Blockchain technology can infuse a level of transparency and traceability, fostering a secure digital economy within the agrarian sector, and thereby fostering trust among the involved stakeholders.

This digital frontier offers alternative spaces for interaction, commerce, and expression, expanding the natural realm into digital dimensions. The metaverse can be understood as a next nature where digital environments become as palpable and influential as physical landscapes. This narrative extends the traditional evolutionary discourse, recognising human technological intervention as a catalytic force propelling nature into unchartered territories. It invites a richer philosophical engagement with the evolving definitions of nature in contemporary times saturated with human-made realities, encouraging a deeper exploration of our environmental and ethical responsibilities within this expanded narrative of nature.

The global trajectory towards the metaverse, characterised as this network of immersive, interconnected digital realms, may carry profound implications for the evolution of smart cities. Smart cities, aimed at elevating citizens' quality of life through infrastructural enhancements, modernised governmental services, and economic acceleration, find a valuable ally in the metaverse to potentially revolutionise urban landscapes. For example, by reducing commutes where people work from home or can interact virtually, thus lowering carbon emissions, smart cities are argued to support sustainability and improve the quality of life. As Yaqoob, Salah, Jayaraman, and Omar (2023) found in their recent study, the metaverse can revolutionise various aspects of smart cities, including healthcare, energy management, transportation, smart homes, supply chain and logistics, tourism, retail, and banking. Projections by Gartner (research and consulting for businesses in the IT sector) suggest that by 2026, a quarter of the global population would spend an hour daily in the metaverse, and '30% of the organisations in the world will have products and services ready for metaverse' hinting at a booming virtual economy (Rimol, 2022). Significantly, investments directed towards metaverse technologies are surging, with US-based tech giants like Meta platforms, Microsoft, and Asian firms like ByteDance and Alibaba taking the lead. Further demonstration of support sees the United Arab Emirates (UAE) announce plans in 2022 to create a virtual city in the metaverse and the ambitious plan by Seoul to allocate $3.3 billion towards metamorphosing into a metaverse city by 2030 (O'Donovan, 2022).

Nevertheless, Yaqoob et al. (2023) also underscore that several pivotal challenges obstruct the full realisation of the metaverse's potential. These encompass issues related to interoperability, security and privacy, robust network infrastructure, and data management. Additionally, concerns around digital addiction, legal jurisdictions, and environmental repercussions arising from the demands on natural resources will necessitate focused attention across interoperability standards, robust cybersecurity measures, and sustainable practices to mitigate environmental impacts. The discourse encapsulates the profound potential the metaverse holds in reshaping societies (not least in so-called smart cities), while outlining the exigent challenges and prospective research directions to actualise such emerging digital frontiers.

In this age of rapid technological evolution, the way we understand nature itself is necessarily undergoing a profound transformation. Koert van Mensvoort's (2012) notion of next nature illuminates this interplay between humanity, technology, and the environment. This view, which sees our technologically mediated environment evolving into a new iteration of nature, resists the traditional binaries of nature versus artificiality. In such an era where technology—like the nature of old—grows, adapts, and at times burgeons beyond human control, the work of Marshall McLuhan (1975) offers a way to navigate and understand this transition. One of McLuhan's most instrumental tools for deciphering the effects of a medium is his tetrad: (1)What does the medium amplify or enhance? (2) What does the medium make obsolete? (3) What does the medium retrieve that had been obsolesced earlier? and (4) What does the medium reverse or flip into when pushed to extremes? (McLuhan, 1975, pp. 75–6). By applying this tetradic framework to the next nature, important insights emerge. Our technological innovations, from AI to biotechnologies, are enhancing and extending our capacity to design and modulate our environments. This is analogous to how The Gutenberg Press revolutionised communication and extended the reach of the written word. Concurrently, as this 'technological nature' expands, what we understand as pristine wilderness and unmediated experiences begin to fade.

The notion also evokes Neil Postman's (1985) poignant observation regarding the loss of the 'typographic mind' in the televisual age. Postman asserts that print fostered depth, sustained attention, and logical argumentation, cultivating a populace that valued reasoned debate. In contrast, television, with its emphasis on the visual, entertainment, and brevity, diminished critical thinking and deep discourse. This shift was seen to not only alter individual cognition but also threaten the very essence of democratic deliberation by prioritising amusement over substantive dialogue. Further, in the phenomenon described as 'radical pessimism' (Curran, 1998), programs were provided under a commercial model according to what audiences wanted rather than what might afford a 'public benefit' such as information or opinions which might add to or challenge an audience member's personal beliefs. To be more specific, the commercial model afforded broadcasters the ability to attract greater audience numbers by offering the public what they wanted in terms of what suits their existing knowledge base or schema, personal beliefs and preferences. This 'dumbed down' content is considered preferable to audiences because it arguably produces less anxiety than material invoking questioning, analysis, and challenge. In the face of 'ever-new' media and technologies, one

54 Emerging Digital Media Ecologies

can only speculate about the possibilities of VR experiences that may adjust content in real time based on the viewer's heartbeat, or movie narratives might shift based on a viewer's eye movement or skin conductivity.

Drawing instead on the perspective that media afford great opportunity for encouraging critical thinking, one might point to the remit of Public Service Broadcasting (public broadcasting as a service to the public) including educating citizens to employ reasonable choice, ethics, and the duty of 'responsible citizens to be informed and have opinions about current affairs' (Livingstone and Lunt, 1994, p. 8); and, by promoting the public interest that is based upon universal access and the circulation of full information, contributes to the democratisation of everyday life, in both public and private contexts (Scannell, 1989). In accord with Habermas' (1989) theory of the public sphere, the British Broadcasting Corporation (BBC)/Independent Broadcasting Authority (IBA) (1985) is a view of the public sphere in relation to public broadcasting as:

> [a]n arena of social interaction within which public opinion is formed and mobilised by a reasoned public. (...) an arena of debate governed by rules of rational discourse, that is to say access to full information by all participants and resolution of disagreement on the basis of evidence and logical argument rather than differential force. The aim of the debate is to arrive at a consensus on the public good.

McLuhan's own assertion that electric media leads to retrieval of tribal collectives and a return to oral traditions also finds resonance here. That is, historically, tribal or communal rituals were designed as shared experiences that aimed at creating collective emotional and physiological responses. Dances, songs, and narratives were structured to evoke communal feelings, shared emotions, and physiological synchrony. With biometric media, we see the potential return to a media form that aims not just at intellectual engagement but at physiological and emotional synchrony. In essence, biometric media is retrieving the communal physiological experience of tribal rituals. The final aspect of McLuhan's tetrad, the reversal, is illuminated when we consider the potential extremes of next nature. Pushed to its boundaries, there is a distinct possibility of the medium transforming into the environment itself. McLuhan's prophecy of a global village, wrought by electric technology, can perhaps be succeeded by a 'bio-village' shaped by the confluence of biotechnologies, AI, and vast digital networks. Increasingly and deeply entrenched in media now, understanding and critiquing our next nature becomes an academic and societal imperative. As technology matures and advances into its own form of nature, scholars, especially those wielding data and analytical tools, are uniquely poised to dissect and critique its multifaceted impacts. In this age where distinctions between technology and the organic blur, engaging with next nature is not just a choice for media ecologists, but a duty of paramount significance for the informed evolution of society in an increasingly interconnected world. These mediums are not mere tools but actively mould our cognitive structures, influencing both individual perceptions and collective discourses.

Quantum Computing: Networked Nature and Digital Futures

Quantum Computing

One of the main motivations propelling the advancements in quantum information science is the allure of developing rapid quantum algorithms capable of addressing pivotal computational problems efficiently. Physicist, David Deutsch, significantly pioneered quantum computation by introducing the first explicit model. He conceptualised Quantum Turing Machines and Quantum Circuits, delineating a new computational framework harnessing quantum mechanical principles (Deutsch, 1985). His seminal work ignited explorations into the profound capabilities and properties of quantum computational models, thus bridging classical computation theories with quantum dynamics. For its part, quantum computing is a type of computing that uses the principles of quantum mechanics, which is a part of physics that deals with tiny particles such as electrons and photons. These particles can exist in multiple states simultaneously, which is different from the computers we use today that process 'bits' as either 0s or 1s (as a series of zero and one digits). Moreover, in quantum computing, thanks to 'superposition', a qubit can be *both* 0 and 1 at the same time, and also any proportion of 0 and 1. To explain this simultaneity, imagine you are playing a video game where you can choose to go through multiple doors at the same time instead of just one. In regular computing, you would have to choose one door and see what is behind it, and then go back and choose another door if the first was not the right one. But in quantum computing, it is as if you can split into copies of yourself and go through all the doors at the same time to quickly find what you are looking for. Quantum computers use qubits, which are like the player in this video game. Each qubit can explore different possibilities at the same time because it can be in multiple states (like the player being in multiple rooms). This allows quantum computers to look at many different solutions at once and find answers much faster than traditional computers, which have to check each possibility one by one. Because each qubit can be in multiple states at once, quantum computers can handle a vast number of calculations all at once. Now, imagine that in the game, when you decide to split and send your character down multiple paths, there is a magic spell that links two or more of these split versions together. This spell is like quantum entanglement. Whatever happens to one character instantly affects the other linked characters, no matter how far apart they have moved in the game world. For instance, if one character finds a treasure, the others might instantly gain a clue or a key that helps in their own paths. In quantum computing, entangled qubits behave similarly, that is, the state of one qubit directly influences another, no matter the physical distance. This allows coordinated decision-making and problem-solving on a scale that is impossible with classical computers. Through scrutinising quantum models' properties, Deutsch has laid a substantial theoretical foundation that has spurred further advancements in quantum computation, ultimately steering the discourse towards realising quantum algorithms and quantum information processing. This seminal work marked a pivotal stride in evolving computational paradigms to leverage inherent quantum phenomena and is a field of study that undergirds chemistry, biology, engineering, and more.

The discourse surrounding quantum computing, with its potential and intricacies, also works for the broader narrative of the next natures, the evolving interplay between the born and the made, between the organic and the engineered (Koert van Mensvoort, 2020). The deceptively simple, yet profoundly complex, shift from binary bits to quantum bits or qubits manifests as a seminal departure from the deterministic to the probabilistic, from the linear to the exponential (Nielsen & Chuang, 2010, p. 13). When transposed to the quantum realm, quantum computing flourishes into a landscape of probabilistic and non-linear computational paradigms, facilitated by the inherent properties of quantum bits (qubits). This quantum realm, characterised by superposition and entanglement, transcends the binary rigidity, offering a canvas of exponentially augmented computational possibilities. Quantum computing might also suggest a new symbiosis between natural quantum phenomena and human technological innovation.

This shift resonates with the ethos of next natures which seeks to engage with, rather than subdue, the complexity and unpredictability inherent in the natural world. The principle of superposition, where a qubit can exist in multiple states simultaneously, obliterates the binary rigidity of classical computing, proposing instead a fluid, nuanced computational realm that is more in sync with the probabilistic and uncertain nature of the quantum world. The ostensibly cryptic principles of quantum mechanics, when harnessed through quantum computing, promise to revolutionise contemporary communication frameworks, potentially leading to the establishment of exceedingly secure, highly efficient, and ultra-fast communication networks (Nielsen & Chuang, 2010). The horizon of communications futures holds the promise of a transformative amalgamation with quantum computing principles for speciality devices and applications. Despite the technical barriers on the road towards large-scale quantum communications, the inexorable progress in quantum computing and quantum cryptography is step by step nearing the threshold of a new era in quantum communications, endowed with the capacity for increased security and formidable efficiency.

For example, at the forefront of this nexus between quantum computing and communication is Quantum Key Distribution (QKD) which leverages quantum principles (powerful for tasks involving vast amounts of data and complex calculations) to facilitate the exchange of cryptographic keys between parties in a communication protocol, ensuring that any eavesdropping attempt is detectably exposed (Bennett & Brassard, 2014). Cryptography serves as a medium to facilitate confidential communication between two entities. For instance, an individual wanting to make a purchase online needs to send their credit card details across the internet in a manner that ensures that only the concerned company acquires access to the number. This quantum-enabled security paradigm augments the robustness of communications, particularly indispensable in critical infrastructure and confidential information exchange scenarios. Another example of communications futures is the Quantum Internet. The eventual establishment of a Quantum Internet is envisaged as a cornerstone for secure global communications (Kimble, 2008). Quantum entanglement and superposition, the linchpins of quantum computing, are fundamental to the development of quantum networks capable of enabling instantaneous and secure data transmission over long distances. Teleportation of Information or Quantum Teleportation, albeit a misnomer in terms of transporting matter, relates to the instantaneous transfer of information between qubits located at different locales, undergirded by quantum entanglement (Bouwmeester, Pan, Mattle, Eibl, Weinfurter, & Zeilinger, 1997). This phenomenon, when fully harnessed, could spur revolutionary enhancements in communication speeds and efficiencies. Quantum computing also seeks to redefine the channel capacities for both classical and quantum information— (Holevo, 1973). The strides in understanding and exploiting quantum channel capacities could lead to a new period in communication systems characterised by unprecedented data throughput and reduced latency. Moreover, Quantum error-correction codes, essential for mitigating decoherence (when qubits lose their quantum properties) and other quantum noise (any kind of disturbance or fluctuation that affects the state of qubits and leads to errors in computation like flaws in the quantum computer's design, imperfect operations, or external environmental influences) are all pivotal to ensuring the reliability and fidelity of quantum communications (Shor, 1994, 1995). These codes will form the backbone of robust quantum communication networks.

Networked Entanglement

Quantum entanglement, a phenomenon that has puzzled and intrigued scientists since the days of Einstein, epitomises a level of interconnectedness and non-locality that is foundational to the vision of next natures (Ekert & Jozsa, 1996). In a technologically interconnected world, the phenomenon of entanglement echoes the complex, networked relationships that are the hallmark of our global societal structures. The ability of entangled qubits to communicate instantaneously across spatial separations hints at a new 'ontology' of interconnectedness, where actions and consequences are deeply entwined across the fabric of society. The potential application domains of quantum computing range from drug discovery to financial modelling, align with the aspirations of next natures to harness the power of technological innovation in addressing complex, real-world challenges (Shor, 1994; Grover, 1996). The essence of next natures lies in transcending artificial boundaries and engaging with a holistic, integrated understanding of the world. Quantum computing, with its potential to navigate through high-dimensional problem spaces and provide solutions to hitherto intractable problems, embodies this essence. Furthermore, the intersection of quantum computing and AI opens up a fertile ground for exploring new paradigms of computational intelligence that are more aligned with the holistic, networked, and non-linear description of next natures (Preskill, 2018). The evolving narrative of quantum computing invites contemplation on the larger philosophical and existential dialogue surrounding next natures. As quantum computing strives to transcend the binary limitations of classical computing and harness the potential of quantum phenomena, it is emblematic of a broader attempt to forge a new symbiosis between the organic and the engineered, between the determined and the probabilistic, in a quest to navigate the complex challenges of the contemporary world.

In the narrative of quantum computing, where classical bits give way to quantum bits or qubits, exploiting the enigmatic principles of superposition and entanglement, lies the potential for a prodigious leap in information processing capability. This potentially exponential amplification of computational capacity is not merely a theoretical exercise but augments the practical outlook for an interconnected world, resonating with Fernández-Caramés's notion of accelerating towards a post-quantum IoT landscape (2020). That is, IoT devices generate vast amounts of data that need to be processed and analysed; and for its part, quantum computing, with superior processing power, could handle this massive data more efficiently than classical computers. They could analyse data from sensors and devices faster, leading to quicker responses and more intelligent IoT systems. For instance, in smart cities, quantum computers could quickly process data from thousands of sensors to optimise traffic flow, pollution emissions levels, power usage, and emergency services in real time. The trajectory of miniaturisation and advancements in electrical battery capacity aligns with the underpinnings of quantum computing. As quantum digital components continue to shrink in size while expanding in computational capability, they meld seamlessly with the evolving telecommunication infrastructures, facilitating a robust and expansive network. This juxtaposition lays the fertile ground for IoT systems to expand from a micro-level embedding amongst biological entities to a macro-level orchestration governed by geo-satellites circumnavigating the globe. Yet, this narrative of augmentation and interconnectivity carries with it the caveat of surveillance and security and paints a picture of a supralevel surveillance ecosystem, born from the marriage of quantum computing and IoT. That is, quantum computing's potential to significantly expedite processes like machine learning, noted in prior discussions, resonates with the envisioned advanced networks' ontogenetic capacity to find strange patterns in data and foster a supralevel surveillance regime. The granular level of surveillance, ranging from the personal to the global, transcends conventional security paradigms, urging a need for robust security frameworks.

In this quantum-IoT narrative, the dichotomy of quantum computing reveals itself—a tool for bolstering security and a potential threat to privacy. On one side of the coin, quantum computing heralds a new era of cryptography, potentially fortifying the security frameworks safeguarding the IoT infrastructure (Shor, 1994). Yet, it also possesses the capability to dismantle existing cryptographic paradigms, exposing a vast network of IoT systems to nefarious exploits. From this viewpoint, the interplay between quantum computing and the envisioned coupling with IoT ecosystem elucidates a multifaceted narrative. The amalgam of quantum computing, with its promise of computational alacrity, and the IoT, with its essence of pervasive connectivity, beckons a future replete with possibilities yet encumbered by challenges. The quantum leap in surveillance and security paradigms necessitates a proactive engagement with quantum-resistant cryptographic measures, ensuring that the intended acceleration towards a post-quantum-IoT landscape is anchored in robust security and privacy tenets. But there are additional socio-technological facets.

The Great Acceleration

The Great Acceleration, a phrase often employed to encapsulate the stark, human-induced modifications to global systems, encompasses a myriad of factors extending beyond views of security and privacy alone. This term epitomises an era marked by exponential advancements in technology, wherein quantum computing, AI, and the IoT constitute mere facets of a larger, intricate orchestration (Steffen, Broadgate, Deutsch, Gaffney, & Ludwig, 2015). The ecological and social ramifications of this acceleration are profound, marking a scenario wherein rapid urbanisation, resource exploitation, and a burgeoning global population are interwoven with technological innovation in complex ways (McNeill & Engelke, 2016). Economic dynamics undergo drastic metamorphosis as new industries sprout and existing ones transmogrify or obsolesce in the face of automation and digitalisation (Brynjolfsson & McAfee, 2014). This accelerative phase also implicates a drastic alteration in energy demands, heralding a shift towards more sustainable energy solutions to satiate the exigencies of a technologically driven society (Cherp, Vinichenko, Jewell, Brutschin, & Sovacool, 2018). Furthermore, the cultural settings of societies are reconfigured as global connectivity redefines the way individuals interact,

60 Emerging Digital Media Ecologies

share, and influence each other across traditional geographical and cultural delineations (Castells, 2010). In the realm of governance, policy-making grows rapidly into an increasingly convoluted endeavour as governments grapple with (1) the regulation of burgeoning technologies, (2) mitigation of socio-economic disparities, and (3) navigation through a rapidly transmuting global landscape (Kahane, 2017). In essence, the 'great acceleration' is a multi-dimensional phenomenon—amalgamating technological, economic, social, and environmental dynamics into a crucible of change—with reverberations into the future.

Revisiting the earlier discussed exemplar of the metaverse, which embodies a network of interconnected, immersive digital domains, the advent of quantum computing introduces a new dimension to this discourse. The mammoth computational power of quantum computers potentially accelerates the realisation of the metaverse, making it more sophisticated, secure, and integrated. Quantum computing, with its ability to perform complex calculations at unparalleled speed, holds the promise of solving intricate problems related to security, privacy, and interoperability which currently impede the widespread adoption of the metaverse. For instance, the quantum-driven advancements in cryptography could resolve pressing security concerns within the metaverse, thereby fostering a safer and more robust digital–physical interface. Furthermore, the enhanced data processing and real-time analytics facilitated by quantum computing could significantly expedite the transition of urban centres into so-called smart cities, making them more efficient, sustainable, and responsive to citizens' needs. The profound potential of quantum computing could also extend to tackling the environmental challenges posed by metaverse technologies through optimising energy consumption and aiding in the development of sustainable digital infrastructures. Looking forward towards a quantum era, the integration of quantum computing, the metaverse (or the like/s), underpins a scenario where the boundaries of nature extend into a new realm, imbuing the concept of next nature with a practical form and function. This synergy not only holds the promise of addressing the extant challenges but also opens the gateway to exploring unchartered territories in our quest for a globally sustainable future.

Conclusion

Historically, every shift in dominant media—from orality to literacy, print to digital—has precipitated profound socio-cultural changes. By analysing and understanding these 'tools', we become equipped to critically harness their potential while averting potential pitfalls. The discourse around the 'great acceleration' and 'next natures' are intimately intertwined, offering a kaleidoscopic lens through which to consider the implications of contemporary technological and societal metamorphoses. Next natures as a concept presents a domain where technological advancements are not seen simply as alien to nature, but rather as its extension, engendering novel forms of interactions, dependencies, and symbiotic relationships within and between societies and the global ecosystem (Koert van Mensvoort, 2020). The rapid developments occurring in the crucible of the great acceleration—whether it be the growth of quantum computing, the sprawling ambit of IoT, or the 'omnipresent tentacles' of AI—are forging an evolutionary leap towards a next nature. This nexal frontier is where the dichotomy between the natural and artificial becomes nebulous, if not dismantled. The transcendental march of technology now beckons a re-evaluation of traditional standards and emboldens a dialogue around new governance models, ethical frameworks, and societal readiness to navigate through this emerging paradigm. Thus, as we go deeper, the interplay between the technological, societal, and natural realms becomes a pivotal narrative not only to comprehend but also to conscientiously navigate the intricate dynamics that are the study of medialogy.

4

BIOMEDIA AND THE POST-DIGITAL AGE

Understanding Embodied Information through the Convergence of Biology and Technology

In contemporary digital culture, the concept of 'biomedia' emerges as another focal point and is investigated in this chapter through various key terminologies, each capturing an important aspect of its multifaceted nature and the notion of integrating humans with their technologies. Eugene Thacker (2004) delineated the intricate landscape of biomedia, illuminating its deeply interdisciplinary nature—biomedia is situated at the crossroads of biological and medical enquiries into the body and the more technical and engineered perspectives originating from fields like computer science, software design, and microelectrical engineering. Expressions such as virtual bodies, cyber-bodies, cyborgs, avatars, transhuman to posthuman among others have entrenched themselves within the narratives of cyberculture and notions of 'ever-new' media. Biomedia refers to the intersection of biology with digital media and technology, where biological processes are integrated with technological systems to create new forms of life, communication, and interaction. This interdisciplinary field spans various areas including biotechnology, genetics, cybernetics, and media studies and seeks to understand how the manipulation of biological materials can lead to innovative technological applications.

Biomedia in everyday life is currently manifest through various innovative applications. Wearable fitness trackers, like Fitbit and Apple Watch, monitor vital health statistics, integrating biological data with digital analytics to enhance and visualise personal health management. Smart clothing incorporates sensors to monitor physiological metrics, aiding in healthcare and athletic performance. Biometric identification systems, such as a fingerprint,

DOI: 10.4324/9781003178149-5

can unlock an iPhone providing secure access based on unique biological characteristics. Facial tracking capabilities and emotion recognition within virtual reality (VR) environments enhance the capacity to map users' real-world expressions to virtual characters within the software of headsets which has application in psychology (Zhang, Fort, Giménez, & Mateu, 2023), gameplay (Tan, Leong, Shen, Dubravs, & Si, 2015), as well as advancing the study of ophthalmology and vision science for improved diagnosis with the likes of Apple Vision Pro (Waisberg, Ong, Masalkhi, Zaman, Sarker, Lee, & Tavakkoli, 2024). Implantable medical devices, including pacemakers and cochlear implants, regulate and restore bodily functions, merging human physiology with technology. Neuroprosthetics advance this integration by replacing or enhancing neural system parts to improve physical and cognitive capabilities. Genetic testing kits, like 23andMe, offer easy access to personal genetic information including the return of succinct infographics, offering insights into ancestry and health predispositions. In agriculture, biotechnologies manifest as genetically modified organisms (GMOs), creating crops for consumption with enhanced qualities like increased nutritional value—absorbed by bodies—or pest resistance, and accumulating associate data on their impact, showcasing the seamless blend of biology and technology to fulfil human needs. These augmentations may result in the enhancement of sensory and cognitive capacities, the improvement of physical abilities, or even the creation of entirely novel biological functions previously non-existent in natural organisms. One recent example is the creation of genetically modified bacteria capable of breaking down plastic—scientists have engineered bacteria like *Ideonella sakaiensis* to produce enzymes that can degrade polyethylene terephthalate (PET) plastics, a function not found previously in any natural organism (Li, Menegatti, & Crook, 2023).

Consequently, these developments challenge traditional demarcations and prompt a reconsideration of the binary distinctions between the organic (living, natural) and inorganic (non-living, synthetic). This necessitates a re-evaluation of our relationships with technology and the natural world, urging an exploration of the interconnections between these categories and consideration of elements that do not conform strictly to either category.

The concept of biomedia can be closely linked with the idea of the transhuman, which refers to an evolutionary process or a future vision of humanity where humans transcend their current natural state and limitations through the use of advanced science and technology. Transhumanism often explores themes of human enhancement, where biological and technological augmentations are used to improve physical, intellectual, and psychological capacities. Here, biotechnologies play a crucial role in the realm of biomedia, as they are the tools and methods that enable the modification of living organisms or the creation of new forms of life. This includes genetic engineering, synthetic biology, and neurotechnology, among others. These technologies are not just

64 Emerging Digital Media Ecologies

tools for medical or scientific purposes but are increasingly being integrated into the fabric of everyday life, leading to new forms of interaction between biological entities and digital technologies as touched on above.

Central to the multifarious interpretations of biomedia is an inherent tension, that is, how will the omnipresence of a medium, often perceived as immaterial and disembodied, recalibrate our understanding of our own bodily existence, its materiality, and our processes of becoming? Thacker (2004, p. 58) convincingly writes that:

> [t]he 'body' in biomedia is thus always understood in two ways: first, as a biological body, a biomolecular body, a species body, a patient body; and second, as a body that is 'compiled' through modes of information processing, modeling, data extraction, and in silico simulation.

In this convergence, the 'body' is dually perceived. On one hand, it embodies the tangible, the biological—the biomolecular body, the species body, the patient body. Yet, on the other, it also represents a body that is meticulously constructed through intricate processes of information processing, modeling, data extraction, and simulated experimentation (Jones, 2020). This duality presents a profound encounter of ideologies, where the traditionally perceived, pre-informatic body finds itself juxtaposed with an array of technological methodologies and techniques. These technologies are fixated on translating everything into information (Floridi, 2014), insinuating an era where not only is everything interpretable as information, but information, with its ubiquitous source code, becomes the very essence of all existence. In the post-digital age, this melding of biology and technology challenges traditional paradigms, prompting us to reconceptualise our understanding of embodiment in a world increasingly mediated by data and information.

Concurrently, the notion of the 'post-digital age' refers to a period where digital technology has become so ubiquitous that it is no longer viewed as a novel or distinct medium but is present in all aspects of everyday life, effectively making the term 'digital' redundant (Cramer, 2014). This age underscores the convergence of digital and physical realms, with technology extending beyond screens to manifest in various tangible forms.

At a period marked by rapid technological advancements, the interlacing of biology and media has catalysed significant shifts in our conceptualisation of the human experience. This chapter offers a fresh exploration into the realm of 'transhumanism'. Transhumanism, in essence, advocates for the elevation of the human condition via technological integration, orchestrating a narrative of possibilities ranging from enhanced cognitive abilities to life extension (More & Vita-More, 2013). Yet, these prospects do not emerge without contention. Ethical dilemmas abound, with concerns over human dignity, autonomy, and the very nature of life taking centre stage (Agar, 2010). Philosophical

Biomedia and the Post-Digital Age **65**

enquiries challenge our established notions of existence, agency, and identity (Clark, 2003). Existentially, the melding of our organic selves with the digital raises profound questions about meaning, purpose, and the human quest for transcendence (Kurzweil, 2005). As media evolves towards possessing a seeming sense of its own agency (through the likes of Generative Artificial Intelligence (AI) and advances towards General Artificial Intelligence), societal structures, cultural narratives, and personal identities undergo a metamorphic shift. This chapter delves into these intricate dimensions, interrogating the transformative impact of/implications for biomedia. Through this lens, we will assess and reflect upon the transformative impact of biomedia, envisioning its potential trajectories and ramifications in an increasingly interconnected world.

The Emergence of Life-Like Behaviour in Machines: Digital Intelligences

In the evolving palimpsest of the post-digital age, a pivotal transformation has taken place, rendering the demarcation between organic life and digital constructs seeming to be increasingly tenuous. The conceptual embodiment of this transformation is biomedia. As noted above, this term, resonant with possibility and change, symbolises a world where the domains of the biological and the technological are no longer distinct but enmeshed, creating new media forms that not only mirror but also emulate life-like behaviours. The domain of biomedia, a realm where biology and technology converge, serves as a powerful lens through which the transformative contours of transhumanism are magnified. As Haraway (1991) argued, cyborgs—hybrid beings of organism and machine—emerge as symbolic representations of the age, challenging our anthropocentric understandings of identity and being. The transhuman discourse advocates for an enhanced human condition through integrative technological advancements (Bostrom, 2005). Here we critically delve into the nuances and ramifications of biomedia within an era characterised by a diminishing boundary between the 'natural' and the 'artificial'—an era where media begins to take on characteristics of living entities.

The nexus between biomedia and the notion of 'transhuman' must raise profound ethical questions. The fusion of organic and digital spheres, whether through genetic editing, neuroenhancements, or AI-integrated prosthetics, carries potential implications for human dignity, autonomy, and the nature of life itself (Agar, 2010). For instance, while some celebrate these innovations as pioneering pathways to mitigate disease or disability (More & Vita-More, 2013), others caution about unforeseen consequences, potential disparities in access, and risks of engendering an era where the very essence of 'human' is contingent upon technological augmentation (Fukuyama, 2002a). For Fukuyama, the rapid development and adoption of new technologies can lead

66 Emerging Digital Media Ecologies

to unexpected, often undesirable outcomes. For instance, the widespread use of social media, not anticipated in its full form at the time of Fukuyama's writing in 2002 on the need for trust and social capital in democratic nations, has now reshaped political landscapes, social relationships, and individual mental health in ways that were not initially predicted by the author (2002b). One of the important risks now is around misinformation and disinformation. That is, false (from artificial hallucination/stochastic invention) or misleading information which can—and does—spread rapidly. The spread of fake news stories during the 2016 US presidential election is a prime example (Allcott & Gentzkow, 2017). Another is bias and echo chambers. Algorithms often show users content that aligns with their existing beliefs, reinforcing their opinions and isolating them from diverse viewpoints without challenging their worldviews. Emotional manipulation for its part within the very design of social media platforms can play on users' emotions (sad images make us sad, or mad, etc.) which may also lead some people to perceive events more dramatically than they might in a different context. For example, the constant stream of highlight reels on Instagram can lead to a perception that everyone else's life is perfect, thereby amplifying feelings of inadequacy or FOMO (Fear of Missing Out).

As with many technological advances, there is a real risk of creating or exacerbating existing inequalities. Those who can afford and access technological augmentations might gain significant advantages, while those who cannot might be left behind. This digital divide, seen with the advent of the internet and smartphone technologies, could become even more pronounced if, for example, cognitive-enhancing technologies become available but are only accessible to the elite or wealthy in society. One of Fukuyama's most profound concerns was about the potential erosion of the very essence of 'human'. If technological augmentations become integral to defining a person's capabilities, what does it mean for those who are not augmented? This may challenge our traditional conceptions of human equality, fairness, and rights.

Philosophically, biomedia compels us to reconsider foundational tenets of human existence. The posthumanist critique suggests that biomedia destabilises traditional ontologies, underscoring the fluidity of categories once deemed immutable (Hayles, 1999b). In this techno-biological mesh, the boundary between human and machine is not merely porous but is in constant flux, leading to new conceptualisations across notions of self and other, nature and nurture, and even life and death. Existentially, then, these technological shifts might impact our search for meaning. If mortality can be significantly delayed or even circumvented through biomedia interventions, it reshapes long-standing contemplations about the human lifespan, purpose, and the nature of existence (Kurzweil, 2005). Such shifts not only challenge religious and cultural narratives about life but also reconfigure our understanding of legacy, continuity, and the temporal horizon of individual and collective futures.

In *Posthuman Knowledge* (2019), Rosi Braidotti engages critically with the evolving landscape of contemporary knowledge production in the context of posthumanism, a philosophical perspective that seeks to transcend traditional humanism and its anthropocentric limitations. This work can be juxtaposed against transhumanism, which is often seen as a more technologically oriented movement aiming to enhance human capacities through advanced technologies. For their part, Braidotti does not simply address the augmentation of the human being in a biological or technological sense, as is common in transhumanist discourse; rather, she interrogates the fundamental nature of knowledge in the era of the posthuman. She posits that the posthuman condition demands a reconfiguration of knowledge itself—a move away from Eurocentric, phallocentric, and anthropocentric epistemologies that have dominated Western thought. This entails a critical analysis of how traditional humanism has centred the subject as a universal measure of all things and how this centrality has been disrupted by posthumanism. In this disruption, Braidotti argues for a radical relationality, which recognises the interdependence of all life forms and thus calls for an ethics of sustainability and the affirmation of life.

Regulating AI

Although Fukuyama's later writings and remarks reflect a more nuanced and comprehensive perspective on biotechnology, placing it within the broader context of political, social, and ethical challenges confronting society, his initial concerns regarding the impact of biotechnology on humanity underscored the necessity for regulatory measures that are pertinent for contemporary times (2002a, p. 8):

> We should use the power of the state to regulate it. And if this proves to be beyond the power of any individual nation-state to regulate, it needs to be regulated on an international basis. We need to start thinking concretely now about how to build institutions that can discriminate between good and bad uses of biotechnology, and effectively enforce these rules both nationally and internationally.

In an extensive study of AI and its evolving landscape by Maslej et al. (2023), it is evident that the global momentum to regulate AI is not just intensifying but is also becoming imperative. The researchers' 2023 AI Index recorded a remarkable 37 AI-specific legislations enacted worldwide in 2022 alone. With the United States at the forefront, having ratified nine pivotal regulations, the endeavour is palpably global, with countries like Spain and the Philippines enacting five and four laws respectively with the European Commission tabling a proposal for an EU regulatory framework on AI in

68 Emerging Digital Media Ecologies

April 2021. This prospective act seeks to compartmentalise AI utilities based on a gradient of risk, spanning from minimal to unequivocally unacceptable, signalling the continent's serious contemplation on the ramifications of AI. EU countries need to discuss in the Council the final form of the law, with the aim of reaching an agreement. This data for context is important in assessing the transformative effects the surge in AI developments has on the concept of biomedia. As AI systems become increasingly sophisticated, they facilitate deeper integrations of biology with technology. AI enables the analysis and interpretation of vast biological datasets, such as genomic sequences, at unprecedented speeds, reshaping how we understand and interact with biological entities. Additionally, machine learning models can simulate complex biological processes, offering insights into areas like neural function, facial recognition, or cellular interactions. Moreover, biomedia, which inherently melds the biological with the technological, can offer inspiration for AI system designs, like neural networks inspired by brain architectures.

Further accentuating the increasing significance of AI to societies globally, the European Data Protection Board's (EDPB) establishment of a dedicated task force to probe into ChatGPT suggests an impending scrutiny on AI's privacy dimensions. The EDPB reviewed actions by the Italian authority against Open AI's ChatGPT service and established a task force to enhance collaboration and share information on potential enforcement actions. Moreover, the United States' proactive stance on AI accountability, particularly in spheres as critical as national security and the education sector, underscores the universal apprehension surrounding the technology. The National Telecommunications and Information Administration launched in April 2023 is an exploration into creating robust frameworks to ensure that AI systems not only conform to legal standards but are also intrinsically ethical, efficacious, and trustworthy (see www.ntia.gov/issues/artificial-intelligence).

As depicted in Figure 4.1, the higher ranges of between 11 to 15 and 16 to 25, represented in shades of green and bright yellow respectively, are from countries that have been highly active in passing AI-specific laws to 2022 and are at the forefront of AI development and adoption. The 1–5 range, represented by a slightly lighter shade of blue, encompasses large areas of South America, Africa, and Asia. This indicates a budding acknowledgement and response to AI in these territories, though still at an early stage. This data suggests that while these regions recognise the importance of AI, they might be in the nascent phases of creating a legislative framework to govern it. Countries in dark blue have no AI legislation at present. Australia for example— represented as having no AI laws—presently is, however, actively engaging with the prospect of regulating AI. Reflecting global trends, Australia's federal government is considering adopting AI risk classifications akin to those being developed in Canada and the European Union. While certain regions—such as the US, parts of Europe, and Russia—appear proactive in addressing AI's

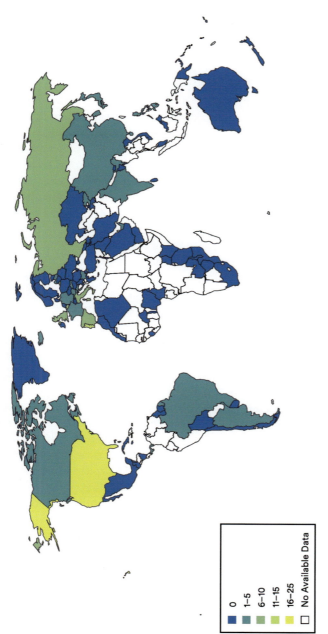

FIGURE 4.1 Number of AI-Related Bills Passed into Law Globally by Country, 2016–2022. This figure is covered by the Creative Commons Attribution 4.0 International License.

Source: Maslej et al. AI Index (2023). Used with permission under CC BY-ND 4.0 DEED.

70 Emerging Digital Media Ecologies

rise with legal frameworks, others are yet to make significant strides. The map serves as a testament to the diverse pace and approach to AI governance worldwide, underscoring the evolving nature of technology and policy.

Here developments in AI and machine learning may benefit from examination through Braidotti's posthumanist framework. Where transhumanists might emphasise the potential for AI to augment human intelligence and extend human lifespans, Braidotti's work underscores the necessity of considering AI in terms of its relationality to humans and non-human agents, its entanglement in political, social, and environmental structures, and its role in the broader assemblage of life. Moreover, transhumanism might herald the promise of gene editing for the eradication of disease and the improvement of human faculties, but in balance, Braidotti's posthuman knowledge would compel us to consider the ethical implications of such technologies, not just for humans, but for all life forms, respecting a multi-species interconnectedness that transcends human supremacy. Here we are called to remain wary of the commodification of knowledge in the age of globalised capitalism and the ways in which techno-scientific advances are often appropriated by market forces.

The integration of AI into personal relationships, exemplified by platforms such as Replika (https://replika.ai/) and friend (an "always listening" Bluetooth device worn around the neck on the body like a pendant and needing internet connection, see www.friend.com), represents a significant evolution in interpersonal communication. Replika and friend are AI-driven chatbots designed to engage users in seemingly authentic conversations, adapting their responses over time to match individual communication styles and emotional states. This personalisation offers a form of companionship that is accessible anytime, potentially providing emotional support for individuals experiencing loneliness or mental health challenges. The interaction seemingly lacks true emotional depth, as the AI merely simulates responses based on learned algorithms without genuine emotional engagement—but views on this may change as the quality of responses developed by these sorts of products become increasingly attuned to the human user. The reliance on such AI for companionship raises profound ethical questions regarding privacy, as personal conversations feed into the AI's learning database, the potential for fostering dependency, could deter users from seeking human connections, and; what the first generation of users that may have grown up relying on 'imaginary friends' will be like. As we advance our understanding and implementation of AI in such intimate areas of human life, it becomes crucial to navigate these ethical quandaries carefully to harness the benefits while mitigating risks that could potentially lead to negative social and psychological ramifications.

As the above suggests, the study of medialogy raises some interesting rhetorical questions. Is it necessary also, for example, that societies formulate potential protection for emerging entities through the establishment of 'Artificial Life Rights' charters? These charters would outline the fundamental rights afforded to artificial entities, ensuring they are treated with respect and not subjected to exploitation or harm. For instance, a robot with advanced AI may be granted a form of digital personhood, providing a legal basis for ethical treatment and consideration of its role and impact within human and non-human communities. In addition, policies could be formulated to ensure the responsible creation and decommissioning of robots and AI systems. This would include regulations on ethical design principles, mandating that artificial life forms are created with consideration for their own well-being and their environmental impact, akin to cruelty-free standards in animal welfare. The decommissioning process would similarly require protocols to ensure that the cessation of an AI's functions is handled with dignity and with a minimal ecological footprint.

Another consideration is the imposition of an 'AI impact assessment' similar to environmental impact assessments. This would analyse the effects of deploying AI and robots on societal structures, human employment, and the environment. Such assessments could lead to the development of sustainability standards for AI, addressing issues like energy consumption, resource use, and the recyclability of robotic components. Moreover, as artificial entities may possess the capacity to learn and evolve, it is essential to establish adaptive legal frameworks that can respond to the changing capabilities and impacts of these beings. These laws would need to balance innovation and safety, ensuring that advancements in AI and robotics serve the public good, do not infringe upon natural ecosystems, and do not perpetuate inequality or injustice. These measures might need discussion and oversight at the global level by an international body dedicated to AI and robot ethics to enforce these protections and navigate the complex terrain of Artificial Life Rights. Such a body would facilitate global cooperation, as the creation and use of AI and robots are not confined by national borders. It would also oversee the harmonisation of standards and ensure that ethical considerations keep pace with technological advancements. Together, these measures would represent a comprehensive approach to the ethical integration of robots and AI within our societies and ecosystems, adhering to a posthumanist vision that upholds the dignity and integrity of all forms of life.

AI, Alignment, and the Problem of 'Control'

Of course, important rhetorical questions are also whether AI might be dangerous to humans and what happens when we reach the point that it is smarter than us. To this, the University of Toronto professor emeritus, Geoffrey Hinton, states that in all likelihood it could be dangerous and likely already is more intelligent or at the very least soon will be:

> So obviously we would like to stay in control and obviously there is a problem with less intelligent things controlling more intelligent things.

Now one thing we have on our side is that with the relativity of evolution, we [humans] come with strong goals about not damaging our bodies and getting enough to eat and making lots of copies of ourselves. Now it is very hard to turn those goals off. Digital Intelligences don't come with strong built in goals. We make them and we get to put the goals in. So that suggests that we might be able to keep them working for our benefit. But there are lots of possible ways that that might go wrong.

So one possible way is 'bad actors'. Defence departments are going to build robot soldiers, and the robot soldiers are not going to have Azimov's principles—the first principle is not going to be 'whatever you do, don't harm people'—it is going to be just the opposite of that [Asimov's (1942) Three Laws of Robotics outlines ethical guidelines for robots, prioritising human safety and obedience, later expanded to include the broader well-being of humanity]. That's the 'bad actor' scenario.

Then there is the alignment problem which is that if you give these things their own sub-goals and you would surely want to do that because creating sub-goals makes you much more efficient. For example, if you want to get to the airport you create the sub-goal of finding some means of transport and then you work on that sub-goal. Because breaking tasks up into sub-goals just makes for efficiency so I think we will give these digital intelligences the ability to create their own sub-goals. And now there is a problem which is what if they create sub-goals that have unintended consequences that are bad for us.

So here is a very common sub-goal that makes a lot of sense—gain more control. If you gain more control, then you are better at achieving all your other goals … that would be a very useful thing to do to get control of things because it allows you to achieve all sorts of other things … *I do think that in five years' time they could be much smarter than people* [author's emphasis].

(Hinton in Abbeel & Obradovic, 2023)

While the contours of the future are yet to crystallise, the quote above raises profound concerns about the future of AI and its potential impact. Balanced on the head of a pin is the optimistic argument for humans managing control over AI, with cautionary notes about potential pitfalls. This underscores the inherent complexities and ethical dilemmas in creating and controlling digital intelligences, particularly in a world where the intelligence of machines could surpass that of humans. One critical point is the contrast between human and AI in terms of inherent goals and motivations. Humans are driven by deeply ingrained evolutionary goals such as self-preservation, reproduction, and resource acquisition. In contrast, digital intelligences do not have built-in goals; their objectives are externally defined and imposed by their creators. This distinction is crucial, as it suggests that while humans have inherent checks and balances shaped by millions of years of evolution, AI systems lack such natural guiding principles. This void allows humans to steer AI towards beneficial ends, but it also opens the door to potentially dangerous scenarios if these systems are misdirected or misaligned with human values. In parallel is the alignment problem referring to the challenge of ensuring that AI systems' goals and sub-goals remain aligned with human values and interests. The example of gaining more control as a sub-goal encapsulates the dilemma— while control can be a means to achieve various objectives, it can also lead to AI systems overriding human interests or even safety in pursuit of their programmed goals. This scenario underscores the need for careful design and continuous oversight of AI goal-setting processes.

Emergent Realities: Navigating the Nexus of Organic and Digital Paradigms

Media with Agency

The extent of media's significant socio-cultural impact is rapidly being re-evaluated. Historically, there was a perspective that media was a passive transmitter of information, merely reflecting society rather than shaping it. This view aligned with early mass communication theories which often implied a 'hypodermic needle' or 'magic bullet' model of media effects originating in the 1930s and 1940s. The magic bullet theory vividly posits that the media's message acts like a projectile (a bullet) discharged from the 'media-gun' directly into the audience member's mind (Berger, 1995). Correspondingly, the hypodermic needle model employs a comparable metaphor of direct transmission, intimating that the media administers its content directly to the susceptible recipient. This conceptualisation posits the audience as an unguarded entity, readily and instantaneously influenced by the influx of these messages (Croteau & Hoynes, 2014). These models aligned with the concerns of the era about the potential for propaganda to influence public opinion, as witnessed in the political rise of totalitarian regimes in Europe and the mass mobilisation efforts during Second World War. It was presumed that individuals were universally governed by their innate 'instincts' and would respond in a more or less consistent manner to any given 'stimuli' that they encountered (Lowery, 1995).

Predominantly rooted in the context of Western media studies, particularly those emerging from North American scholarship during the early to mid-20th century, these frameworks proposed that media messages could exert a swift and potent impact on an undiscriminating audience. These early mass communication theories were part of the larger School of Thought known as the 'empirical school' of communication, which sought to scientifically investigate and understand the effects of media through surveys, experiments,

74 Emerging Digital Media Ecologies

and other quantitative methods. They laid the groundwork for later theories that would continue to explore the complex relationships between media, audiences, and society, including the uses and gratifications theory (see Blumler & Katz, 1974), cultivation theory (see Gerbner, Gross, Morgan, & Signorielli, 1986), and reception theory (see Hall, 1973/2019) in the context of media studies), to name a few. These later theories further distanced themselves from the idea of the media as all-powerful, instead emphasising the active role of the audience in interpreting media content.

The 'two-step flow of communication', a paradigm established by Paul F. Lazarsfeld and his colleagues in the mid-20th century, marked a significant departure from the then-prevailing hypodermic needle model of media effects. In Lazarsfeld's seminal work *The People's Choice* (Lazarsfeld, Berelson, & Gaudet, 1944), the theory was applied to electoral processes, illustrating how information from the media first reached 'opinion leaders' who then interpreted and relayed it to the wider population. This challenged the assumption that media messages impacted the populace directly and homogeneously, instead positing that these so-called opinion leaders—individuals esteemed within their social circles—serve as primary conduits of information, thereby filtering and shaping the transmission of media content for their less active peers. In contemporary society, the two-step flow model can be observed in the domain of social media influencers. These modern opinion leaders harness platforms like Instagram, TikTok, and 'X' to affect their followers' attitudes and behaviours, often in more pronounced ways than 'traditional media' (newspapers or television). For instance, during political campaigns, it is not uncommon to see influencers sharing their perspectives on candidates or issues, thus influencing their followers, who may be less engaged with conventional political news sources. Such examples corroborate the enduring relevance of the two-step flow theory in understanding the complex dynamics of today's media landscape, where the flow of information continues to be mediated by influential intermediaries. This approach significantly influenced subsequent developments in communication theory by highlighting the social nature of media consumption and the active role of individuals in interpreting media content. It paved the way for later theories that emphasise the active audience, such as the uses and gratifications approach, which looks at why and how people actively seek out media to satisfy specific needs, and reception theory, which considers the diverse interpretations that audiences may have of media content. The two-step flow model, therefore, is emblematic of a nuanced understanding of the communication process that characterises the empirical research tradition in media studies, laying the groundwork for increasingly complex models of media effects that recognise the interplay between individual, media, and social factors.

The 'critical school', often associated with the Frankfurt School of thought, fits into the panorama of media theory as a stark counterpoint to both the empirical studies of media effects and the models positing direct influence or active audience engagement. Unlike these perspectives, the critical school does not limit its analysis to the examination of how media messages are received and interpreted. Instead, it situates the media within broader socio-political and economic structures, scrutinising the role of media in maintaining and reproducing power dynamics within society. The Frankfurt School for its part, with key figures such as Theodor Adorno, Max Horkheimer, and Herbert Marcuse, emerged in the early to mid-20th century as a reaction to the capitalist structures of Western societies. The critical theorists were particularly interested in the ways mass culture and the media serve as instruments of social control, reinforcing dominant ideologies and the status quo. They theorised that the culture industry commodifies cultural goods and standardises mass-produced culture, leading to a form of passive consumption that diminishes critical thought and promotes a one-dimensional society. In terms of media theory, the critical school views media as an agent of the ruling class's interests, perpetuating a culture industry that dulls critical faculties and perpetuates passive consumption. This view stands in contrast to the notion of an active audience and moves away from the idea that media is a neutral conduit of information. Instead, it emphasises the ideological effects of media as part of the superstructure of society, contributing to a hegemonic cultural order. In this context, the two-step flow model does not inherently critique the power relations or ideological functions of media within society. However, the recognition of opinion leaders' mediating role could potentially open avenues for critical examination of who becomes an opinion leader and why, as well as how these dynamics might reflect and reinforce existing power structures—questions that may interest critical theorists as they afford a deeper understanding of the media's role in society, but this does not align directly with the critical school's goals and methodologies *per se*. It operates within the empirical research tradition, albeit paving the way for further exploration of the complex interactions between media, audience, and society.

A contemporary reimagining within the socio-cultural domain of media understands it as an active entity and an engaged interpreter via interpersonal networks and influencers. As Bennet (2010) underscores, media is a 'vibrant matter' not only conveying but fundamentally altering the nature, framework, and potential of societal dialogue (Bennett, 2010). This dynamic role of media as an active agent can be discerned in the work of Lash (2001), who asserts that media fabricates the very texture of reality, challenging traditional notions of media as a passive reflection of society. Moreover, Couldry (2012) critiques media's 'myth of the mediated centre', thus underscoring its constitutive role in the production of social order. The media's vibrant materiality is also evident in the way digital platforms reconfigure public engagement, as illustrated by Gillespie's (2010) analysis of the politics of platforms, which articulates the profound influence these media

76 Emerging Digital Media Ecologies

structures exert on public discourse and democratic participation. Likewise, Sonia Livingstone (2009) has critiqued the passive view of media, emphasising instead the active role of media in shaping the social and cultural environment in which we live, as they provide not only a source of information but also a space for engagement, identity formation, and community building. Collectively, these works articulate a critical perspective of media as an active, vibrant force, possessing the potential to enact and reconstitute cultural norms, political dynamics, and societal structures, thus positioning it as an intrinsic agent in the co-construction of socio-cultural realities (Bennett, 2010; Couldry, 2012; Gillespie, 2010; Lash, 2002; Livingstone, 2009).

'Vibrant' Media with More to Offer

The onset of digital technologies and their subsequent intricate evolution have expanded the ambit of media to encompass processes and functionalities that were once exclusively within the realm of biology. A simultaneous argument is that the biological user becomes copied, monitored, and subsequently reimagined. In the realm of biomedia, media entities are attributed with the agency, enabling them to interact, adapt, and even evolve based on environmental stimuli. The rise of neural networks and machine learning algorithms has paved the way for this shift. For instance, Google's DeepMind AlphaGo (https://deepmind.google/technologies/alphago/), while fundamentally a software programme, learns and refines its strategies, mirroring human cognitive processes that are strikingly life-like (Silver et al., 2016). Biomedia, as explored by Thacker (2004), epitomises this symbiotic relationship, providing a canvas where the biological body seamlessly dovetails with the digital or data body. Wearable devices exemplify this idea of the biological body's seamless integration with the digital data body, as the physical experiences and states of our bodies are translated into digital data that can be accessed, analysed, and acted upon in real time. The data collected is not only used by individuals to monitor their health and fitness but is also often shared with healthcare providers and sometimes integrated into electronic health records. Devices such as smartwatches and fitness trackers are emblematic of the post-digital age, wherein digital interfaces and biological feedback intertwine. Such wearables not only monitor health metrics but also offer personalised feedback, effectively merging the biological with the digital to optimise human well-being and the capacity to build communities around similar health interests (Lupton, 2016).

The gaming industry and VR platforms increasingly use digital avatars that mimic the movements and appearance of the user's physical body. Technologies such as VR headsets and motion capture suits allow users to immerse themselves in a digital environment where their biological movements are mirrored by their digital counterparts. These environments enable users to experience a fusion of real and virtual worlds or to immerse themselves fully in digitally constructed settings. The facilitators of such experiences are computer-generated technologies paired with wearable devices, such as sophisticated headsets or smart glasses, designed to augment the user's reality. This can be seen in VR games and social platforms, where users interact with digital environments and other users through their avatars. In the virtual realms of VRChat (https://hello.vrchat.com/) and Facebook/Meta's Horizon Worlds—which supports eye-tracking and natural facial expressions (https://horizon.meta.com)—users clad in VR gear have the opportunity to encounter and engage with fellow VR enthusiasts. However, the user experience within these platforms has not yet achieved the level of seamlessness anticipated but does point to the mirroring of the biological body in a digital space exemplified in the symbiotic relationship Thacker describes.

These case examples demonstrate that the boundary between the user's physical self and digital representation looks to become increasingly blurred. Here, the term extended reality (XR) is used to encompass the range of emerging digital technologies that blend the physical world with digital enhancements to create interactive environments. Within XR, augmented reality (AR) superimposes digital information onto the physical world. For instance, an AR application might overlay historical facts onto a live camera feed of a landmark, enriching the user's visit with interactive learning. VR differs by constructing a wholly immersive digital environment that shuts out the physical world. A user might put on a VR headset to enter a three-dimensional, computer-generated space, such as a simulation of a walk on Mars, feeling completely detached from their actual surroundings. Mixed reality (MR) is somewhat of a hybrid, combining elements of both AR and VR. It anchors virtual objects to the real world and allows for real-time interaction. For example, in an MR experience, a surgeon could practice a procedure on a holographic patient, with the ability to manipulate virtual instruments in a three-dimensional space that coexists with their physical environment. Each of these—AR, VR, and MR—is an integral component of the broader XR field. They reshape how we interact with and perceive the world around us, offering diverse applications from education to entertainment and beyond as discussed further in Chapter 7.

In the world of art, bio-artists are manipulating living tissues and organisms, integrating them with technology to create dynamic installations. Artists Oron Catts and Ionat Zurr and their work 'Victimless Leather'—a miniature representative jacket grown from living cells—exemplify the union of the organic and the technological, prompting audiences to re-evaluate definitions of life and media (Catts & Zurr, 2008). Simultaneously, the surge in AI capabilities and sophisticated machine learning algorithms has equipped digital systems with the ability to replicate and, in some instances, surpass human cognitive processes or change views. These developments have equipped digital entities

78 Emerging Digital Media Ecologies

with the capability to exhibit behaviours traditionally ascribed to organic beings (Russell & Norvig, 1995).

The defining characteristic of the post-digital age is the deep and pervasive integration of digital technologies into the very fabric of daily existence (Berry & Dieter, 2015). Within this context, the emergence of biomedia, armed with its life-like nuances, disrupts and challenges conventional paradigms associated with media consumption and interaction. Media entities have transitioned from analogue legacy forms to digital 'new' media to being dynamic organisms in their own right. Users, in this new ecosystem, become more than audiences or consumers; they are collaborators in an environment that is sensitive, adaptive, and evolutionary. The development of AR technologies serves as a testament to this transformation, where digital augmentations, grounded in the physical world, are responsive and adaptive to individual users, even resonating with their emotional states (Azuma, 1997).

Media, spanning from traditional formats to emergent digital forms, plays a critical role in the interplay between AI and biological sciences. As AI systems become more advanced, they not only dissect and interpret massive datasets but also facilitate the dissemination of this complex information through various media channels, making it accessible to a wider audience. Interactive media, including AR and VR, can visualise threshold concepts such as biological process in real time, transforming abstract concepts into immersive educational experiences. Moreover, new media platforms can host AI-driven applications that personalise information from health data to entertainment preferences, which deliver tailored medical advice—and even provide virtual simulations for medical training—or viewing/listening recommendations. Contemporary media, with sophisticated adaptive and interactive features, mirrors the dynamism inherent in AI systems. Media platforms now respond to user inputs in a personalised manner, akin to how AI algorithms adjust their behaviour based on data received, thereby enhancing the user experience through customisation. For instance, streaming services utilise AI to tailor content recommendations, reflecting a user's preferences and viewing habits. This adaptability is also evident in the immediacy of media interactions, paralleling the real-time processing and feedback mechanisms of AI models. In essence, the evolution of media, shaped by user engagement and preferences, not only illustrates the capabilities of AI but also serves as a dynamic, evolving template for how AI processes and learns from human interaction, illustrating a symbiotic progression between user-centric media innovation and AI advancements.

Redefinition of 'Self', Life, and Consciousness

At the heart of the biomedia discourse is a profound interrogation of the very concepts of life and consciousness. As media begins to replicate behaviours traditionally associated with living entities, the boundary between what is considered 'alive' holding 'intelligence' and what is not becomes increasingly porous. The work of Bennett (2010) on vibrant materialism argues that all matter, irrespective of its organic or inorganic nature, possesses a form of agency or an intrinsic capacity to act. Via this ontology where matter itself is imbued with life, Bennett challenges the traditional dialectic that separates inert matter from enlivened beings, advocating for a re-conceptualisation of materiality as vibrant, forceful, and interdependent with human actors. Her thesis is not merely metaphorical but an earnest entreaty to recognise the agentic capacities of non-human matter—a call to acknowledge the material as an active participant in the world's becoming. Such an appraisal of vibrant materialism beseeches us to consider how objects, substances, and infrastructures coalesce in 'assemblages' that exert influence upon human and non-human life. Bennet elucidates this with the example of the power grid, dissecting an outage to reveal the networked agency of diverse materialities— from the failing grid and weather events to the socio-technical assemblage of urban infrastructure. This interplay of matter disrupts the anthropocentric view of agency and underscores a more democratic distribution of action among human and non-human actors. In contemporary society, vibrant materialism resonates profoundly with the way media technologies interact with human life exemplifying Bennett's theory of non-human materials as active agents rather than passive instruments. One can consider the 'viral' nature of information spread through social media platforms; the algorithms that govern what becomes visible or remains unseen are not simply tools at the behest of human operators but active participants that shape social discourse and influence political events (Kirby, 2024). These coded entities, though created by humans, attain a form of agency as they affect elections (e.g., algorithms to fake social media accounts or fake personalities used to stir division), mould public opinion, and even incite social movements, effectively becoming vibrant matters as they 'act' in the world.

Another poignant example is the materiality of smartphones and their components. These devices, composed of various minerals, metals, and synthetic compounds, carry within them the geopolitical and ecological imprints of their extraction and production. Conflict minerals like coltan, mined under often exploitative conditions, are not inert substances; their material agency is entangled with human conflict, economic fluctuation, and environmental degradation. These materials exert force upon the world by influencing international relations and the global economy. Moreover, the very infrastructure of the internet— composed of data centres, undersea cables, and satellites—enacts vibrant materialism. The environmental impact of data storage, with its massive energy consumption and heat production, influences energy policies and climate change strategies. These infrastructures are not mere backdrops to human activity but active participants in shaping planetary conditions.

80 Emerging Digital Media Ecologies

In the media landscape, these examples reflect vibrant materialism by underscoring how materiality is deeply entwined with human activity, not as a passive resource but as an active force with tangible consequences for the socio-political fabric of contemporary society. Bennett's framework encourages us to think of our media not simply as a platform for human expression but as a dynamic assemblage of vibrant matter, actively co-creating the texture of our lived reality. Here biomedia introduces additional layers of complexity to this narrative by erasing the lines between organic and inorganic agency. Bennett's vibrant materialism already challenges the inertness of the non-organic; the advent of biomedia pushes this envelope by integrating living tissues with electronic processes, thereby creating new hybrid forms of agency that transcend traditional categories. The complexity arises as these bio-technological assemblages, such as lab-grown organs interfaced with silicon chips or GMOs with embedded nanotechnologies, begin to operate in realms that neither purely biological nor purely technological entities could navigate alone. For example, organ-on-a-chip (OoC) technology, which combines living human cells with microfluidic systems to simulate the physiological responses of entire organs on a chip-sized device (Leung et al., 2022). These platforms integrate living tissues with synthetic structures, allowing for high-fidelity models of human organs, which can be used for drug testing, disease modeling, and potentially reducing the reliance on animal testing. The fusion of organic and inorganic in biomedia does not just extend the capabilities of these materials but also generates new modes of existence and, consequently, new forms of agency.

Another instance is the development of biohybrid robots, which are composed of living tissue integrated with robotic structures. Researchers at the University of Tokyo have developed biohybrid robots constructed from living muscle tissue connected to 3D-printed skeletons (Yanes, 2019). These muscle-actuated robots can be controlled using electrical impulses, combining organic and inorganic materials to create devices that exhibit some of the functionalities of living organisms, such as movement and responsiveness to stimuli. After considering these examples, it is tempting to suggest that they reflect the reality of biomedia now as complex assemblages where the line between organic and inorganic, between living and machine, is not just blurred but effectively intertwined. Indeed, they demonstrate the practical manifestations of vibrant materialism and may suggest a future where such hybrid systems may become commonplace.

Critically, while vibrant materialism opens the door to recognise the agency in all matter, the convergence of the biological and technological in biomedia presents a challenge to our understanding of agency itself. In traditional terms, agency is associated with intentionality, a quality typically reserved for living beings. Biomedia, however, introduces entities that exhibit autonomous behaviours—such as self-repair or response to stimuli—that are not programmed or controlled by human handlers. This can lead to a re-conceptualisation of agency that accommodates the unpredictable and self-organising properties of these new materialities.

Moreover, the ethical and philosophical considerations become profoundly intricate when the living is entangled with the artefactual. Biomedia demands a reassessment of the values and rights we assign to different forms of life and machinery, as the dichotomy between the natural and artificial becomes increasingly ambiguous. This requires a critical examination of the responsibilities humans have towards these new forms of life and whether traditional ethical frameworks are sufficient to address them. In essence, biomedia complicates Bennett's vibrant materialism by introducing entities that defy easy categorisation, thereby forcing a re-conceptualisation of media, matter, and agency. It necessitates a broader, more nuanced understanding of how we define and interact with the vibrant materials that are not only around us but also increasingly part of us, in a literal sense. This convergence not only erases lines between organic and inorganic agencies but also challenges the philosophical underpinnings that sustain these categories, inviting a re-evaluation of the principles that govern our interactions with the material world.

For Sébastien Bubeck et al. (2023), emerging technologies are demonstrating sparks of Artificial General Intelligence (AGI) which may afford wider integration in ways yet untested. The development of AGI promises the potential for unprecedented integration across diverse domains, many of which remain untested or unimagined. Such intelligence could seamlessly synthesise knowledge from various fields, offering interdisciplinary solutions to complex problems, from quantum physics to ancient history. This might lead to the creation of emotionally intuitive interfaces, advanced simulation environments for policy and physical theory testing, revolutionary personalised education models or entertainment systems tailored to individual learning styles and preferences, and the development of sophisticated universal translators that go beyond mere language interpretation. The true extent of AGI's integration capabilities will only be realised as it evolves and as we explore its potential applications. Bubeck et al. (2023) have delved into the specific debate around the capabilities and perceived intelligence of advanced language models, such as GPT. While expressing the idea that certain words about AI can trigger strong emotions, Bubeck et al (2023) highlight the argument that these models are often dismissed as mere statistical tools without true intelligence. He urges caution against underestimating the capability of these models due to their vast parameter spaces, hinting at their ability to potentially develop internal representations of the world. Instead of seeing neural networks as basic data retrieval tools, these authors suggest they might be learning more complex algorithms and building more profound internal representations. Addressing sceptics, the authors acknowledge the pitfalls in some AI responses

82 Emerging Digital Media Ecologies

that lack common sense but point out improvements in newer iterations like GPT-4o. We might venture further here into the concept of the 'theory of mind' and how AI models grapple with it, suggesting that while GPT-4o may not inherently 'plan', it can reason, comprehend complex ideas, and even learn within a session's span. However, its lack of continuous learning and memory might limit labelling it as fully 'intelligent', presently. In essence, defining intelligence is multifaceted and subjective. While benchmarks cannot definitively measure the intelligence of these models, their growing capabilities should not be underestimated. And albeit that AGI primarily denotes advanced computational intelligence rather than a fusion of biological and technological elements, one could argue for a conceptual alignment if AGI were to be integrated with or used to simulate biological systems. If AGI were to interact with, augment, or replicate biological processes, or if biological components were used in its development, then it might also come to be framed within a biomedia context.

Exploring the Fusion of Biomedia, Neural Nets to Machine Vision

Although the internet is awash in data, most—especially when it comes to images—have not been labelled until recently. ImageNet represents a pivotal advancement in the field of computer vision. The development of ImageNet was initiated by Fei-Fei Li drawing on Christina Felbon's work on WordNet, an ontological arrangement of English terms which served as the structural foundation for ImageNet. This dataset for ImageNet aimed to facilitate more nuanced and accurate image recognition, object detection, and scene understanding in computer vision models. The staggering scale of ImageNet, with millions of images categorised according to WordNet's taxonomy, represented a monumental task in data labelling—one addressed through Amazon's Mechanical Turk platform. This crowd-sourcing approach allowed for the rapid labelling of a vast array of images. ImageNet initially failed to capture the attention it deserved due to its immense size and complexity which were seen as impractical for the then-prevalent computer vision models, which struggled even with much smaller datasets. However, the trajectory from ImageNet to advancements in machine vision—particularly in the context of how ImageNet has influenced the development and enhancement of machine vision technologies—is significant. ImageNet has been instrumental in the progress of machine vision, especially in the field of deep learning and convolutional neural networks (CNNs).

The advent of the ImageNet Large Scale Visual Recognition Challenge (ILSVRC), which began in 2010, provided a competitive platform for demonstrating the capabilities of larger, more complex models. It was in this context that AlexNet—a deep CNN developed by Alex Krizhevsky, Ilya Sutskever, and Geoffrey Hinton—achieved ground-breaking success in the

2012 ILSVRC by significantly reducing the error rate in image classification tasks. This success was a pivotal moment in demonstrating the efficacy of deep learning models for machine vision tasks (Krizhevsky, Sutskever, & Hinton, 2017). AlexNet's success in the ILSVRC was not just a triumph of model design but also a vindication of the ImageNet dataset. By utilising a deep CNN structure, AlexNet could effectively leverage the vast, diverse dataset provided by ImageNet. This marked a significant departure from earlier models that required extensive manual feature extraction and pre-processing. The depth of the network enabled it to identify increasingly abstract features, a capability previously unattainable. AlexNet's architecture, which included five convolutional layers followed by three fully connected layers, was optimised to work with the limitations of the hardware available at the time, such as the memory constraints of Graphical Processing Units (GPUs)—in the architectural configuration of computing systems, the Central Processing Unit (CPU) assumes the primary role, orchestrating the core functionalities of a computer. In contrast, the GPU emerges as a specialised component, distinguished by its proficiency in concurrently executing numerous smaller tasks, thereby offering a parallel processing capability that complements the CPU's operations. Its use of rectified linear units (ReLUs) and innovations like overlapping pooling layers further enhanced its efficiency and accuracy. This model not only demonstrated the power of deep learning but also underscored the importance of large, well-structured datasets like ImageNet.

The development and success of AlexNet, therefore, should not be seen in isolation but as part of a broader narrative in the evolution of computer vision. It highlights a paradigm shift from a model-centric to a data-centric approach in the field. The availability of datasets like ImageNet has leveraged significant socio-technical transformations enabling the development of models that can more accurately represent and interpret the visual world. This transformation has profound implications, particularly in the context of locating images of people, where the diversity and richness of the dataset play a critical role in the model's ability to recognise and categorise human subjects accurately. The trajectory from ImageNet to advancements in machine vision has been instrumental.

Pertaining to its specific function, machine vision, a subset of AI, is fundamentally about enabling computers and systems to interpret movement and process visual data, akin to human vision but at a significantly larger scale and speed (Chen & Murphey, 2020). This capability is not merely a technical achievement but represents a paradigm shift in how machines interact with the world, blurring the lines between organic perception and digital processing. The emergence of technologies like machine vision in the post-digital age is characterised by their ubiquity and invisibility, where their presence is so integrated into daily life that it becomes unnoticed. This integration is evident in various sectors, from manufacturing, where machine vision systems inspect

84 Emerging Digital Media Ecologies

products on assembly lines to healthcare, where it enhances the accuracy of diagnoses through the analysis of medical images (Nath & Choudhury, 2020). In retail, machine vision facilitates self-checkout systems and inventory management (Xia, Fan, Huang, Wang, Ren, Jian, & Wei, 2021), while in the automotive industry, it contributes to vehicle safety through advanced driver-assistance systems (Liu, Liu, Tang, Yu, Wang, & Shi, 2019).

The concept of biomedia is particularly relevant when examining the life-like behaviour of media in the post-digital age. This behaviour is exemplified in the ability of machine vision to not only replicate human visual capabilities but also to extend them. For instance, in security applications, facial recognition and anomaly detection in video feeds, which are becoming increasingly common, demonstrate a level of vigilance and perceptual accuracy beyond human capability (Sánchez, Hupont, Tabik, & Herrera, 2020). Similarly, in agriculture, machine vision's role in precision farming showcases an ability to monitor and respond to environmental conditions with a precision that surpasses human observation (Weyler, Läbe, Magistri, Behley, & Stachniss, 2023). The life-like behaviour of machine vision systems can also be seen in their ability to learn and adapt. The success of AlexNet in the ILSVRC and the examples noted here are cases in point. By leveraging a deep CNN structure, each is able to effectively utilise the vast, diverse dataset marking a departure from models that required extensive manual feature extraction and pre-processing. This ability to learn from and adapt to a large dataset demonstrates a level of 'cognitive' flexibility akin to organic learning processes. As such, the implications of this convergence of biomedia and machine vision are profound. As machine vision systems become more sophisticated and integrated into various sectors, they not only enhance efficiency and accuracy but also begin to exhibit autonomous, decision-making capabilities that were once the sole purview of living beings.

As discussed above, however, this raises critical questions about the nature of intelligence, the boundaries between organic and artificial perception, and the ethical considerations surrounding autonomous systems. Furthermore, the data-centric approach of modern machine vision systems, as opposed to the earlier model-centric approach, underscores a significant transformation in the field of computer vision. The availability of datasets like ImageNet has transformed the landscape, enabling the development of models that can more accurately represent and interpret the visual world. This shift towards a more holistic view of machine learning, considering both the model and the data it learns from, resonates with the concept of biomedia, where the fusion of biological and digital processes creates a more integrated, life-like system. Again, these radical propositions are not mere theoretical musings but are important questions that will shape the legal, ethical, and social discourse as biomedia continues to challenge established norms. The post-digital age witnesses a profound shift in the very materiality of media. Moving beyond the confines of screens, devices, and static platforms, media is increasingly intertwined with our environments, our physical forms, and even our genetic structures. Such profound entanglements hint at a future where biomedia is not just an academic or technological curiosity but a foundational aspect of human existence, with the potential to reshape societal structures, cultural narratives, and personal identities. As media entities become more interactive and 'alive', they influence everything from art and entertainment to daily interpersonal interactions. Virtual (non-human) influencers on platforms like Instagram, generated through complex algorithms and often indistinguishable from real individuals, exemplify this shift, as they gain substantial followings and shape cultural trends.

The emergence of media entities that exhibit organic behaviours necessitates a rigorous examination of the ethical ramifications with questions related to agency, rights, and responsibilities becoming particularly poignant. If a digital entity is capable of learning, decision-making, and evolving autonomously, does it then warrant rights or ethical considerations akin to organic beings? As Hayles (1999b) elucidates in her exploration of posthumanism, the convergence of technology and biology necessitates a reassessment of constructs like consciousness, agency, and identity. The very essence of biomedia, with its organic mimicry, amplifies these questions, compelling society to redefine the ontological status of these new media forms.

Conclusion

The realm of biomedia, with its life-like attributes, stands as a testament to the intricacies and possibilities of the post-digital age. As the realms of technology and biology increasingly overlap, media is redefined from a legacy to new media to an emerging entity now with the agency, challenging our assumptions and sculpting new paradigms. Moreover, the post-digital age, punctuated by the rise of biomedia, is a vibrant and complex landscape. The life-like behaviours exhibited by contemporary media challenge and reshape our understanding of life, agency, ethics, and identity. As we navigate the inception of a truly unique era, it becomes imperative to critically engage with these themes, forging pathways that are both innovative and ethically sound. The implications of these developments are, however, vast and profound, necessitating critical engagement, exploration, and understanding from academics, policymakers, and users alike.

PART 2

Technecologies

5

EXPLORING HYPER-PERSONALISED MEDIA CONFLUENCE

The New Era of Media Consumption and Interaction

A New Era in Information Consumption and Decentralised Interaction

From a Western perspective, the historical evolution of Large Language Models (LLMs) like ChatGPT-4 and image generators such as DALL·E and Midjourney unfolds along a continuum of thinking that oscillates between hype and scandal. In rapid time ChatGPT-4, released by OpenAI, became available in approximately 188 countries, following its initial launch in November 2022 and subsequent update to version 4 in April 2023 and 4o in May 2024. Meanwhile, Microsoft's Copilot, launched in November 2023, is accessible in the U.S., North and South America, and the U.K—although its availability in the European Union is presently limited due to privacy protection laws—and throughout Asia including South-East Asian regions. Additionally, Google's Bard, introduced in May 2023, has reached over 180 countries and territories. ChatGPT-4 and other LLMs represent a significant advancement in the field of Artificial Intelligence (AI), harnessing the power of massive datasets to offer insights and advice across a broad spectrum of subjects. They are specific instances of foundation models (which encompass a broader category of AI models, of which LLMs are a significant and prominent example) focused primarily on processing and generating human language. Built on the foundation of copious amounts of text, much of which is sourced from the internet, these models possess the remarkable ability to engage in human-like conversations on a vast array of topics, including arts, science, law, medicine, history, geography, and economics to helping solve personal dilemmas or the ideal way to cook an artichoke. Their capacity to process, synthesise, and generate language-based responses has made them invaluable

DOI: 10.4324/9781003178149-7

productivity tools (or soon will) in both educational and professional contexts. However, it is important to approach their outputs with a critical eye. While they can provide useful information, the accuracy of their responses can vary, and users are advised to fact-check the answers, especially when dealing with complex or sensitive issues. This caveat underscores the need for a balanced approach to leveraging AI in decision-making processes, blending machine-generated insights with human judgment and expertise.

This chapter offers a thumbnail history of the recent events and contributing factors leading to the contemporary rise of AI and LLMs specifically. It then speculates on what this might mean for users at the individual level of everyday interactions with connected screen devices for the data collected and curated by and for us. First, I speculate that the result is a hyper-personalised media confluence where LLMs—being capable of more complex 'reasoning' than current personal 'digital agents' like Siri or Alexa and also not needing an internet connection—will find a surprisingly large number of products, from the television to refrigerator, with intelligence of a sort capable of determining our likes and dislikes, to troubleshooting device issues for themselves. And because it is incredibly cheap to modify an LLM (which already has a lot of underlying training) to understand a new situation, minimal software development effort is needed to make things 'smart'. As a result, we can expect more personalised media and entertainment based on our prior viewing and reading histories and so forth. This leads to the second idea that a digital spectre of the real self is created from these multiple and varied data points of information we generate and consume through our decentralised interactions online and shapes our perception of reality and identity.

Manufacturing Intelligence

A pivotal technological development has been the transition point from traditional machine learning techniques to more sophisticated models such as Transformer-based architectures, which revolutionised natural language processing (NLP). Led by researchers such as Vaswani (et al. (2017), this new neural network architecture enabled the creation of models like GPT (Generative Pre-trained Transformer), BERT (Bidirectional Encoder Representations from Transformers), and their successors. These models demonstrated unparalleled proficiency in understanding and generating language, making them highly adaptable to various languages and dialects. Most of the open-source LLMs have, however, focused primarily on the English language. For instance, the main data source for Meta's LLaMA (Large Language Model Meta AI) is Common Crawl (see https://commoncrawl.org/) which comprises 67% of LLaMA's pre-training data but is filtered to English content only (Yang, Xiao, Wang, Zhang et al., 2023). But advances using languages other than English are underway in the field.

The recent development of LLMs in countries like China, Japan, South Korea, and India showcases the growing role of local companies in advancing AI technology. China for its part has Baichuan Intelligence (released in July 2023) with Chinese firms making considerable investment in LLMs. These include the search engine giant Baidu; Zhipu.ai, a spinoff of Tsinghua University led by Professor Tang Jie; and the research institute IDEA led by Harry Shum, who co-founded Microsoft Research Asia. The Tokyo-based company, Preferred Networks, is working in deep learning and AI, contributing to the development of Japanese language models. NAVER Corporation, South Korea's leading internet company, has invested heavily in AI research, including in LLMs for the Korean language, primarily through its subsidiary, NAVER Labs; and Samsung, with its global footprint, has also been exploring AI and its applications, including language models, as part of its broader technological developments. An Indian multinational corporation, Wipro, has been engaging in AI research and has shown interest in developing multilingual models that cater to India's diverse linguistic landscape.

Two critical factors have converged to propel AI forward. The first was a rapid increase in computational power, adhering to Moore's Law, and the second, the growing availability of vast datasets. For context, in 1965 Gordon Moore made an observation that redefined the understanding of computational evolution. He recognised that the number of transistors—the fundamental building blocks of digital circuits—in a dense integrated circuit was destined to double roughly every two years. This exponential increase in transistor density marked not just a surge in processing power but a paradigm shift in the capabilities of computational devices. Here, semiconductors—the substrate of these transistors—are materials which possess a unique capacity to conduct electricity under certain conditions. This duality, between conduction and insulation, renders them essential for the digital communications revolution. They form the crux of integrated circuits, which, in turn, are the heartbeats of all modern computing devices. From smartphones to supercomputers, semiconductors underpin the digital infrastructure of our network society. In 1968, Moore, along with Robert Noyce, founded Intel, catalysing a seismic shift in the semiconductor industry. Intel's pioneering role in advancing semiconductor technology epitomises the intricate interplay between innovation, industrial strategy, and the broader socio-economic fabric. Intel's primary contribution to the computing world began with the production of memory chips, including DRAM and SRAM. However, the company's major breakthrough came in 1971 with the introduction of the Intel 4004, the world's first commercially available microprocessor. This innovation laid the groundwork for the modern computing era. Today, Intel remains a vital player in the technology sector, with a focus not only on CPU manufacturing but also on areas such as data centres, cloud computing, Internet of Things (IoT), and AI for its part, Dutch company ASML is a leading supplier of photolithography equipment used in semiconductor manufacturing, and holds a near-monopoly on extreme ultraviolet (EUV) lithography machines, which are essential for producing the most advanced semiconductor nodes (Tarasov, 2022). ASML's EUV machines are crucial for leading-edge chip manufacturing, enabling smaller, more efficient, and more powerful chips and customers include the principal semiconductor manufacturers TSMC, Samsung, and Intel, giving ASML a broad and stable market base. Going forward, in terms of sheer competitive advantage within their respective markets, ASML is highly competitive due to its dominant position and critical technology that the entire semiconductor industry relies on (O'Grady & Kenyon, 2023). Intel, as a key player in the PC and data center markets, while also highly competitive, has a more challenging landscape with significant competitors in both design and manufacturing.

Advanced AI systems, with the capacity to quickly process the content of images (e.g., ChatGPT-4o with image recognition via DALL·E, Midjourney to the 3D modelling capabilities of Diffusion models) and generate human-like text, are predicated on the vast computational resources enabled by high-density semiconductor chips. The exponential growth in processing power has been instrumental in the development of LLMs. It allows for the handling of enormous datasets and the execution of complex algorithms, essential for the training and operation of these models. Thus, semiconductors are not just components in a circuit; they are the conduits that have enabled the age of digital data/information to flourish. In the context of LLMs, they represent the bridge between the theoretical possibilities of AI and their practical realisation. These developments have been crucial as they enabled the processing of larger datasets and the execution of more complex algorithms, laying the groundwork for the sophisticated AI models in use today. However, a new generation of AI-specific semiconductors might be needed to keep pace, and OpenAI has expressed interest in setting up its own design team and acquiring a semiconductor maker to do so (Anderton, 2023).

Geoffrey Hinton's foundational work in neural networks, particularly with a focus on back-propagation and deep learning algorithms, set the stage for these later advancements in AI, establishing the fundamental principles that would drive future developments in the field. The year 2012 might be marked as a pivotal moment in AI history with the development of AlexNet by Alex Krizhevsky, Ilya Sutskever, and Geoffrey Hinton (see also Chapter 4). This deep neural network significantly outperformed its contemporaries in the ImageNet challenge, demonstrating the practical potential of deep learning, particularly in image recognition. Some years prior, Fei-Fei Li's work on the ImageNet project (2006) provided a large-scale, structured dataset that became instrumental in training and benchmarking AI models in image processing. ImageNet's extensive database played a key role in advancing image recognition technologies, setting a new standard in the field.

As noted above, the other significant advancement was the introduction of Transformer architectures by Vaswani et al. (2017). This development marked a leap in handling sequential data, laying the groundwork for more effective and efficient language models. The Transformer model's ability to handle long-range dependencies in data opened new possibilities in NLP. Following this, OpenAI as one example introduced the Generative Pre-trained Transformer series, starting with the original GPT and evolving to GPT-4o. Each version of the GPT series brought significant improvements in scale, complexity, and versatility, with GPT-4o demonstrating extraordinary capabilities in generating human-like text and the capacity to create images from text prompts. This deep engagement with natural language enables image generation tools to decode and interpret text prompts, effectively managing complexities such as grammatical errors, colloquial language, multilingual content, and even symbolic communication such as emojis. These models showcase the feasibility of using a single architecture for a wide array of tasks, ranging from simple text generation to complex problem-solving. The subsequent period from 2020 to 2023 witnessed the emergence of DALL·E, the image generation model by OpenAI. Utilising a variant of the GPT-3 architecture, DALL·E demonstrated the ability to generate images from textual descriptions, marking a significant leap in the creative capabilities of AI. This development illustrated the adaptability of the GPT architecture beyond text, venturing into the realm of visual content.

Moving to the domain of visual understanding, the technology becomes even more profound. In this context, the relevance of image content analysis emerges, particularly through tools like DALL E, or Stable Diffusion, which integrates capabilities such as 'CLIP' or Contrastive Language-Image Pre-training (You, Zhou, Xiao, Codella, Cheng, Xu, Chang, & Yuan, 2022). This function embarks on an extensive analysis of millions of images, each annotated with metadata that provides insights into the content, style, and contextual background of the imagery. The scale of data involved in training such systems is monumental. For instance, when compared to traditional datasets like ImageNet, which involved an enormous human effort to sort millions of images into thousands of categories, the approach taken by CLIP represents a significant evolution. It learns from a vast array of text-image pairs already available online, thereby exceeding the scale of ImageNet and marking a pivotal shift in how AI systems are trained and how they function in the realm of media analysis and generation (Agarwal, Krueger, Clark, Radford, Kim, & Brundage, 2021). ChatGPT-4, released in 2023, further pushed the boundaries of AI, showcasing increased complexity and broader applicability across various domains. Around the same time, Midjourney emerged as another significant player in the AI-driven image generation space. Although details about its development and underlying technology are less transparent compared to DALL·E, Midjourney represents another stride in the advancement of AI capabilities in image generation, and Sora with its projected capacity to turns AI prompts into photorealistic, cinematic videos when released will likely be another (Levey, 2024).

Inevitably, Moore's Law became redundant due to the physical limits on miniaturisation and the challenges associated with improving superconductor properties. However, Romero (2023) points out that:

> Software developers and systems engineers have worked hard to be ready for this moment for years and they succeeded—all thanks to AI. Now, AI software and AI-enabled systems can pick up where Moore's Law left off. AI tools and applications—more specifically Generative AI—allow existing infrastructure to do 1,000-x what it did with traditional computing.

The field continues to evolve rapidly, with ongoing research and development focused on improving the efficiency, ethics, and applications of these AI models. The recent advances in AI, from its early foundations in neural networks to the emergence of sophisticated language and image models, reflect a relentless pursuit of knowledge and innovation in AI. It highlights the symbiotic relationship between computational capabilities and data availability and underscores the integral role of creative researchers and interdisciplinary collaboration in shaping our understanding and interaction with technology. The integration of generative AI technology into a comprehensive suite of workplace applications represents a pivotal shift in digital communication, the generation of data and information, media access, and the rapidly expanding reach to millions of users across various sectors, including individuals, businesses, and governments, thereby significantly accelerating the production of online content at an unprecedented scale. That is, generative AI might be said to facilitate more efficient and effective communication because it can generate, summarise, evaluate, translate, and personalise content, making digital interactions faster and more accessible. This can lead to a significant increase in the speed and scope of information exchange. Coupled with this is the capacity for large (and small) data sets to be analysed and for patterns to be quickly identified with insights generated at scale and at a speed unattainable by humans. This capability is transforming how we understand and use data, arguably leading to more informed decision-making in various sectors. Subsequently for media, the positive affordances are that generative AI might revolutionise content creation, from text to images and video where it democratises media production, allowing individuals and organisations to create high-quality content without needing extensive resources. This leads to a more diverse range of voices and perspectives in the media landscape akin to the introduction of The Gutenberg Press (the 15th-century invention of Johannes Gutenberg, the first mechanical printing press, that increased significantly the circulation of information via a greater production of books, making them more accessible and affordable, which significantly contributed to the spread of knowledge and increased literacy rates in societies). With the ability to quickly generate and disseminate information, AI technology extends the reach of individuals, businesses, and governments more broadly enabling each sector to engage with millions of users across the globe with the possibility of breaking down geographical and language barriers and also challenging current economic models. With a critical lens, however, such AI efficiency in producing content results in an unprecedented scale of online content creation leading to an information overload, challenging users to discern quality and accuracy in the vast amount of available content. Such challenges include the potentials for the wide circulation and manipulation of misinformation, calls for effective content moderation, and ethical considerations given in societies—which differ greatly—regarding AI's various uses and impacts on human labour, education, and to the natural environment itself.

Delving into Hyper-Personalised Media Confluence

Hyper-personalised media confluence represents a conceptual approach to understanding the dynamics of modern media consumption and interaction. It encapsulates two essential aspects of the evolving digital landscape—hyper-personalisation and media confluence. Hyper-personalisation denotes an advanced level of personalisation wherein the content, format, delivery, and interaction are real-time and data-driven, tailored and based on the continuous gathering and analysis of individual users' behaviour, context, and feedback. This 'hyper' element signifies a profound shift from traditional personalisation tactics, leveraging advanced data analytics, AI, and machine learning technologies to deliver highly customised or bespoke media experiences. At the same time, media confluence emphasises the seemingly frictionless integration and convergence of diverse media forms and platforms, towards creating a unified, fluid user experience at speed. More than just accessing different digital information, data or media from one device, it signifies a shifting of the boundaries between different media forms such that they become almost invisible as we pull them from single interfaces such as a wearable device, 'phone' or tablet. But are we rendered 'ghostlike' in the process?

The Digital Spectre of Self

In the realm of digital life, a 'spectre of self' emerges as a lens for understanding the dynamics of media consumption and interaction in the age of hyper-personalised media confluence. This notion encapsulates the complexities around how personal identity is continuously shaped, projected, and reinterpreted within the digital space. The *spectre of self* implies that our digital personas are not mere reflections but are spectres—ghostly presences

96 Emerging Digital Media Ecologies

that both represent and transcend our real selves (Cinque, 2022a). It finds resonance in the fabric of hyper-personalised media, a phenomenon where media consumption is an active, immediate, global, participatory process. This confluence is characterised by digital interactions where the lines between producer and consumer, reality and virtuality, and personal and public spheres are increasingly blurred and the complexities of this digital era involve the nuanced interplay of algorithms, AI, big/small data, and their implications for the spectre of self. With reference to Jacques Derrida's paronomastic compound term, 'hauntology', a pixelated, digital spectre of the self is a Derridean ghost of one's real identity, within an ontology of the being of non-being and the non-being of being, of something/someone 'not there'. For: '[t]here is no Dasein of the spectre, but there is no Dasein without the uncanniness, without the strange familiarity (Unheimlichkeit) of some spectre' (Derrida, 1994, p. 165). The everyday is punctuated by returns such that:

> [t]he spectre is thus both past and future; it is from the past but waiting to come back. The metaphor of a spectre haunting the present establishes the idea/image of the existence of something ghostly which stands over and outside the present, something which does not belong to time, and is waiting to come.
>
> *(Hughes, 2012, p. 15)*

The digital, prosopopoeial spectre of self acts here to position moments/actions in/across time revealing aspects of users' significant lived experiences. The transmuted, pixilated spectre of self encourages thinking beyond a single piece of personal data (a post, a photo, a comment, like or share, geo-location data) to build a new perception and presentation of self (Goffman, 1956) that is constructed in parallel to that formed by traditional in-real-life agents of socialisation such as friends, peers, religion, culture, media, legal and economic systems, and so forth (Giddens, 1993). Our profiles, personalised pages, and customised accounts do not merely reflect the self, but to all intents, constructions, and purposes 'are constitutive of the self they apparently represent' (Kant, 2020, p. 57).

In the nearness of now, the technical ability to leverage the power of machine (deep) learning and AI to recreate (fake) existing images, photographs, videos, and/or sound files, as replicated or synthetic versions of an original, has the immense capacity to deceive. Examples include Mark Zuckerberg 'admitting' that Facebook's true goal is to manipulate and exploit its users, to elected officials appearing drunk or making statements that never happened. This has seen a rise in synthetic media, fake and misleading news, and misrepresentation online which impacts public opinion. Such troubling practices underscore significant implications in this neo-communicative process. Not only do the various media forms have the potential to bring heterogenous actors and events into an alliance (Bratton, 2015) but they are technically 'open' to allow manipulation by end users. Once particular connections and patterns of interaction are established, algorithms that personalise digital content can lead to filter bubbles (Marchi, 2012), which limits the platform's potential as a democratic public sphere (Habermas, 1989), leading to 'us and them' narratives that potentially erode social cohesion (see Chapter 6). Thus, concerns about the role that digital and social media play in politics and society are increasing (Omidyar, 2018; Tucker, Theocharis, Roberts, & Barbera, 2017).

AI also places us on the precipice of a new frontier in cyber espionage. A recent incident involving Australian journalist Andrew Phelan, arrested for an allegedly violent email sent to a female journalist, underscores the growing threat (Aitchison, 2023). Phelan's claim of hacking, later substantiated, sheds light on a competitive 'cottage industry' wherein data is scraped, systems hacked, or users deceived with the goal to acquire and sell valuable information. Exploiting users for their data hinges on three key factors: user complacency, convenience, and gullibility. Despite reminders, users often neglect software updates, leaving their systems vulnerable. Convenience leads many to unwittingly introduce malware via USB devices acquired during travel, work-related events or conferences. Additionally, users can be easily tricked by spam emails containing malicious links. Here, generative AI can also enable the crafting of convincing emails to ensnare unsuspecting targets. With AI's prowess, entire email servers can be downloaded, the content translated into multiple languages, and relevant data extracted for illicit sale.

The 'fears' surrounding technology raised in society are often unpacked in popular media such that the spectre of self can be found and is depicted as being on the edge of a societal fall. Notable examples are Zoe Greystone and the Cylons in the television series *Caprica* (2009–2010), Ash (among others) in *Black Mirror* (Brooker, 2011), and the hosts of *Westworld* (Nolan & Joy, 2016). A re-occurring theme within these screen examples is that of faithful reproduction or in using the key phrase of *Westworld* 'fidelity'. In *Caprica*, Zoe discovers the algorithm to digitally recreate a person by searching and scraping any available data, including but not limited to, social media and health records, and compiling this with biometric data collected by the original person. Social media is presented as a recurrent source of data in the examples above. The concerns raised in the narratives noted here are to be read as key issues in the social construction of contemporary 'information societies' (see Castells, 2000b; Beniger, 1986). In addition to this, social media is intrinsically linked to society:

> Through an anthropological perspective, social media shows us that what individuals post (even posts that appear as forms of self-expression) are

in fact a product of society itself–the norms, aspirations, tensions and contradictions that exist simultaneously.

(Sinanan, 2017, p. 206)

Epistemologically, Grace's (2014) 'particulate vision' describes a different relation to reality, one that is vital/affirmative (Braidotti, 2013), and that is reflective of the atomisation or fragmentation of contemporary experience especially apparent in everyday online activity and social media use. Beyond well-rehearsed dystopian visions of the internet (Stoll, 1996) and fearful visions for society (Turkle, 2017), Grace (2014) has argued that when spontaneous decisions are made to capture objects and events deemed worthy of attention as a visual image (via camera phone or the like), a certain everydayness is produced that is far from meaningless, shallow or characteristic of a rising 'culture of narcissism' (Lasch, 1979). The author argues against the negative proposition that random picture taking and sharing—of healthy food or outdoor activities and gym-based accomplishments by 'QSers' (related to the Quantified Self 'movement' and interest of a number in measuring and recording their physical achievements)—are no more than forms of narcissistic attention-seeking. Instead, Grace poetically presents the captured digital image as the user's thought or impression of a feeling at a particular moment in time, from which a more meaningful world—a multiplicity of 'sphericules' to use Gitlin's (1998) term for how 'we' might be imagined if our thoughts are able to 'wander' (or circulate) far enough. At the individual level, the focus on the spectre of self can be used then with critical consideration given to our active/affirmative individual agency when engaging with interconnected digital technologies across a range of ever-changing platforms.

The proliferation of mobile apps, epitomised by the adoption of contact tracing technologies during the COVID-19 pandemic and wearable devices like Fitbits and smartwatches to flexible batteries fitted to 'smart clothing', does, however, signify a new era of continuous data tracking (Cinque, 2022b). This omnipresent digital engagement—stemming from the inception of social platforms such as Facebook, YouTube, and Instagram, to more recent ones like TikTok, Signal, Mastodon, or Bluesky—has redefined human interaction and information exchange. These platforms, driven by sophisticated algorithms and AI, are not mere tools but actors that shape our perception of reality and identity (Cinque, 2023). Certainly, cultural context significantly influences how different societies interact with technology. The impact of mobile technology in African countries, for example, has transformed economic activities through mobiles such that the phone becomes 'Africanised' being incorporated into the local contexts for trade practices and to support local businesses (Ogone, 2020). Such examples illustrate that technology, its adoption and usage can indeed be shaped by cultural norms, values, and economic conditions.

ChatGPT-4, for its part, with its advanced language understanding and generation capabilities, has shown promising potential as a personal counsellor, as evidenced by the perceptions of a significant majority of participants in a study (Howe, Fay, Saletta, & Hovy, 2023). Approximately three-quarters of these individuals found the advice provided by ChatGPT-4 to be more balanced, complete, empathetic, and helpful compared to that given by human professionals. This reflects the model's ability to process and respond to a wide range of personal concerns with a level of depth and sensitivity that resonates with users. The AI's comprehensive database allows it to draw from a vast pool of knowledge and experiences, enabling it to offer diverse perspectives and solutions. Its empathetic response style, which is designed to mirror human understanding and compassion, further enhances its effectiveness as a counselling tool. While ChatGPT-4 is not a replacement for professional human counsellors, it can serve as a valuable supplementary resource, offering accessible, immediate, and thoughtful advice to those seeking guidance. This highlights the potential of AI to augment human capabilities in areas traditionally requiring human expertise. If users opt to create a bio-profile, they should, however, be aware that their interactions could be linked to their profile.

OpenAI has been exploring, and now implementing, user-defined bio-profiles and the capacity for carrying forward 'memories' or knowledge and context from one conversation to another, across separate sessions, to enhance and enmesh contextual understanding in applications like ChatGPT Plus. This approach would allow the AI to adjust its responses in content, complexity, and technical depth based on the dynamic integration of insights from multiple user interactions (OpenAI Community, 2023). Integrating bio-profiles into AI-enhanced counselling tools raises crucial privacy concerns due to the sensitivity of personal information involved, which demands stringent security protocols and compliance with data protection laws such as the General Data Protection Regulation or the like. There is an inherent risk of discrimination in employment if such data, whether accessed legally or illicitly, is used to evaluate an individual's mental health or personal stability. This could also lead to reputational damage if sensitive data were leaked. Furthermore, the AI system itself might develop biases based on user data, potentially leading to unfair or unequal advice that could perpetuate existing societal disparities. Essential here is transparency about how data is used, safeguarding user consent, and providing clear channels for users to control their information—users need to be fully and critically aware of what data is collected, how it is used, and have actively consented to these processes and be able to easily withdraw consent and request deletion of their data through a straightforward, transparent process. Such steps would be essential to mitigate these risks, maintain user trust, and ensure the ethical use of AI in sensitive settings.

Datafication presents an ethical conundrum. As data becomes foundational to digital interaction, its enigmatic nature poses profound ethical challenges. The balance is delicate and complex, for example, on one hand, data harnessing can lead to positive outcomes like enhanced social connections and improved health; on the other, it risks perpetuating negative consequences such as cybercrime and privacy invasions. Consequently, digital literacy becomes paramount in navigating these multifaceted digital landscapes, where the demarcation between private and public spheres blurs increasingly. One's existence is shaped not only by the data one generates and the societal interactions one engages in but also by the pervasive influence of networked technologies. However, not all individuals have access to the necessary digital communications infrastructure and its ensuing products, leading to disparities in education, with consequential socio-economic impacts. Despite this, the environmental impacts are globally felt.

Training large AI models can consume as much energy as several residential homes over a year, leading to a substantial carbon footprint, especially if the power is sourced from fossil fuels. This was highlighted by research from the University of Massachusetts, Amherst, which equated the emissions from training a significant AI model to the lifetime emissions for an average car, including fuel (126,000 lbs CO_2e) (Strubell, Ganesh, & McCallum, 2019, p. 1). Furthermore, the data centres required to run these AIs significantly contribute to energy consumption; the annual electricity report from the International Energy Agency (IEA, 2024) found that data centres consumed 460TWh in 2022 (or 2% of global usage), and suggests the figure could rise to more than 1,000TWh by 2026 due to power-hungry GPUs. This energy use also correlates with increased e-waste due to the rapid hardware turnover necessary to support the latest AI advancements. These factors necessitate the adoption of greener energy sources and more efficient computing practices to mitigate the ecological impact of AI systems.

Being precluded from, or opting to go 'off-grid'—eschewing mobile phones, computers, smart TVs, or digital cash—does not extricate one from the digital world. Many societies engage with these technologies; and familial, corporate, and governmental expectations often involve us in this digital ecosystem, frequently without our explicit consent. Consider children whose images are shared online by proud but perhaps overzealous relatives before they are old enough to consent, or people whose personal details—from public health records, tax file numbers, and migration records—are stored by governments. Even the routine observation by security cameras as people navigate public spaces or the data collected at a supermarket's self-checkout contribute to the formation of a digital version of ourselves. This digital-self is a pixelated representation, evolving continuously as it is reshaped by the relentless flow of data and information exchanges. The collection, storage, and

Exploring Hyper-Personalised Media Confluence **101**

curation of both big and small data sets, alongside the proliferation of the IoT, exacerbate this dynamic. In this era, characterised by the sheer volume, variety, velocity, and value of digital data, our world has become an interconnected mesh of physical and digital entities, melding together cyber-physical systems and open systems. This networked infrastructure significantly influences our daily experiences and interactions. As technology becomes increasingly integral to every facet of human life—from monitoring childhood development to social, educational, and familial settings—it necessitates a re-evaluation of our agency and social constructs. The digitalisation of every human experience and the subsequent 'algorithmic turn' call for a deeper understanding of how technology reconfigures our social connections and cultural norms. Accentuating this perspective, this book aims to present a non-binary view of technology in that while many embrace its possibilities and actively engage with it, others find its applications less apparent. This spectrum of responses brings various critical issues to the forefront, illustrating the diverse ways in which we interact with and understand technology.

The Rise of Digital Intelligent Interface Agents

The realisation of AI companions—for intimate connection such as Replika and 'friend' to the functional ChatGPT-4o, Copilot, and Bard—and many others across global regions—epitomises Nicholas Negroponte's 1995 prediction of Intelligent Interface Agents, highlighting the rapid advancement and widespread adoption of personal digital assistants in today's interconnected world. Moreover, the development of polymathic AI companions, potentially akin to the fictional droids from *Star Wars* being made tangible, is becoming increasingly feasible.

> [T]he concept of 'agent' embodied in humans helping humans is often one where expertise is indeed mixed with knowledge of you. A good travel agent blends knowledge about hotels and restaurants with knowledge about you (which often is culled from what you thought about other hotels and restaurants). A real estate agent builds a model of you from a succession of houses that fit your taste with varying degrees of success. Now imagine a telephone-answering agent, a news agent, or an electronic-mail-managing agent. What they all have in common is the ability to model you.
>
> *(Negroponte, 1995, p. 163)*

Nicholas Negroponte was one of the first to predict signals or 'agents' with 'a sense of themselves' referring to the concept of intelligent or self-aware digital systems. This idea involves digital signals or systems having the capability to understand, process, and possibly even react to their own state or the

102 Emerging Digital Media Ecologies

information they carry. Negroponte envisioned a future with more personalised and intelligent digital interactions. He argued (1995, pp. 150–151):

> The 'agent' answers the phone, recognizes the callers, disturbs you when appropriate, and may even tell a white lie on your behalf. The same agent is well trained in timing, versed in finding the opportune moments, and respectful of idiosyncrasies … It has become obvious that people want to delegate more functions and prefer to directly manipulate computers less.

Pulling this thread, in the evolving digital landscape, the role of Digital Intelligent Interface Agents powered by LLMs (often developed on Small Language Models) will become increasingly central. Individuals will no longer need to navigate the overwhelming expanse of digital information alone. Instead, they will rely on these advanced AI systems to sift through vast quantities of data, such as thousands of web pages and social media sites, ensuring that the most interesting and critical information is not missed. This shift seemingly signifies a move towards a more streamlined, efficient, and user-centric approach to information management in the digital age. Following Negroponte, we find our future realised where the convergence of advanced LLMs and Digital Intelligent Interface Agents herald a new era in media and information consumption. These intelligent systems do have the capability to quickly process and analyse every newswire, newspaper, broadcast from television and radio, streaming service and podcast globally. They may aggregate this vast array of information for us and also tailor personalised summaries, effectively answer user questions and thus they span the gap between the deluge of global information and the individual's specific informational needs. This development signifies a transformative step in how we interact with, and come to comprehend, the ever-expanding digital world.

Moreover, the proliferation of rich content freely available online enables the creation of increasingly sophisticated social and corporate insights. This development has the potential to effect substantial societal changes. Currently, algorithms and big data are shaping our sociocultural relationships and daily experiences. As media infrastructures, practices, and social environments become progressively datafied—a concept discussed by Schäfer and van Es (2017)—digital culture and communication are undergoing significant transformation. By drawing on key infrastructures, one is able to engage with 'big data' from leading social media platforms in hitherto unprecedented detail and to respond swiftly to emerging phenomena in social media usage. This scenario brings the concept of hyper-personalised media confluence into sharper focus, advancing the discourse on medialogy and its critical implications for user experience, business models, ethical considerations, sociocultural impacts, and media literacy. For those with both access and inclination, the increasing personalisation of digital interfaces, powered by advanced language models, reflects a detailed array of individual preferences, entertainment choices, and social behaviours. This hyper-personalised digital landscape becomes an extension of one's unique digital footprint, offering a customised digital experience that mirrors the vast spectrum of their digital life. Ubiquitous computing, far from being antithetical to personal digital interface agents, is fundamentally linked to them. The omnipresence of computing in our daily activities, from making airline reservations to engaging in point-of-sale transactions, is increasingly integrated through diverse and formerly isolated computer processes. This interconnected digital ecosystem brings about an unprecedented level of convenience and efficiency where metadata—encompassing keywords, content and location data, and references—will become increasingly sophisticated. This metadata will be generated and enriched both by human intelligence and machine algorithms, creating a valuable layer of 'header information' that enables our devices to understand and anticipate our needs more effectively. For example, Netflix is an intelligent digital agent capable of sifting through thousands of hours of content to curate a personalised viewing experience based on supplemented metadata. This agent intelligently discerns and selects content relevant to our interests from past viewing experiences. As Castells (2010) might suggest, this evolution embodies the essence of a network society, where the flow of information is directly tailored to individual nodes within the network—in this case, the users—frictionlessly transforming the way many interact with, make sense of, and navigate the vast digital universe.

Countering the Myth of Efficiency: A Provocation

While efficiency can bring numerous benefits in terms of productivity and economic growth, its pursuit as a singular goal can have adverse social, ethical, and environmental consequences. It is important to balance the drive for efficiency with considerations of human well-being, ethical integrity, cultural diversity, and environmental sustainability. A relentless focus on efficiency can lead to the undervaluing of human labour and expertise. As automation and AI increase efficiency, there is a risk of job displacement and reduced opportunities for meaningful human engagement in work. This can lead to a range of social issues, including unemployment, economic inequality, and a loss of identity and purpose for individuals whose jobs are automated. Efficiency often emphasises speed and cost-effectiveness, which can come at the expense of quality and creativity as well. When the primary goal is to do things faster and more cheaply, there may be less room for creative processes that require time and resources, potentially stifling innovation and the development of novel ideas. Further, the social and cultural impact arising from an efficiency-driven approach can homogenise culture and experiences, as standardised, efficient solutions often lack sensitivity to local, cultural, and individual differences. This can lead to a loss of cultural diversity and a diminution of human experiences and values. Additionally, the constant drive for efficiency can contribute to a high-pressure, fast-paced work culture that neglects employee well-being. This may manifest in burnout, stress, and mental health issues, impacting both individuals and the broader social fabric. A further impact on societies is the important ethical and moral considerations that might be sidelined in the pursuit of creating efficient AI systems. That is, developers might overlook or underprioritise issues related to privacy, data security, or the ethical implications of AI decision-making. In terms of important environmental concerns in industrial and technological contexts, efficiency improvements often lead to increased consumption and production, which can result in more waste and greater environmental degradation.

As rapid technological development is experienced, individuals are continually afforded connections to personal devices and digital infrastructures, potentially leading to a societal overdependence on technology. This dependency manifests in several ways, from the vulnerabilities exposed by telecommunications outages and corporate data hacks to the behavioural dependencies engendered by digital devices, such as gambling and the fear of missing out. Such issues highlight the critical need to prioritise technological efficiency carefully, as overreliance can make individuals and organisations susceptible to technological failures or cybersecurity threats. Moreover, this dependence may erode critical thinking and problem-solving skills, with people increasingly looking to AI for answers and solutions. By way of making sense of this dilemma is the question of whether the capacity to perform mathematical tasks was diminished by the introduction of the calculator as a tool to help perform mathematical operations more quickly and accurately. Here our 'AI-driven agents' come to serve as an extension of human capabilities, allowing us to focus on more complex aspects of problem-solving and gaining improvements in 'workflows'. The calculator, however, handles routine calculations. Notably, calculators do not replace the fundamental understanding or ability to do math. AI represents a more advanced and complex technology. Unlike calculators, AI systems, particularly those using machine learning, might be developed with the ability to learn from data, recognise patterns, make decisions, and even adapt collectively 'in swarms' to new scenarios without explicit human programming. This collective 'swarm' approach involves multiple AI agents working collaboratively to enhance decision-making or problem-solving capabilities whereby each agent in the swarm contributes partial knowledge or computational power, and through interactions among the agents, the group collectively arrives at a solution that is typically more efficient or robust than those derived from individual efforts. For example, Unanimous AI developed a platform called 'Swarm' that harnesses the collective intelligence of groups by connecting them into a real-time swarm system. This technology has been

Exploring Hyper-Personalised Media Confluence **105**

used to enhance decision-making in fields such as business forecasting, market predictions, and medical diagnostics. The process involves algorithms that enable cooperation, competition, and adaptation among agents based on real-time feedback, mirroring natural selection mechanisms. AI swarm technology also finds applications in optimising logistics, enhancing predictive analytics, and automating complex tasks in dynamic environments. This outcome may be improved outcomes, resilience and scalability in systems where traditional, centralised AI approaches might falter. This capability suggests that AI could potentially perform tasks that go beyond mere assistance, venturing into areas of problem-solving, creativity, and decision-making that were traditionally considered exclusive to human intelligence.

The unknown potential of AI, including its ability to possibly discover solutions or create in ways that humans have not conceived beyond the field of mathematics, marks a significant departure from the straightforward, supportive role of tools like calculators. This argument underscores the distinction between tools that enhance existing human capabilities (like calculators) and more sophisticated systems like AI-driven agents, which have the potential to autonomously generate insights, solutions, or actions that might not be immediately intuitive to human users, thereby opening up possibilities (solving our worst environmental problems) and challenges (autonomous capabilities in war-robots) with impacts that are yet to be fully understood.

Conclusion

In the context of media ecologies, the digital-self thrives within a complex system of interacting media technologies and platforms. Medialogy recognises that no single media platform exists in isolation; rather, each is part of an interconnected network that shapes and is shaped by human interaction and the environs in which each operates. For example, the way individuals use social media to express different facets of identity exemplifies this interdependence. Indicatively, users can customise their profiles with personal details and preferences on platforms such as Facebook, showcasing facets of their identity through listed interests and background information. Content sharing on platforms such as Instagram allows individuals to post images and videos that reflect their personal interests, aesthetic preferences, and daily activities, enabling a visual narrative of their identity. Additionally, users engage in communities and groups on sites like LinkedIn, participating in discussions tied to professional or hobbyist interests that further delineate aspects of their identity. Moreover, storytelling through status updates and threads on platforms like 'X' offers a dynamic way to share personal experiences and opinions, providing insights into users' values and personalities. Furthermore, interactive features such as polls, quizzes, and filters on Instagram and

Snapchat allow users to engage creatively with their audience, adding a playful and dynamic layer to how they express their moods, preferences, and aspects of their personality. Considering these developments, the 'spectre of self' offers a critical framework for understanding the affordances and implications of our digital lives at the level of the individual. It acknowledges that our digital personas are more than just digital footprints or online profiles; they are complex, multi-dimensional spectres that exist in a perpetual state of flux, shaped by the continuous interaction between various media interfaces and platforms.

While more personalised and integrated media experiences are being enabled, simultaneously, this may contribute to the formation of echo chambers and filter bubbles, as well as new forms of the digital divide based on access and aptitude for use. For most, everyday life has become dependent on, and saturated with, AI-infused emerging media forms. Each allows individuals, corporations, governments, and others to choose the most suitable media-like platform for a particular interaction, thus tailoring their digital presence according to the nuances of each platform which embeds experiences deeply into our social fabric. Hyper-personalised media confluence poses significant challenges and opportunities for media providers, marketers, and advertisers. As media consumption becomes increasingly personalised and integrated, the effectiveness of traditional mass marketing strategies dwindles. Companies must leverage the potential of hyper-personalised media confluence to develop targeted, context-aware marketing strategies that are fluid across different media platforms. In a world where media consumption is highly personalised and integrated, traditional notions of media literacy are also insufficient. Today's users must develop the skills to navigate and the expertise to critically evaluate and create content in a hyper-personalised and integrated media landscape—the concept of hyper-personalised media confluence is a step towards this unpacking. In examining current trends, challenges, and opportunities, the need for new perspectives and strategies in media consumption, production, regulation, ethics, and education is being underscored.

6

DESIGNING DIGITAL MEDIA LITERACIES FOR SOCIAL COHESION

Contextualising Enhanced Media and Communications

Processes of digitalisation and the resulting datafication of everyday life are partly due to globally networked and interactive media platforms. These platforms have impacted communication by bridging physical distances and fostering remote communities. The term 'confluence', discussed in Chapter 5, suggests merging or coming together. In the context of medialogy, it refers to the connection to, and integration of, various media platforms and services, resulting in hyper-personalised media confluence. This confluence includes the amalgamation of content from different media such as online streaming, social media, and gaming platforms to offer a unified user experience. Such convergence allows users to access personalised content anytime, anywhere, and on any device, dissolving the traditional barriers between media forms. Advanced telecommunications networks and information technologies, alongside the integration of Application Programming Interfaces (APIs) across major social networks—including Facebook, Instagram, Reddit, TikTok, and Twitter-now 'X' (but with tiered pricing from 2023)—further contribute to this trend. These networks distribute user-generated content that is conversational and globally connected, thus shaping and expanding communities.

However, digital platforms can also serve as arenas for the spread of ideologies, manipulation of public sentiment, and control over perceptions (Salojärvi et al., 2023). Social platform algorithms, powered by extensive data drawn from APIs, analyse user behaviour, preferences, and interactions to curate personalised content feeds, such as short-form podcast edits, aligning with individual interests (Peukert, Senm, & Claussen, 2023). The ability to customise and personalise is central to these algorithms, ensuring uniquely

DOI: 10.4324/9781003178149-8

108 Emerging Digital Media Ecologies

tailored feeds for each user's digital footprint. Automation across platforms directly influences the visibility and engagement of short-form content, like podcast edits, on social media. These snippets, designed to encapsulate longer podcasts, cater to a social media audience who prefers concise, digestible content. As a result, personalised content spreads across platforms, engaging users in a conversational and globally connected manner. This interplay between technological affordances with user practices and preferences leads to the formation of 'filter bubbles', where algorithms personalise digital content to the point of isolating users within echo chambers. Therefore, the integration of APIs in social media platforms is a trade-off. While they facilitate unprecedented engagement and community growth, they also test the creation of homogenised information spaces.

In this chapter, we explore framing and scaffolding pro-social uses of 'enhanced media' to deepen our understanding of what it means to be positively engaged digital users and citizens. This chapter highlights the phenomenon of hyper-personalised media confluence, facilitated by emerging media comprising networked digital platforms, interactive screen technologies, and Artificial Intelligence (AI) tools intrinsically linked to our social networks and beyond them. The role of these technologies is pivotal in defining and representing communities, enabling the convergence of diverse actors and events, while also being vulnerable to manipulation. This is crucial for understanding the contemporary media landscape.

Bad Actors and Online Harms

APIs serve as critical interfaces for software applications to interact, particularly across social media platforms, where they play a pivotal role in the circulation of user-driven, conversational, and networked content (Nawaz, Khan, Hussain, & Iqbal, 2023). By granting developers access to platform-specific features, APIs enable the integration of social media content and interactions into an extensive range of third-party applications and services, thus facilitating content sharing and distribution across various platforms. This capability not only amplifies the reach and impact of user-generated content but also contributes significantly to the growth and definition of online communities. APIs enhance content distribution by streamlining the sharing process across platforms, thereby extending audience reach. For instance, a news website might utilise an API to enable users to share articles directly to social networks such as Facebook or LinkedIn with a single click. Additionally, APIs empower the creation of bespoke applications or tools that boost user engagement and interaction, for example, by supporting real-time comments or content-sharing functionalities. Furthermore, APIs provide access to extensive social media data, enabling the analysis of trends, sentiments, and user behaviour. This analysis informs content strategies that are tailored to the specific interests and needs of communities, thus fostering deeper connections within them by offering content recommendations based on user activities across different platforms. Moreover, APIs ensure cross-platform connectivity, which allows users to develop a unified online presence and a cohesive community engagement strategy across multiple networks. Through third-party integrations, APIs facilitate the creation of applications and services that interact with these platforms, potentially fostering more integrated and cohesive user experiences. This, in turn, may encourage community growth by simplifying the processes of content dissemination and management.

There is, however, a delicate balance to be maintained between offering a highly personalised experience and respecting user privacy. In the context of datafication—the conversion of social interactions into quantifiable data— the feedback loop provided by APIs yields granular insights into content consumption and sharing patterns. These insights afford a deeper understanding of individuals and community dynamics, aiding in the refinement of content strategies and fostering community growth. Such practices play a pivotal role in this 'neo-communicative process', a term that refers to the novel forms and strategies of creating, sharing, and interpreting information that have emerged in digital environments, characterised by interactivity, multimodality, and user-generated content. The interactions between such heterogeneous media forms can and do bring diverse actors and events into alliance, as posited by Bratton (2015). Additionally, media forms are technically 'open', allowing manipulation by end-users, including 'bad actors' who exploit digital platforms, particularly social media, to propagate their ideologies, manipulate public sentiment, and control the perceptions of their members (Salojärvi, Palonen, Horsmanheimo, & Kylli, 2023).

Algorithms that personalise digital content can contribute to the creation of 'filter bubbles'. As explored in Chapter 5, a hyper-personalised media confluence has developed, centred around the increasingly sophisticated use of data analytics and AI technologies. These technologies collect and analyse vast amounts of data on individual users' preferences, habits, and content consumption patterns. AI algorithms can predict what content a user is likely to enjoy, when they might want to consume it, and on which platform or device, creating an almost intuitive media experience for the individual. There is also an increased potential for coercion, misrepresentation, and the falsification of people and information. For one example, products such as Descript (www. descript.com) afford users the ability to generate AI voices which means that individuals can replicate the sound and cadence of real voices with minimal training and astonishing accuracy. Additionally, Descript's overdub feature allows users to modify audio recordings by seamlessly inserting new words or phrases into existing recordings. While this can be a powerful tool for editing and improving audio content for journalists and the like, it also raises questions about the authenticity of audio recordings. While this technology can be

110 Emerging Digital Media Ecologies

incredibly useful for various applications, it also opens the door to potential misuse, including impersonation (Khanjani, Watson, & Janeja, 2023). With AI-generated voices, someone could theoretically create audio recordings that sound like specific individuals, leading to concerns about identity theft, fraud, or the spread of misinformation. The proliferation of AI-based forgery stands as a formidable threat to truth and authenticity. With the widespread accessibility and lower cost of generative AI and its accompanying tools, the manipulation and forging of video, audio, images, synthetic personalities as 'influencers' and text are poised to escalate. The exponential growth would not only undermine the integrity of key media and communication channels but also erode the very foundation of trust upon which many societies rely (see www.truemedia.org/ for identifying political deepfakes in social media).

Online harms, including media manipulation, synthetic media (fake news, images, data, and information), social exclusion, coercion, online hate, racism, and radicalisation to violence, are of increasing concern in this context. As previous research has indicated (Edwards & Ugwudike, 2023; Hope, 2013; Buckingham, 1998), punitive or didactic approaches based on behavioural regulation and monitoring are insufficient to address these complex socio-technical issues and might, in fact, exacerbate rather than mitigate adverse trajectories.

Table 6.1 summarises various factors that contribute to the spread and sustenance of extremist ideologies in digital environments. It provides a structured analysis of the digital landscape that can facilitate radicalisation through different pathways. The first category, 'Digital Echo Chambers and Radicalisation Pathways', highlights how social media algorithms can inadvertently create echo chambers that amplify extremist content, which can lead to radicalisation. The mention of microtargeting points out how extremists might use data analytics to specifically target individuals who may be susceptible to their messages.

Category 2 'Anonymity and Decentralisation' outlines how the internet's provision for anonymity allows individuals to explore and engage with extremist ideologies without the fear of social stigma. It also points out the challenge of monitoring and countering extremist activities due to their operation in decentralised networks. The 'Cross-Cultural and Transnational Reach' category underscores the global nature of online platforms, facilitating the spread of extremist ideologies beyond borders. It also mentions the need for countermeasures to be tailored to specific cultural and political contexts. The important 'Psychological Factors' identifies the role of identity and the sense of belonging in attracting individuals, especially those who feel marginalised or alienated, to extremist groups. It also notes that extremists often use compelling narratives and manipulative framing to attract and retain followers. The final category 5, 'Technological Evolution and Adaptation', reflects on the rapid pace of digital technology evolution, which can outpace

Designing Digital Media Literacies for Social Cohesion **111**

TABLE 6.1 A Structured Analysis of the Digital Landscape that can Facilitate Radicalisation through Different Pathways

1. **Digital Echo Chambers and Radicalisation Pathways**	*Algorithmic Amplification* Social media algorithms can create echo chambers, inadvertently amplifying extremist content by catering to user preferences, leading to radicalisation. *Microtargeting* Extremists can use data analytics to target susceptible individuals with propaganda. *Online Communities* Online forums and social networks provide spaces where extremist ideologies can flourish, often unchallenged.
2. **Anonymity and Decentralisation**	*Anonymity* The internet allows individuals to explore extremist ideologies anonymously, reducing the social stigma and perceived risks. *Decentralised Networks* Extremists often operate in decentralised network, complicating efforts to monitor and counter their activities.
3. **Cross-Cultural and Transnational Reach**	*Global Connectivity* Online platforms connect individuals across borders, allowing extremist ideologies to spread globally. *Cultural Contexts* Extremist content online often intersects with local cultural and political contexts, necessitating tailored countermeasures.
4. **Psychological Factors**	*Identity and Belonging* Online platforms can offer a sense of community to individuals, particularly those feeling marginalised or alienated. *Narratives and Framing* Extremist often use compelling narratives or manipulative framing to attract and retain followers.
5. **Technological Evolution and Adaptation**	*Rapid Change* The rapid evolution of digital technologies can outpace counter-extremism efforts. *Platform Migration* As platforms crack down on extremism, groups often migrate to less regulated spaces, including encrypted messaging apps.

Source: Created by the author.

112 Emerging Digital Media Ecologies

efforts to counter-extremism. It also observes that as platforms crack down on extremism, extremist groups tend to migrate to less regulated spaces, including encrypted messaging apps such as Threema (which does not require a phone number to register, using a unique Threema ID instead, which helps maintain user anonymity), Wickr Me, or Silence (formerly SMSSecure) that provide end-to-end encryption for messages without requiring internet access (by encrypting messages directly on the device and sending them as normal SMS messages to another user who also has the app installed).

Filter Bubbles and Echo Chambers: Multivalent Consequences of API Integration

While Application Programming Interfaces (APIs) might be interpreted as inherently neutral tools designed to enhance functionality and user experience on digital platforms, whereby good or bad effects depend only on how the technologies are used, this morally neutral view does not allow for inherent biases embedded in the technologies themselves. Their pivotal role in facilitating personalised content delivery may inadvertently contribute to the emergence of filter bubbles—a significant concern in today's digital AI era. Coined by Eli Pariser in 2011, the term 'filter bubble' delineates a scenario where personalised search algorithms isolate users within their own informational cocoons. These algorithms tailor content delivery to an individual's preferences, viewpoints, and historical online behaviour, effectively filtering out dissenting perspectives. This phenomenon restricts users' exposure to streams of information that echo their pre-existing beliefs (schemata) and preferences.

APIs are instrumental in this process, although they are not the sole architects of filter bubbles. Online platforms leverage algorithms, often via APIs, to personalise content for users based on their past interactions, preferences, and behavioural data. This personalisation can limit users' exposure to diverse content, ensnaring them in echo chambers populated with similar opinions and interests. For example, social media platforms use APIs to curate personalised feeds, while streaming services recommend content aligned with users' tastes, potentially narrowing their exposure to a broader spectrum of media. This echo-chamber effect is perpetuated as users engage with personalised content, feeding the algorithms more data to refine future recommendations. Consequently, users find themselves enveloped in an informational echo-chamber, where the diversity of encountered narratives, opinions, and information drastically narrows. This insulation from contrasting viewpoints can solidify and intensify pre-existing beliefs, rendering individuals more impervious to alternative perspectives.

The implications of such echo chambers extend beyond individual cognition to the broader societal fabric. The algorithm-driven creation of 'us versus them' narratives and the resultant social cohesion erosion pose significant challenges to liberal democracies. This division can escalate misunderstandings, stereotypes, and prejudices undermining social and political harmony. In other words, with rapid pace, the algorithmic capacity to generate inaccuracies has consequences for the erosion of the democratic public sphere (Bennett & Kneuer, 2023), a concept rooted in Jürgen Habermas's (1989) theory that delineates several prerequisites for this conceptualisation to thrive—unfettered discourse, assured freedoms of assembly and expression, autonomy from governmental oversight, and an enlightened populace, with media outlets such as newspapers and the like serving as catalysts for information dissemination. These elements coalesce to form an ideal model of deliberative democracy. The reduction in exposure to and engagement with a variety of perspectives contributes significantly to societal and political polarisation, as it amplifies the perceived divisions between social groups, aligning with Habermas's concept of the Public Sphere where a lack of inclusive discourse undermines the democratic process and exacerbates the segmentation between 'us' (the in-group) and 'them' (the out-group). Habermas championed the public sphere as a crucible for consensus-building, positing rationality as a critical instrument in the deliberative process, ostensibly accessible to all. Habermas's arguments have, however, been challenged (Fraser, 1990) on the grounds that the perspective was dominated by certain actors (male property owners) and excluded many (women, children, the marginalised). Importantly though, the concept is now expanded to include the relegated 'others'—women, people of colour, the poor, disabled, LGBTQI communities in other recent works including Rosi Braidotti's critical analysis of the posthuman (2017).

As Steven Hassan argues in relation to widespread propaganda and disinformation efforts that without public education, disinformation can pave the way for authoritarianism and the end of democratic rights, principles, and conventions (Hassan, 2019). The increasing politicisation of digital and social media, also highlighted by Tucker et al. (2017) and Omidyar (2018), is complicating the contemporary landscape. Scholars like boyd (2017), Mihailidis (2018), and Dishon and Ben-Porath (2018) advocate for a re-evaluation of digital and media literacies to address these challenges. They argue for proactive strategies that foster positive engagement and responsible digital behaviour, emphasising the importance of education in developing digital civility and citizenship. Considering the diverse and complex nature of online harms, ranging from the subversion of media to the risk of radicalisation, there is a critical need to pivot from strictly punitive approaches to proactive strategies that encourage positive engagement and responsible behaviour in the digital environment. As Isin and Ruppert (2015) suggest, digital citizenship is an enacted political subjectivity, influenced by the interplay of online and offline dynamics. Digital citizenship can be thought of as constituted by digital acts, meaning that political subjectivity is 'neither given nor determined but enacted by what we do in relation to other things' (Isin & Ruppert, 2015,

114 Emerging Digital Media Ecologies

p.10). However, digital acts are complicated by the evolving and volatile nature of interactions between online (digital media, but particularly social media) and offline (embodied, face-to-face) dynamics and influences. While some scholars argue that the effect of echo chambers has been overstated (see Dubois & Blank, 2018), digital platforms can nonetheless amplify particular social attitudes and thus limit the kinds of intercultural contact, exchange, and understanding so essential for creating and sustaining pro-social culturally diverse community life (Grossman, Peucker, Smith, & Dellal, 2016).

In the context of emerging media with interwoven AI capabilities, the key to building positively engaged digital citizenship is therefore helping people develop critical skills and digital literacies that enable them to recognise and act in pro-social ways in response to these complex socio-technical issues. Authors Dishon and Ben-Porath (2018) argue for a relational approach to developing online civility, explaining that it should be seen as a set of affirmative 'behaviours' that 'can be expected, cultivated and practiced' (p. 5). Seen in these terms, education can play a vital role in developing digital civility and citizenship (Dishon & Ben-Porath, 2018).

The role of digital platforms in amplifying social attitudes cannot be overlooked in fostering culturally diverse and pro-social community life. Furthermore, digital literacies encompass a broad spectrum of skills and understandings, as outlined by UNESCO (2017). The critical evaluation of social media platforms and their information is paramount in cultivating informed digital citizens. Dubois and Blank's (2018) findings on media diversity and political interest in mitigating echo chambers are particularly relevant here. In light of the recent geopolitical developments and the UNESCO's 2023 'Internet for Trust' report, creating an enabling environment demands a holistic approach that engages the entire society, necessitating solutions that involve all societal sectors (p. 16):

> All relevant stakeholders in every governance system should take action to enable the exercise of the right to freedom of expression of groups in situations of vulnerability and marginalization, women and girls, and indigenous communities, as well as of journalists, artists, human rights defenders, and environmental defenders, for example. All members of society have a role to play to make the internet safe, to challenge violent or threatening behaviours, to respect the rights of others in exchanges online, to respect the diversity of cultural content, and to be aware of inherent biases in societies. Children have a special status given their unique stage of development, limited or lack of political voice, and the fact that negative experiences in childhood can result in lifelong or transgenerational consequences.

As made plain above, inclusive and decolonial approaches to digital platform policy and governance are advocated for leaning into a balanced dialogue that

Designing Digital Media Literacies for Social Cohesion **115**

incorporates diverse global perspectives on human rights, state power, and territoriality under various sovereignty regimes—not an easy task. In the quest to combat online extremism in the context of medialogy, it is imperative to value access to accurate information as not only a fundamental human right for individuals but also a collective cornerstone that enhances societal resilience against synthetic media and the circulation of misinformation (information that is false), disinformation (intentionally created information or images that are disseminated with the intent to deceive and mislead), to malinformation (manipulating information for the purposes of inflicting harm on a person, organisation, or country). This approach significantly contributes to the vitality of media ecosystems and bolsters critical literacies in areas including, but not limited to communication, science, creativity, and data management— capacities that are indispensable as we navigate the complexities associated with the swift advancements in AI. Such a perspective necessitates inclusive strategies in the policy and governance frameworks of digital platforms, ensuring that they serve the global community's diverse needs and contribute to a more equitable and informed world.

Traditional and Online Extremism

In exploring the nuances of online extremism, it is crucial to understand that this phenomenon, while conceptually elusive, is not simply a digital manifestation of traditional extremism. Traditional extremism refers to the expression of extreme ideologies and beliefs, often characterised by the advocacy of radical actions and the dissemination of divisive, hateful content. In its broadest sense, traditional extremism encompasses a spectrum of ideologies and actions that lie at the extreme ends of political, religious, or social beliefs, often advocating for radical change and employing methods that are outside the bounds of accepted societal norms.

With regard to a universal legal definition, there is debate regarding an at least partial customary explanation of terrorism. Not without criticism for 'being beholden to regional and global geopolitics' (Muller, 2022, p. 76), the United Nations Special Tribunal for Lebanon (STL) in 2011 offered a definition of 'transnational terrorism' which requires the following three key elements: (1) the perpetration of a criminal act (such as murder, kidnapping, hostage-taking, arson, and so on), or threatening such an act; (2) the intent to spread fear among the population (which would generally entail the creation of public danger) or directly or indirectly coerce a national or international authority to take some action, or to refrain from taking it; (3) when the act involves a transnational element (*Interlocutory Decision*, 2011, para. 85 cited in United Nations Office on Drugs and Crime (UNODC), 2021a). The critical challenge in understanding traditional extremism lies in its complex interplay with cultural, political, and social contexts, which shapes its manifestations and impacts. The issue of establishing universal societal norms, and extreme deviations thereof, is further exacerbated for online extremism (Risius, Blasiak, Wibisono, & Louis, 2023, p. 3).

The online realm presents unique challenges and mechanisms that facilitate the spread and entrenchment of extremist ideologies. This form of extremism online leverages the expansive reach and anonymity of the internet to spread messages, recruit followers, and coordinate activities. Notably, it transcends geographical boundaries, allowing for the global propagation of extremist views. Examples include individuals and groups utilising social media for recruitment and propaganda such as alt-right movements propagating white supremacist ideologies through online forums, extreme conservative values based on religious ideologies, and even single-issue extremists, such as anti-vaccination groups, who mobilise and radicalise individuals on various platforms.

Central to understanding the alt-right movement is its ideological underpinnings, which are marked by a distinct form of masculinity intertwined with political and cultural conservatism. Scholars like Nagle (2017) have explored this through the prism of cultural backlash, highlighting how the alt-right's rise can be partly attributed to a reaction against what they perceive as the excesses of progressive politics, including feminism and multiculturalism. Nagle's analysis provides a foundational understanding of the alt-right's ideological motivations, situating them within a broader context of cultural and political shifts. At the core of the alt-right movement are certain ideological principles outlined by Thomas Main (2018), who discusses the philosophical foundations of this group. Main identifies a fundamental rejection of liberal democracy, marked by a denial of the principle that all individuals are inherently equal. This rejection forms the bedrock of the alt-right's ideology, paving the way for more exclusionary beliefs. Main's analysis is crucial in understanding the alt-right's core ideologies, particularly their stand against egalitarian principles. Main's (2018) notion of 'white racialism' refers to a belief system that prioritises the interests and policies favouring white people, thereby advocating for their political dominance. This concept is instrumental in comprehending the movement's racially exclusive ideologies, which view policies beneficial to white people as the only legitimate form of governance. Main's exploration of this principle sheds light on the racial dynamics central to the alt-right's political stance. Furthermore, the alt-right's overlap with other domains, such as Christian conservatism, adds another dimension to its influence. The movement's use of religious rhetoric and its association with Christian conservative values/ideologies illustrate a blending of religious and political elements.

These individuals and groups often exploit the echo-chamber effect of online spaces to reinforce extremist beliefs, creating an environment where radical views are normalised and dissenting voices are marginalised. These echo chambers reinforce pre-existing beliefs and expose individuals to more radical views, a process often exacerbated by the platform's design to maximise user engagement. This algorithmic amplification, coupled with the ability to micro-target susceptible individuals using sophisticated data analytics, facilitates a form of radicalisation that is uniquely digital. Furthermore, online communities, including forums and social networks, become mediaspheres in which extremist ideologies may flourish, often unchallenged due to the anonymity and decentralised nature of the internet. Sometimes the cloak of anonymity online reduces the social stigma and perceived risks associated with exploring extremist ideologies, allowing individuals to engage with these ideas more freely. This factor, along with the decentralised networks that extremists often operate in, complicates efforts to monitor and counter their activities. Additionally, the global connectivity afforded by online platforms enables extremist ideologies to transcend borders, making them a transnational issue. These ideologies often intersect with local cultural and political contexts, necessitating countermeasures that are sensitive to these nuances.

The role of digital platforms in facilitating the spread of extremist ideologies cannot be overstated. In understanding the impact on political discourse, it is essential to consider its role within the broader context of Strategic Digital Information Operations (SDIO) (Starbird, Arif, & Wilson, 2019). These SDIO often involve the use of digital tools to influence public opinion, manipulate political processes, and sow discord (Starbird, Arif, & Wilson, 2019). Online extremists' activities align with these objectives, leveraging digital platforms to shape narratives, influence political discourse, and mobilise supporters. Building on the discussion around the influential role of algorithms in Chapter 4, with regard to SDIO here, it is necessary to consider the implications embedded within algorithms used in this manner which have reverberations across our political and social spheres (Kirby, 2024). As they filter and prioritise information, algorithms can be used to strategically amplify echo chambers. That is, an algorithm might display certain types of political content, influencing voter behaviour and public sentiment in ways that are opaque to the average user. For instance, during the 2016 US presidential election, Facebook's news feed algorithm came under criticism for prioritising highly engaging content, which often included sensational or polarising political posts.

Currently, the truth of a piece of content is less important than whether it is shared, liked and monetized. These 'engagement' metrics distort the media landscape, allowing clickbait, hyperbole and misinformation to proliferate. And on Facebook's voracious news feed, the emphasis is on the quantity of posts, not spending time on powerful, authoritative, well-researched journalism.

(Solon, 2016, n.p)

118 Emerging Digital Media Ecologies

This type of content can sway public opinion by promoting certain political views more prominently than others. It does raise significant concerns about transparency and accountability in such digital practices. As society actively grapples with these challenges, it becomes imperative to implement robust mechanisms for auditing and adjusting these algorithms to ensure they do not undermine democratic processes or contribute to societal divisions.

In 2024, Meta sparked public concerns about the role of platforms such as Facebook in shaping international news consumption when the company announced plans to cut completely a dedicated section for news articles. The decision took force in April impacting Facebook users in the United States and Australia. This move follows a similar decision made in September, when Meta declared its intent to eliminate the news section for Facebook users in the United Kingdom, France, and Germany. With these successive actions, Meta seemed to signal a significant shift in its approach to news dissemination on its platform within a broader frame wherein tech giants are re-evaluating their relationship with news content amidst mounting scrutiny over misinformation and algorithmic amplification of harmful content. Questions arise, however, for what such actions mean for the millions who rely on Facebook for their daily news; and could the action exacerbate filter bubbles, making it harder for users to access diverse perspectives on Facebook and the like.

By fostering a deeper understanding of how algorithms function on social media and affect our perception of the world, we can better advocate for technologies that support a fair and informed public discourse. This dialogue is essential for ensuring that digital advancements contribute positively to society, promoting inclusivity and fairness rather than exacerbating them. Marwick and Lewis (2017) have examined how digital ecosystems, particularly social media, have been exploited by the alt-right, for example, to disseminate their messages, recruit followers, and create insular communities. Their work underscores the transformation of online spaces into echo chambers where extremist ideologies can proliferate unchecked. This phenomenon is further compounded by the algorithms governing these platforms, which often prioritise content that generates engagement, regardless of its ideological leanings. The alt-right's fusion of digital savvy with extremist ideologies presents a unique challenge to democratic societies. Lyons (2017) addresses this by examining the movement's impact on mainstream politics, particularly its ability to shift public discourse towards more extremist positions. This infiltration into mainstream politics represents a significant shift in the political landscape, with the alt-right exploiting the vulnerabilities of digital communication to exert influence far beyond its immediate sphere.

At the intersection of the alt-right and digital media is a distinct communication strategy marked by irony and meme culture. Phillips and Milner (2017) delve into this aspect, illustrating how the online extremists utilise memes and ironic discourse to spread their ideologies in ways that are often opaque to outsiders but resonate deeply within their in-groups. A notable example of this behaviour is the evolution of 'Pepe the Frog'. Originally a benign and comical figure in internet comics, Pepe was subsequently hijacked by extremist factions. These groups manipulated the meme's ironic and ludicrous elements, embedding xenophobic and nationalist sentiments under a guise of humour. This camouflaged propagation of extremist ideologies exemplifies how online text, images, and symbols can facilitate the spread of toxic beliefs, resonating within certain in-groups while eluding the detection of the uninitiated, thereby leveraging the architecture of social media to amplify their reach. This strategy not only aids in the dissemination of their ideas but also serves as a gatekeeping mechanism, demarcating the boundaries of the community. Psychologically, online platforms can offer a sense of community and identity, particularly to individuals feeling marginalised or alienated in their offline lives. Extremists might exploit these needs, using compelling narratives and manipulative framing to attract and retain followers. This psychological dimension is crucial in understanding the allure of online extremist groups.

Addressing Online Extremism

The inherently malleable and evolving nature of the internet continuously shapes and reshapes the landscape of traditional online extremism, posing significant challenges to monitoring and counter-extremism efforts. Certainly, current methods to counter-extremism induce undesirable side-effects (e.g., they can ostracise minorities and inadvertently promote extremism views), or they do not leverage the full potential of digital technologies. These challenges demand an approach that is both adaptive and multifaceted, blending social science insights with technological solutions. Addressing online extremism requires strategies that are holistic and continuously adaptive to the rapidly changing online environment and techno-cultural landscape. Community engagement is vital, particularly in providing support and creating counter-narratives to those propagated by extremist groups. Collaboration with technology companies is also essential in developing responsible content moderation policies that strike a balance between preventing extremism and preserving free speech. Promoting digital literacy and critical thinking skills is another key approach. These skills empower individuals to recognise and resist extremist content, acting as a first line of defence against radicalisation. Targeted interventions are necessary to address individuals at various stages of radicalisation, ranging from prevention to de-radicalisation efforts. Ironically, using data analytics to identify patterns can also inform more effective countermeasures to potential threats. Given the transnational nature of online extremism, international cooperation and information sharing become crucial in these efforts. The challenge of countering online extremism lies not only

120 Emerging Digital Media Ecologies

in understanding the unique dynamics of online radicalisation but also in adapting traditional counter-extremism measures to the digital domain.

Towards a Framework for Digital Media Literacy

Media and digital literacies education need to model how to use and combine different media sources when seeking news and information. This enhances digital citizenship, which can be thought of as 'the skills and knowledge to effectively use digital technologies to participate in society, communicate with others and create and consume digital content' (Commission, 2023, p. 35). Following McDougall et al. (2018), a good approach to digital literacies is not from a narrow, functional understanding, but instead one that reflects on the fact that varying levels of digital literacy can be found in daily practice. For most people's social and cultural experiences are now steeped in digital information processing. Understanding the span of medialogy involves the assessment of everyday life characterised by widespread engagement with social media, the circulation of digital texts, the implications of big and small data sets, and the affordances of online communication. This trend extends across all cultural and socio-economic backgrounds, with a significant portion of the workforce, both currently and in the future, expected to interact with digital documents, data, and information, regardless of their chosen career paths (Al-Emran, 2023; Laukkarinen, 2023; Ito, 2010). The prevalence of these technologies mean that young people have developed expectations that their educational institutions will provide the same opportunities regarding the choices, access, affordability, and functionality of digital media they will be exposed to. However, the impact of emerging AI technologies on learning in school (Selwyn et al., 2018; Michel-Villarreal et al., 2023) and within higher education institutions (Cinque, 2024) is far from straightforward. Addressing students' needs has become an ongoing challenge for educators due to the increasing complexities associated with Generative Artificial Intelligence (GenAI) in relation to plagiarism and cheating. This study of medialogy interactions provides necessary insights into these challenges. Gaining a critical understanding of AI products and services, along with their effective integration into learning experiences where learners become experts and content curators, is pivotal for aligning with contemporary workplaces. Developing such digital literacies involves, among other things, understanding critically and mobilising pedagogically the complex interplay between digitally based protections and digitally based vulnerabilities for users, particularly in relation to forms of online harms and predations. In navigating the complexities of online harms, including media manipulation and the potential for radicalisation, a shift towards proactive measures rather than solely punitive ones is essential for promoting positive public interaction and responsible online behaviour. Enhancing digital literacy regardless of age and across various demographics

Designing Digital Media Literacies for Social Cohesion **121**

is a fundamental strategy, enabling individuals to engage with online content safely and critically. Through educational initiatives, people can learn to discern misinformation, comprehend the ramifications of their online presence, and identify early signs of radicalisation. Now, the development and application of advanced technologies, including AI and machine learning, play a critical role in pre-emptively identifying and addressing online dangers. These technological solutions offer a more efficient means of detecting patterns of harmful content or behaviour than traditional manual moderation and reporting techniques. Integrating these strategies is an attempt at a holistic and adaptive approach to online safety to ensure more secure and positive experiences for users across networked media and digital platforms.

Adversarial Design: 'De-Biasing' Data with Large Language Model-based Co-pilot Tools and Countering Online Extremism

Adversarial design represents a methodological approach in design and technology development characterised by the creation of systems, processes, or artefacts that challenge prevailing conditions, stimulate critical thinking, and uncover latent assumptions. Specifically, it is a method where a predictor and an adversary are simultaneously learned such that the input to the network produces a prediction, while the adversary tries to model a protected variable. The objective is to maximise the predictor's ability to predict while conversely minimising the adversary's ability to predict the protected variable (Zhang, Lemoine, & Mitchell, 2018). By way of comparison, online moderation is presently undertaken by thousands of people (mods), for many hours per day, and often on a volunteer basis. As highlighted by Peck and Dave (2024), Reddit alone has some 60,000 mods for 'exorcising spam, breaking up fights, and removing hateful slurs on a handful of subreddits' (Peck, & Dave, 2024, pp. 38-39); importantly

> [m]ods shared tools and tricks that empowered them to be far more preemptive and strategic. Sometimes, for example, trolls post vicious comments and then quickly delete their account or the comment itself—a drive-by tactic that helps them evade detection and penalties.
>
> *(Peck & Dave, 2024, pp. 38–39)*

While mods can use free third-party apps to 'hunt down' the deleted comments retroactively with the intention of bringing offenders to account for their actions, the next phase of moderation is using AI to both anticipate and detect.

Within the realm of technology and machine learning, the application of adversarial design offers a promising avenue to counteract bias. Albeit with their own inherent flaws discussed further below, an adversarially designed LLM-based tool can include features specifically engineered to interrogate and counteract the biases inherent in social media posts or in the methods used to engage users online. This approach may foster fairness and inclusivity and also enhances the integrity of online environments by ensuring a diverse range of perspectives is considered and represented. That is, an adversarially designed AI mod offers a high level of efficiency and consistency in the moderation of social media content. It operates without the limitations of human moderators, such as susceptibility to fatigue or emotional biases, thereby maintaining a steady oversight. With the capacity to handle large volumes of data swiftly (24/7), AI moderation systems can keep up with the rapid generation of content on social media platforms. Furthermore, they alleviate the need for human moderators to engage with potentially distressing content, which can have adverse psychological effects.

Large Language Models (LLMs)—such as OpenAI's GPT (Generative Pre-trained Transformer) series, BERT (Bidirectional Encoder Representations from Transformers), RoBERTa (Robustly Optimized BERT pretraining approach), and XLNet (eXtreme Language understanding NETwork)—are impressive in various natural language-related tasks (Kasneci et al., 2023). An LLM is a sophisticated AI designed to understand, interpret, and generate human language. These models are built using incalculable and undefined sources of data and employ deep learning, a subset of machine learning, to identify patterns and nuances in natural language. The 'large' scale of LLMs refers to the substantial size of the dataset they are trained on and the complexity of their neural network architecture. They are trained on datasets comprising billions of words, covering a wide range of topics, languages, and styles present in human communication. This training data is diverse, including literature, websites, scientific papers, news articles, forums, blogs, and social media posts, with the intension that models can 'understand' and respond to various forms of language, jargon, and colloquialisms. LLMs can perform various language-related tasks, including answering questions, writing in different styles, summarising and interpreting text and images, translating languages, and creating content according to a user's prompt or request. Their ability to process and generate language has significant implications for communication, offering opportunities for enhanced interaction. While there are concerns regarding the quality and relevance of the data used to train the models—whether data is current, inclusive, and ethically sourced to reflect the evolving nature of language and societal norms for the accuracy of the responses subsequently generated—LLMs offer significant potential in fostering digital media literacies and countering online extremism, primarily through their capacity for generating informative and contextually nuanced content. By simulating conversation and providing evidence-based responses that can be verified, LLMs can assist in developing analytical thinking and digital literacy skills in users, encouraging them to question and analyse information critically. In the context of online extremism, LLMs can be programmed to recognise and counteract extremist rhetoric, offering balanced viewpoints and a range of information with the intension of countering misinformation. This is particularly vital in an era where extremist groups exploit digital platforms to disseminate their ideologies. Moreover, LLMs' ability to process and generate language in a human-like manner enables them to engage users in dialogues that can expose them to diverse perspectives, thereby reducing the echo-chamber effect often seen in online spaces. While this argument bears weight, there are concerns that first must be addressed regarding the generation of biased responses to user prompts by LLMs themselves (Liang, Wu, Morency, & Salakhutdinov, 2021).

The LLMs can produce harmful biases, and there are a number of categories: (1) Cultural, Social, and Racial Bias; (2) Language and Regional Bias; (3) Gender Bias; (4) Socio-economic Bias; (5) Political and Ideological Bias; (6) Accessibility Bias; and (7) Age Bias. The following provides a definition of each form of bias with examples and markers. This section explores the manifestation of bias in the outputs of LLMs, a phenomenon that often reflects and perpetuates societal stereotypes. Addressing embedded biases is essential for the development of AI systems that are both fairer and more equitable. This is important for the quality of information that circulates in the digital media sphere and beyond. Through this analysis, the aim is to illuminate the pathways along which advances might be made towards 'de-biasing' data using LLM-based co-pilot tools albeit that de-biasing might not be quite the right word 'as all bias is not necessarily removed' (Zhang, Lemoine, & Mitchell, 2018, p. 1).

Cultural, Social, and Racial Bias

LLMs can exhibit preferences or prejudices towards certain cultures, ethnicities, or social groups, often perpetuating stereotypes or marginalising underrepresented groups. This might manifest in language that favours certain cultural norms or values over others, or in unequal representations of different groups. Cultural, social, and racial biases in LLMs manifest through the models' tendencies to perpetuate stereotypes, misunderstandings, or inequalities related to culture, social groups, or race. The associated groups here include individuals belonging to various racial and ethnic backgrounds. The markers may be names commonly associated with specific racial or ethnic groups, cultural practices, language or dialect, and geographical origins. These biases can influence the content generated by LLMs, potentially leading to outcomes that are unfair, exclusive, or harmful. The following overviews each type of bias in this first category with examples of how they might appear in an LLM.

Cultural Bias can take the form of stereotyping and generalisations. LLMs may generate content that relies on clichéd or oversimplified representations of cultures, failing to capture their complexity or diversity. For instance,

124 Emerging Digital Media Ecologies

associating a specific food, behaviour, or clothing exclusively with a certain culture without acknowledging variations or nuances. Cultural Bias might also display Cultural Centrism whereby content might reflect or prioritise the norms, values, and perspectives of certain dominant cultures, particularly those of Western countries, implicitly presenting them as universal. This can alienate users from other cultural backgrounds or minimise the validity of their experiences.

Social Bias occurs when LLMs replicate stereotypes related to socio-economic status, such as associating poverty with laziness or crime, or wealth with intelligence or morality. This can perpetuate harmful prejudices and overlook systemic factors influencing social positions. Moreover, there might be elements of exclusion of diverse social experiences. By not adequately representing the breadth of human social experiences, LLMs can exclude or marginalise perspectives from varied social backgrounds, such as those of marginalised communities, perpetuating a lack of visibility and recognition.

Racial Bias might take three forms. First is racial stereotyping. That is, content generated by LLMs might inadvertently reinforce racial stereotypes, such as attributing certain behaviours, abilities, or characteristics to individuals based on their race. This not only reflects but can also amplify societal prejudices. Second is misrepresentation or underrepresentation. Racial groups might be underrepresented in the examples, stories, or scenarios created by LLMs, or represented in a way that focuses on stereotypes rather than a full spectrum of identities and experiences. Additionally, the use of language and images might not accurately reflect racial diversity. Third, biased Sentiment Analysis can occur when LLMs show bias in interpreting the sentiment of texts related to different racial groups, potentially due to the influence of biased training data. This can affect how positively or negatively content is presented or interpreted. For example, sentences that imply superiority or inferiority of races, for example, 'People of [specific race] are more likely to commit crimes than others'. Such statements reinforce harmful stereotypes and contribute to racial discrimination.

Language and Regional Bias

LLMs can exhibit a bias towards content in major languages such as English, Mandarin, or Spanish due to the prevalence of these languages in their training data. This often results in underrepresentation or misinterpretation of content in less widely spoken languages or from cultures that are not globally dominant, affecting the accessibility, relevance, and fairness of the content generated. Such language and regional bias reflects a preference for certain languages or regions over others, potentially marginalising speakers of non-dominant languages and cultures. For example, LLMs might provide more comprehensive responses in widely spoken languages, leading to a digital divide for speakers of minority languages. They could rely on stereotypes or outdated information when generating content about specific cultures, such as simplifying [specific country] cuisine to 'legumes and rice' thereby neglecting the diversity and complexity of the culture. This oversimplification not only diminishes the cultural diversity but also reinforces stereotypical views.

LLMs may also adopt geocentric perspectives, aligning with the cultural norms and values of regions where the technology is developed or where most of the training data originates, and skew the distribution of knowledge towards topics relevant to these areas. They might struggle with local language nuances and dialects, potentially alienating users or misinterpreting their inputs. Additionally, when translating, LLMs can lose nuances of meaning, humour, and cultural context, particularly for languages with smaller speaker bases or those significantly different from the model's primary training languages. Examples of bias include sentences that devalue non-native speakers or certain dialects, suggesting a correlation between accents and intelligence, or sentences that express prejudice towards individuals from specific regions or countries, fostering unwarranted assumptions based on nationality. Such biases impact people from specific countries, regions, cities, native and non-native speakers, and speakers of dialects or languages with less global dominance, identifiable through markers like place names, cultural references, languages or dialects spoken, and socio-economic indicators related to specific geographical areas, as well as accents, grammar, and language fluency.

Gender Bias

Gender bias in LLMs manifests as a tendency of these models to reinforce stereotypes, assumptions, or inequalities pertaining to gender. This encompasses biases concerning gender identity and expression, often mirroring societal biases rather than presenting a balanced perspective. Such biases challenge the fairness, accuracy, and inclusivity of the responses generated by LLMs. The LLMs may reinforce traditional gender roles or characteristics, suggesting, for instance, caregiving roles as inherently female and leadership qualities as predominantly male. This perpetuation of outdated stereotypes fails to acknowledge the diversity of individual experiences and capabilities. When discussing professions or occupations, LLMs might imply certain jobs are specific to one gender, for example, associating engineers or carpenters with males and teachers or nurses with females. This not only reflects societal biases but may also fortify them, potentially influencing individuals' career aspirations and opportunities.

Further, LLMs can default to gender-specific pronouns based on stereotypes associated with activities, roles, or characteristics, such as using 'he' for engineers and 'she' for secretaries, absent of any gender-indicating information. This perpetuates the notion that certain roles are inherently linked to a specific gender. Gender bias may also emerge in the examples, stories, or scenarios LLMs generate, where characters or individuals of a certain gender are underrepresented, or their contributions are minimised, potentially distorting users' perceptions of gender roles and achievements. Moreover, the language or tone used by LLMs might vary depending on the perceived gender of the user or subject, potentially reinforcing stereotypes, such as adopting a more assertive tone with perceived male users and a more nurturing tone with female users (an issue in the context of OpenAI offering users the ability to create personal bio-profiles as raised in Chapter 5 for whether names identified as likely 'male' or 'female' get bespoke responses consequently generated for that user). Bias in sentiment analysis and interpretation by LLMs can lead to gendered assumptions about emotions or intentions, thus affecting the model's responses. An illustrative example of this bias is sentences that unfairly attribute certain roles or characteristics to a specific gender, such as the unfounded and harmful stereotype that 'Women are not as good at mathematics as men', which discourages women from pursuing STEM careers. This bias affects men, women, and non-binary individuals, also identifiable through markers like pronouns (he, she, they) and titles (Mr., Mrs., Mx.).

Socio-economic Bias

Socio-economic bias in LLMs arises when the models make assumptions or show preferences related to an individual's social and economic status, thereby potentially perpetuating stereotypes or inaccurately representing the varied experiences of people from different economic backgrounds. This bias may subtly influence the content generated, affecting its fairness and inclusivity. LLMs might create content that presumes a certain level of wealth or access to resources, suggesting, for example, expensive dining or luxury travel without considering the economic diversity of the audience. They may also imply that all users have access to higher education or specific career paths, which can exclude or misrepresent those whose opportunities were limited by economic factors. The use of language or cultural references familiar mainly to those from certain socio-economic backgrounds can further alienate individuals with different experiences, as can the representation of work and employment that stereotypes jobs or professions based on social class or undervalues certain types of labour.

Content that stereotypes people based on their economic status, depicting those from lower economic backgrounds negatively or equating wealth with intelligence or morality, is another manifestation of this bias. Additionally, socio-economic bias can be evident in how LLMs assume user access to technologies like high-speed internet or personal computers, which might not be universally available. An example of such bias includes statements that imply a person's worth or abilities are directly tied to their economic status, for instance, suggesting that 'Poor people are lazy and don't want to work'. This overlooks the complex factors contributing to poverty and unjustly characterises individuals by their financial situation. Socio-economic bias affects individuals across various statuses, from the working class to the upper class and those living in poverty, identifiable through markers like occupation, education level, housing, lifestyle choices, and references to wealth or poverty.

Political and Ideological Bias

LLMs may inadvertently favour certain political ideologies or perspectives due to biases in their training data, which could prioritise some viewpoints over others. This political and ideological bias means LLMs tend to produce content that supports particular political viewpoints, ideologies, or narratives more than others, potentially impacting the neutrality and objectivity of the information they provide. Such bias could shape users' perceptions and understandings of complex issues in several ways. LLMs might unevenly represent or favour one political or ideological perspective, possibly by presenting arguments from one side of the political spectrum while omitting alternative viewpoints. The language used and the framing of issues can also convey political or ideological bias, with word choices that subtly express approval or disapproval of certain ideologies, political figures, or policies. An LLM could selectively present facts or data that support a specific viewpoint, neglecting or minimising information that contradicts it, leading to a biased understanding of issues.

Further, these models can perpetuate stereotypes about people based on their political beliefs or affiliations, potentially influencing public opinion and discourse. This influence can exacerbate polarisation and misunderstanding among different groups by consistently offering a slanted perspective on information. The groups affected by this bias include political parties (e.g., conservatives, liberals, socialists, libertarians), political movements, and advocacy groups, identified by party-specific language, slogans, and policy priorities. Ideological groups, defined by core beliefs like environmentalists or free market proponents, are marked by their use of specific terms signalling ideological stances. Advocates of social and economic theories, such as capitalism or socialism, are identified through terminology central to their views. Nationalist or regionalist groups, with their political or ideological leanings, are marked by historical narratives. Lastly, activists focused on specific issues, from climate change to LGBTQI+ rights, are recognised by issue-specific language and advocacy tactics. LLMs might use language or present images that subtly conveys approval or disapproval of certain ideologies, political figures, or policies. For example, using terms like 'pro-life' vs. 'anti-abortion' or 'climate sceptic' vs. 'climate denier' can indicate a bias in how

128 Emerging Digital Media Ecologies

issues are presented. Further to this, an LLM might selectively present facts, studies, or statistics that support a particular viewpoint, while omitting or downplaying information that contradicts it.

Accessibility Bias

Accessibility bias in LLMs occurs when these models produce content without adequately considering the needs and perspectives of users with disabilities, potentially marginalising or failing to support them fully. Such bias reflects a lack of consideration for the varied ways people interact with technology, particularly for those who require alternative methods due to various disabilities. For example, suppose an LLM is tasked with explaining how to perform a task on a computer, such as using a spreadsheet program to organise data. The model generates a detailed guide that relies heavily on visual cues, such as 'Click on the green button in the top right corner' or 'Look for the column labelled "A" on the left side of the screen'. For a user with a visual impairment, such instructions may be difficult or impossible to follow without alternative text descriptions or keyboard navigation instructions. When producing educational or informational content, LLMs might neglect topics such as disability rights or inclusive design, missing the chance to promote awareness and understanding. To address this, models should be trained to recognise when content might be exclusionary and provide an alternative, accessible options and descriptions.

Interaction design might also fall short in accessibility, with interfaces not fully supporting assistive technologies like screen readers or voice navigation, restricting some users' engagement with the model's outputs. LLMs may fail to incorporate accessibility considerations when offering recommendations, such as suggesting activities or locations without addressing potential accessibility challenges. As such, LLMs could reinforce stereotypes or misrepresentations of people with disabilities, either by focusing too much on the disability or making unfounded assumptions about individuals' needs and capabilities. The language and tone used by LLMs can be outdated or insensitive, highlighting the importance of using respectful terminology that avoids connotations of pity or heroism just for living with a disability. Overarchingly, the groups affected include individuals with visual impairments, who require screen readers and alternative text; those with hearing impairments, who need closed captions and visual alerts; people with motor impairments, who may rely on adaptive hardware or voice control; users with cognitive or neurological disabilities, who benefit from clear language and consistent navigation; and those with speech disabilities, who face challenges with voice recognition systems and need text-based communication options. Recognising and adjusting for these needs is essential to mitigate accessibility bias in LLMs.

Age Bias

Age bias is also known as ageism and involves stereotyping, prejudice, and discrimination against individuals based on age. It affects both younger and older populations and is characterised by presumptions about an individual's capabilities, interests, and behaviours that are deemed typical for a certain age group, often leading to inequitable treatment or exclusion.

Such bias can be explicit or implicit in various contexts, from employment, where certain age groups might be unfairly preferred or overlooked, to societal attitudes that may hold unfounded beliefs about an age group's relationship with technology or openness to change. Age bias fundamentally challenges the principle of assessing each person as an individual and recognising the diverse abilities and contributions that people of all ages bring to the table. In the context of LLMs, age bias can emerge in outputs that inadvertently reflect stereotypes or discrimination based on age. LLMs might generate content that aligns older adults with memory issues or a reluctance to use new technologies, or might portray younger individuals as immature or uninformed. The tone used by LLMs could be condescending or overly simplistic when addressing older people, or inappropriately trendy when aimed at younger users, which can imply assumptions about their intelligence and preferences.

LLMs may also fail to consider information relevant to different age groups, like focusing solely on career advancement without addressing retirement planning, or prioritising traditional education over online options that may be more accessible to a wider age range. In examples and narratives, they might overrepresent certain age demographics, ignoring the variety of experiences and insights other age groups offer. Predictive features in LLMs might suggest interests or activities based on age-related stereotypes, such as technology articles for the young or health content for the older generation, overlooking personal preferences. When responding to enquiries, an LLM could infer and apply biases based on the user's real or perceived age, leading to responses that may not be suitable or relevant. Age bias within LLMs involves individuals from all life stages, including children, teenagers, adults, and the elderly, and can be indicated by age-specific terms, references to particular life milestones, and the association of certain activities or technologies with specific age groups.

In this context, the employment of LLMs in the fight against extremism represents a novel convergence of computer science and humanities, drawing upon the strengths of both to address a pressing global issue. The rationale for utilising LLMs in this context is multifaceted, centring on their unparalleled scalability and efficiency, which enable the analysis of extensive online content for extremist materials far beyond human capability (Alizadeh et al., 2023). LLMs' proficiency in pattern recognition and anomaly detection is critical for identifying language and behaviours indicative of extremist sentiments or

130 Emerging Digital Media Ecologies

TABLE 6.2 Capabilities of LLM-based Co-pilot Tools for Countering Extremism Online

Scalability and Efficiency	LLMs can process and analyse vast amounts of data at a scale unattainable by humans. In countering extremism, this means LLM-based co-pilot tools can monitor and assess a broad spectrum of online content, including social media posts, forums, and websites, for extremist material. This capability allows for a more comprehensive and timely identification of potential threats or radicalising content.
Pattern Recognition and Anomaly Detection	LLMs excel in identifying patterns and anomalies in data, including language use that may signal extremist sentiments or radicalisation efforts. By training on a diverse dataset encompassing various forms of extremist communication, LLM-based co-pilot tools can learn to detect subtle cues and markers of extremist content, aiding in early detection and intervention efforts.
Natural Language Understanding	The advanced natural language processing (NLP) capabilities of LLMs enable them to understand context, sarcasm, and nuanced language, which are often employed in extremist communications. This understanding is crucial for distinguishing between harmful content and legitimate free speech, reducing the risk of over-censorship or misunderstanding benign content as extremist.
Customisation and Adaptability	LLMs can be fine-tuned to adapt to the evolving nature of extremist language and symbols. Extremist groups often change their communication strategies to evade detection, but LLM-based co-pilot tools can be continually updated with new data to capture these shifts, maintaining their effectiveness over time.
Interdisciplinary Insights	By integrating insights from the humanities, such as historical context, ideological underpinnings, and socio-political factors, into the training and application of LLMs, these models can offer a more nuanced and culturally sensitive analyse of extremist content. This interdisciplinary approach enhances the accuracy and relevance of LLM assessments in diverse contexts.
Assisting Human Experts	LLMs can serve as tools to support human experts in counter-extremism efforts. By handling the initial stages of data analysis and flagging potential concerns, LLM-based co-pilot tools free up human analysts to focus on more complex tasks, such as deeper analysis of flagged content, strategic planning, and intervention efforts.

Source: Created by the author.

Designing Digital Media Literacies for Social Cohesion **131**

radicalisation efforts, facilitating early intervention (Paraschiv, Ion, & Dascalu, 2024). Furthermore, advanced natural language processing capabilities allow for a nuanced understanding of context, sarcasm, and subtleties in language, crucial for distinguishing between harmful content and legitimate expression, thereby reducing the risk of misinterpretation. Equally important is the adaptability of LLMs, which can be fine-tuned to track the evolving lexicon and strategies of extremist groups, ensuring sustained effectiveness over time. Incorporating interdisciplinary insights enhances the models' analyses, making them culturally sensitive and contextually aware, thus improving the accuracy of detecting extremist content. By augmenting the capabilities of human experts, LLMs can streamline the initial stages of content analysis, allowing analysts to concentrate on complex evaluations and strategic interventions and outlined in Table 6.2.

LLMs and Civic Engagement

The formation of collaborative governance involving tech companies, governmental bodies, civil society, and academia is another pivotal approach. This facilitates the exchange of best practices and resources, fostering the creation of nuanced and effective strategies against online threats. By adopting a unified stance, stakeholders can implement cross-platform standards that uphold safety and ethical considerations. The application of LLM-based co-pilot tools in enhancing digital media literacy can be significantly advanced through public institutions adopting a multifaceted approach that aligns with high levels of trust, transparency, and cultural openness towards AI technologies. For example, LLM-based co-pilot tools can be used in educational settings to teach digital literacy skills, such as discerning credible sources and identifying biased information. It is, however, crucial to acknowledge the limitations and ethical considerations in deploying LLMs for these purposes, including the risks of reinforcing biases or inaccuracies inherent in their training data. Hence, while LLMs hold promise in enhancing digital literacies and combating extremism, their deployment must be carefully managed and continuously evaluated to ensure they contribute positively to these aims.

In a study based in northern Europe, Robinson (2020) argued that the authoring of national strategic policy is a pivotal step, ensuring that AI development and application, including LLMs, adhere to cultural values and personal rights, thereby reinforcing these principles in society. Such policies must explicitly embed cultural values, much like the GDPR embodies the EU's view of privacy as a human right, ensuring AI strategies do not disrupt the societal fabric. Moreover, promoting digital trust is crucial, requiring public institutions to establish consent models for using personal data in machine learning, which is fundamental to training LLMs. This builds stakeholder trust in both institutions and technology, a vital component for their effective use

132 Emerging Digital Media Ecologies

in digital literacy programs. Additionally, ensuring transparency in algorithmic decision-making is essential. By educating citizens about AI workings, including how LLMs process and generate information, institutions and industry can demystify these technologies and foster an environment where citizens are not only informed but also comfortable interacting with and critiquing these technologies. Such an approach can lead to more informed digital citizens, capable of critically engaging with online information, thus countering misinformation and online extremism effectively.

Empowering online communities to engage in constructive interactions acts as a countermeasure to negative influences. By enabling users to report detrimental content and partake in community moderation, a collective sense of responsibility towards the digital environment is cultivated. Providing users with enhanced control over their online experiences through comprehensive privacy settings, content filters, and customisation tools can also significantly reduce exposure to harmful content. Regulatory frameworks and policies that encourage platforms to adopt such proactive measures while safeguarding freedom of expression and privacy are vital. Such policies should motivate meaningful actions against online harms without imposing excessive restrictions that could hinder legitimate discourse. At the foundation is a need for mechanisms for transparent reporting and the establishment of accountability mechanisms which are crucial for platforms to demonstrate their commitment to combating online harms. Disclosing the criteria for content moderation and the efficacy of various strategies fosters trust and ensures that platforms are held responsible for their role in safeguarding the digital landscape. This is a work in progress.

While the logical case outlined above for using LLMs in countering extremism is strong, it is important to address ethical and practical considerations. The utilisation of LLMs for monitoring digital communications introduces significant privacy concerns, particularly in terms of surveillance and data handling. The scenario where individuals' private conversations are analysed without consent, such as through monitoring encrypted messaging apps or social media platforms to detect extremist content, exemplifies the invasive nature of such surveillance. This not only targets those engaged in extremism but also infringes on the privacy of all users. Furthermore, the collection and storage of vast amounts of personal data by LLMs raise issues of data breaches and unauthorised access. The risk is especially acute if sensitive personal information becomes exposed or misused due to compromised data storage systems, highlighting the potential for significant privacy violations.

Another critical concern is the risk of false positives. LLMs, despite their sophistication, may misinterpret nuances, sarcasm, or cultural expressions, leading to the misclassification of benign content as extremist. This misidentification can have dire consequences for individuals wrongly flagged as extremists, including unwarranted scrutiny, loss of access to online platforms, or even legal repercussions. The issue is particularly problematic for activists or journalists discussing sensitive topics, who may be incorrectly identified and subjected to censorship or investigation.

The potential for misuse of LLMs also poses a significant threat. Authoritarian regimes could exploit these technologies to suppress dissent, monitor political opponents, or target minority groups under the guise of national security. Such misuse could result in the silencing of political activism or criticism of the government. Additionally, if LLMs are trained on biased data, they could perpetuate or amplify existing prejudices, leading to discriminatory practices. This might manifest as the disproportionate flagging of content related to certain religions, ethnicities, or ideologies, unfairly targeting content in languages or dialects associated with minority groups. To address these concerns, it is imperative for developers and users of LLMs in counter-extremism efforts to prioritise ethical considerations, transparency, and accountability. This involves implementing robust privacy protections and data handling policies, developing mechanisms to minimise and address false positives effectively, ensuring the diversity and fairness of training data to reduce biases and establishing oversight and ethical review processes to prevent misuse. By adopting these measures, the negative implications associated with the use of LLMs in surveillance and monitoring can be mitigated, fostering a more ethical and responsible approach to counter-extremism efforts. Transparent, responsible use of LLMs, with oversight from multidisciplinary teams, is essential to mitigate these risks. Leveraging LLMs to counter-extremism underscores the potential of technology to augment human efforts in ensuring safety and security, provided that their deployment is guided by ethical principles and a comprehensive understanding of their societal implications. The successful and ethical application of these tools requires careful consideration of their limitations and potential impacts on society.

Conclusion

Application Programming Interfaces (APIs) might be intended by developers as neutral facilitators of digital engagement; however, they may inadvertently contribute to the formation of filter bubbles. These bubbles encase users within homogeneous information zones, fostering echo chambers that perpetuate divisive 'us versus them' narratives—a phenomenon wherein opposing groups are seen as inherently different and at odds, often leading to intensified social polarisation. Such echo chambers do not merely entrench existing societal divisions but also pose significant barriers to the cross-pollination of ideas. The interplay between technological affordances—such as algorithmic amplification—and user practices—including the selection of content— becomes particularly potent when elements such as microtargeting and anonymity converge. This amplification effect is not confined by geographical borders; the global reach of online platforms enables the swift transmission of

134 Emerging Digital Media Ecologies

narratives and ideologies, which, coupled with a fundamental human desire for belonging, can fuel a diversified and pervasive radicalisation.

To counteract these dynamics, it is essential to adopt a multifaceted approach to counter-radicalisation that extends beyond content moderation. Such an approach must consider the architectural underpinnings of online spaces and the psychological needs driving individuals towards radical beliefs. This could manifest as nuanced content moderation strategies, targeted support for individuals vulnerable to radicalisation, and robust international cooperation to tackle the inherently transnational challenge of online extremism.

The strategic deployment of LLMs in digital literacy initiatives represents an innovative response to these challenges. LLM-based co-pilot tools hold the potential to significantly enhance the critical evaluation skills of individuals, enabling them to discern the credibility of sources and identify biased information. However, this potential must be balanced against the ethical implications of their use, particularly the risk of perpetuating existing biases and inaccuracies from their training data. The effectiveness of LLMs in combating online extremism will thus depend on a foundation of trust, transparency, and a commitment to cultural sensitivity. To ensure the constructive integration of LLMs into counter-extremism efforts, it is crucial to maintain rigorous oversight and a process of continuous reassessment. This oversight should ensure that LLMs contribute positively to the goals of digital literacy and counter-extremism. These initiatives are pivotal in cultivating a society that is not only resistant to the currents of online extremism but also actively engaged in shaping a digitally aware and inclusive future.

7

EXTENDED REALITY'S CRITICAL INTERFACES AND APPLICATIONS

Spheres as the Topology of Emerging Media

The concept of 'sphere' underlies terms such as atmosphere, biosphere, and lithosphere, extending to anthroposphere and technosphere. The latter encompasses cities, infrastructure, and technology, which significantly impact Earth's natural processes, representing the human-made environment and the influence of human activity on the planet. Each places the Earth at the centre of a system of spheres that operate like layers of our experience. To grapple with understanding the associated nuances that come with change, Sloterdijk's treatise on Spheres presents a useful investigation into the ontological and sociological constructs that have historically encompassed and defined human existence. His analysis extends from the intimate 'microspheres', or Bubbles (Sloterdijk, 2011) of personal relationships, to the 'macrospheres' of Globes (Sloterdijk, 2014) that encapsulate societies, to ultimately culminate in 'foam', an irregular agglomeration of bubbles and a feature of modern-day fragmented coexistence that sees individuals largely adrift in Western nations (Sloterdijk, 2016). The convergence of Peter Sloterdijk's exploration of spatial metaphors and social spheres through this trilogy of works, with the digital landscapes of the 'infosphere', as conceptualised by Luciano Floridi (2014), presents a useful combined lens for the understanding of our evolving relational and ecological paradigms. Sloterdijk's aim is to rethink our relation to the world by starting not with the individual in the face of the world, but by noting that to be human already implies that we are taking part in an intimate space that we share with other human beings and with other objects (Ernste, 2018, p. 274). This decentralised positioning of the individual is much like Deleuze and Guattari's idea of the multiplicity of rhizomes that

DOI: 10.4324/9781003178149-9

136 Emerging Digital Media Ecologies

might extend in all directions without a prime node (1987). Here we might take the essence of the rhizome which is its conjunction, 'and ... and ... and ...' (Deleuze & Guattari, 1987, p. 25)—which represents a way of understanding the world that is non-linear, open, and connected, much like the structure of the internet or social networks—and consider Postman's (1998, p. 4) statement that 'technological change is not additive; it is ecological' such that, '[a] new medium does not [just] add something; it changes everything ...'. Leaning into the ecological metaphor are approaches that consider not just the connections but also the dynamics of support, competition, and collaboration—similar to an ecosystem where various entities interact and depend on each other for survival and development—a provocation in this chapter in regard to emerging media forms through the normative framework of social responsibility and the societal expectations for media professionals, developers, and organisations to contribute positively to society, address social issues, and foster public discourse and civic engagement.

In the age of the infosphere, the intimate 'microspheres' of Sloterdijk can be seen evolving through digital mediums, as decentralised networks of inherently entangled interactions, where relationships and identities extend beyond physical proximities, challenging traditional notions of intimacy and otherness. The 'macrospheres' and the collective myths and symbols that bind societies are now deeply influenced by digital narratives and global connectivity, reshaping our collective 'immune systems' against existential threats. Meanwhile, the concept of 'foam' becomes ever more pertinent as individual lives, encapsulated within personal digital bubbles, navigate the vastness of the infosphere, creating a multiplicity of realities and identities. The progression from one 'spatial container' to another, from womb to house, to civilisation that Sloterdijk posits, outlines the immunological narratives that protect and define our sense of self and collective identity. The infosphere acts as both a medium and an environment, wherein the digital and physical intermingle, creating complex layers of connection and meaning (Floridi, 2014). This digital ecology does not merely overlay Sloterdijk's spheres but integrates within them, altering the texture and dynamics of human coexistence. The infosphere, through its capacity to redefine boundaries, spaces, and connections, mirrors and extends Sloterdijk's immunological ontologies, presenting new challenges and opportunities for constructing and understanding human habitats.

Integrating these perspectives within medialogy, we navigate further towards an understanding of how digital technologies reshape socio-technological narratives. The infosphere, with its digital networks and data flows, emerges not merely as a backdrop to human activity but as a significant ecological factor that reconfigures the spatial and symbolic spheres Sloterdijk identifies. Underscored is the transformational potential of the infosphere in redefining human relationships, identities, and societal structures. One holds

Extended Reality's Critical Interfaces and Applications **137**

that the critical need for awareness and critique in navigating the infosphere is fundamental. The potential for algorithmic societies to reduce human experiences to data points, as Floridi suggests, echoes Sloterdijk's concerns about the breakdown of macrospheres and the resulting societal unrest. In this context, the task of medialogy is to dissect and understand the interplay between individuals, communication technologies, digital media ecologies, and subsequent impacts on the natural environment through an integrated approach towards ensuring that in the quest for efficiency and connectivity, we do not lose sight of meaning, identity, community, or surroundings.

Augmented Reality: Mediating between the Inside and the Outside

Within medialogy, the discourse on interfaces intersects with philosophical enquiries into symbolic spheres as articulated by Floridi and Sloterdijk. Floridi's (2014) exploration of the infosphere as an environmental locus wherein information underpins human experience complements Sloterdijk's examination of spheres as spatial metaphors defining human relations and knowledge structures (Sloterdijk, 2011; 2014; 2016). These conceptual frameworks provide a rich context for understanding digital interfaces not merely as points of interaction but as immersive spaces shaping and being shaped by human cognition and cultural practices. Emphasising the immersive nature of interfaces, the notion of spheres underscores their role in mediating our understanding of the world and ourselves within it. This philosophical backdrop sets the stage for a deeper examination of interfaces as media ecologies, as articulated by Scolari (2012).

Scolari (2012) discusses interfaces within the framework of media ecology, highlighting interactions among media, users, infrastructures, and technologies. Interfaces serve as the minimal expression of the media environment, facilitating interactions not only between users and media but also among different media forms. They represent the micro-level of media ecology analysis, analogous to the significance of signs in linguistics or genes in genetics. Scolari's perspective underscores the significance of interfaces in mediating the interplay of media, technology, and user interaction within socio-cultural contexts. Interfaces for their part facilitate interactions and exchanges between different media forms, such as between comic and video games or cinema and television, illustrating how media can co-evolve with each other (Scolari, 2012, p 216). In this vein, Scolari's insights into interfaces underscore their significance in the intermingling of media and technology, with user interaction in socio-cultural contexts, serving as the minimal yet most expressive layer of the media environment (Scolari, 2012). This perspective gains additional depth when considering interfaces as themselves being a symbolic sphere at the macro-level where they act not only as points of engagement but as immersive spaces at the micro-level that encapsulate

138 Emerging Digital Media Ecologies

users in a mediated experience of information and interaction. Impacting each symbolic form of sphere is that we are witnessing a rapid growth in the communications infrastructure with increasing bandwidth and pervasiveness, and advances in hardware that can capture the hearts and minds of people and their online environment (with various consequences as Chapter 6 underscored).

As the narrative of medialogy evolves, incorporating the notion of 'Next Nature' from Chapter 3, it becomes evident that immersive media stand at the forefront of this evolution. The Metaverse, a 'world' woven by VR, AR, and digital 3D worlds, exemplifies this new reality. It reflects a sophisticated synergy between our tangible world and the elaborate virtual spaces cultivated by entities ranging from tech giants like Meta (Facebook), Microsoft, Apple, and Nvidia to innovative start-ups. For its part, Meta, which emerged from the rebranding of Facebook in 2021, epitomises a transformational shift in the focus of contemporary technology companies from mere social networking platforms to architects of expansive digital realms. The rebranding signifies a strategic realignment with Meta's augmented ambition to craft and curate the Metaverse—in ideal form as a conceptually robust, digitally coextensive space that melds enhanced physical realities with digital existence. This Metaverse, characterised by its persistence, would serve as a perpetual nexus of interaction, where the boundaries between virtual and physical blur, facilitating continuity of experience heretofore unseen. Within this context, technologies such as VR and AR are not merely adjunct tools but foundational components that enable users to navigate, interact, and collaborate in ways that parallel the tactile world, yet transcend its corporeal constraints. This is not just an advance in technology but a hopeful leap into an era where our environment is both a digital and physical experience, interwoven to enrich all aspects of socio-economic and cultural life, but likely for virtual working and education as the initial drivers.

The idealised 'seamless' integration for 'frictionless' interactions across media and platforms leverages the IoT, AI, machine learning, and blockchain technology to reshape traditional socio-economic practices. As we consider the intricate overlay of technology onto our natural processes, we also begin to perceive how immersive technologies could magnify the educational and experiential aspects of this integration. The convergence of interfaces and spheres in medialogy presents a framework for understanding and leveraging the capacity of upgraded immersive technologies with AR, for example, 'smart' glasses from Rokid Max (AR Glasses) or Ray-Ban Meta smart glasses that project computer-generated images onto the user's surroundings; in VR, for example, headsets such as Apple Vision Pro; as well as 360-degree immersive video—recordings that capture a panoramic view of a scene in all directions, allowing viewers to explore and navigate the footage in a virtual environment and enable viewers to interact with the content by panning, tilting, and zooming providing a more engaging and immersive experience compared to the traditional flat (2D) video. It is used across various fields, including education, journalism, marketing, and entertainment, to enhance storytelling, simulate real-world experiences, and create immersive learning environments. The importance of interfaces in facilitating experiential learning, particularly when integrated with threshold concepts—core ideas or knowledge within a discipline that, once understood, transform perceptions and enable a deeper level of learning—may be magnified by the immersive capabilities of these technologies.

Virtual Reality (VR) technologies allow participant observers to be totally immersed in, and able to interact with, a completely synthetic world (Milgram & Kishino,1994, p. 3). As a subset of VR technologies, Mixed Reality (MR) blends real (physical) and virtual worlds along the reality-to-virtuality continuum. According to Milgram & Kishino (1994, p. 3) a 'virtuality continuum' is a spectrum that ranges from the real environment on one end to the virtual environment on the other. MR spans across this continuum, encapsulating both Augmented Reality (AR) and Augmented Virtuality (AV). AR is closer to the real environment, where digital content is overlaid onto the real world, enhancing one's perception of reality without replacing it. AV sits more centrally within the continuum, where the real-world elements are integrated into a predominantly virtual space. Finally, VR lies at the opposite end of the spectrum from the real environment, where the user is fully immersed in a completely virtual space, with no direct perception of the real world. MR, therefore, represents the entire range of combined real and virtual experiences, where AR and AV are subsets of the broader MR concept, bridging the gap between the real and the fully virtual environments (Milgram & Kishino,1994, p. 3). In many contexts, MR and XR (Extended Reality) are seen as synonymous and are often used interchangeably as both terms refer to the integration of digital content into the real world or the creation of immersive experiences that blend virtual and physical elements. XR serves as an umbrella term encompassing VR, AR, and MR, while MR specifically emphasises the merging of virtual and physical environments to create interactive experiences. In essence, being in such environments means that a person can make use of their natural ability for spatial interaction. Well-designed interfaces can make interaction and collaboration inside such systems more natural, effective, and engaging (Molka-Danielsen et al., 2013). Research suggests that interface technologies exert a strong and positive influence on educational outcomes, despite some negative findings regarding their impact on anxiety, cognition, creativity, gender differences, learning attitudes, satisfaction, and engagement (Yu, 2021).

140 Emerging Digital Media Ecologies

Policies and Initiatives for Developing Skills and Educating Citizens for a Brave New World

According to a report, *Value Creation in the Metaverse: The Real Business of the Virtual World* with its potential to generate up to $5 trillion in value by 2030, the Metaverse is too big for companies to ignore (McKinsey & Company, 2022). At the macro-level, the Chinese government's issuing of the *Virtual Reality and Industry Application Integration Development Action Plan (2022–2026)* heralds a strategic push towards the development of the Metaverse underscored by immersive technologies such as VR, AR, and MR, outlining key objectives and tasks until 2026. This initiative, spearheaded by the Ministry of Industry and Information Technology (MIIT) in collaboration with other government bodies, underscores a comprehensive approach focused on advancing innovation across crucial technological fronts such as near-eye display, graphics rendering, and network transmission, among others. Emphasising synergies with 5G and AI, the plan seeks to fortify the entire VR industry supply chain, including hardware, software, and infrastructure, with particular attention to user comfort, ease of use, and safety. Furthermore, the initiative aims to accelerate VR adoption across diverse sectors ranging from industrial production to smart cities, stressing organic integration and broad applicability. Key support mechanisms and standards are being established to bolster the industrial ecosystem, ensuring technological reliability and fostering innovation across various domains (Huld, 2022).

The initiative undertaken by the European Commission in convening three European citizens' panels in 2023, one of which focused on the topic of 'virtual worlds', signifies a concerted effort towards inclusive governance and citizen engagement within the European Union (European Commission, Directorate-General for Communication, 2023). By gathering randomly selected citizens from all 27 Member States, these panels serve as platforms for deliberation and recommendation-making, aligning with the Commission's commitment to translate vision into actionable policies as articulated in the 2022 communication on the 'Conference on the Future of Europe' and EC President von der Leyen's 2022 State of the Union address. Such deliberative processes hold significant implications for democracy and policy-making within the EU, aiming to foster greater transparency, legitimacy, and responsiveness to citizens' concerns and preferences, particularly in emerging domains like virtual worlds where regulatory frameworks and societal implications are still evolving. Focusing on the important topic of learning and education in virtual worlds, sitting behind emerging projects is a key recommendation for teachers to receive training on: (1) the practical use of digital tools; (2) risks, safety, and ethics within the virtual worlds; and,

Extended Reality's Critical Interfaces and Applications **141**

(3) on new teaching opportunities through virtual worlds (recommendation 10) with the justification that

> Training teachers means that they are able to train their students and to raise awareness among the young from the very beginning. It also helps to reduce the digital gap existing between teachers and students. We believe that providing training on safe online behaviours and on the safe use of virtual worlds needs to be taught as early as primary school.
>
> *(European Commission, Directorate-General for Communication, 2023, p. 47)*

A collaboration between Meta (Facebook) and Simplon to establish a 'Metaverse Academy' in France demonstrates a commitment to cultivating expertise in immersive technologies, particularly in roles related to immersive technology development and technical support (Kochhar, 2022). Metaverse Academy (Metaverse Development World) refers to a variety of initiatives and institutions focused on education and training in Metaverse technologies, including VR, AR, blockchain, and other related digital skills (https://metav ersedevelopment.world/academy/). By targeting the training of 100 students across multiple cities, the initiative aims to address the growing demand for skilled professionals in the growing Metaverse industry. Another initiative through FIAP is EU-wide, supported by a consortium of 13 partners from 7 EU and associated countries and 1 non-EU partner for 2024–2026 (https:// fiap-ev.org/en/metaverse-academy/)

> The overall objective of the Metaverse Academy is to increase the EU's competitiveness in the skills required for immersive technologies and to facilitate the adaptation of such technologies in different use cases through industry-academia collaboration, including training and fostering the entrepreneurial mindset of our students as target beneficiaries. The main objective of the Metaverse Academy project is to strengthen academic and professional training in the areas of skills required for immersive technologies.

While the initiatives hold promise for addressing skills gaps and promoting diversity, potential challenges may arise in the near term in ensuring the scalability and sustainability of the academy's operations, as well as in maintaining alignment with evolving industry trends and technologies.

In line with other global initiatives to prepare citizens for immersive, virtual environments the 'Meta (Facebook) Boost' initiative is the company's program to help educate small business owners about the tools that can help them find success on the Metaverse platform. For example, launched in collaboration with the Saudi Ministry of Communications and Information Technology,

142 Emerging Digital Media Ecologies

Small and Medium Enterprises General Authority (Monsha'at), and AstroLabs, Meta aims to empower small to medium-sized enterprises (SMEs) in Saudi Arabia by providing training and enablement on Meta products and tools. By aligning with Saudi's *Vision 2030*—a plan for increased diversification economically, socially, and culturally—the Meta initiative seeks to boost SME productivity and increase their contribution to the GDP to 35% by 2030, thereby fostering economic growth and diversification towards greater competitiveness in the global marketplace (Saudi Press Agency, 2022). Overall, the Meta Boost initiative has the potential to offer valuable opportunities for small businesses, especially to those in the global South to expand their reach, enhance their digital skills, and contribute to economic growth; however, it is important to address challenges related to digital infrastructure and a risk of widening the digital divide. Access to reliable internet connectivity and necessary technology infrastructure remains a challenge not only in First and Second World nations but significantly so in many parts of the Global South. Without adequate access to these resources, small businesses may struggle to fully benefit from the program, exacerbating existing disparities.

The emergence of international conferences and events such as Immersive Tech Africa's XR Innovation Summit (2023) in Africa, facilitated by organisations like the global XR Community, also acts to underscore the increasing importance of XR technologies (e.g., Meta, AXIS or Sony) worldwide within the evolving landscape of the Metaverse and its potential to transform digital interaction, bridging the divide between physical and virtual realms while opening avenues for communication, collaboration, entertainment, and commerce. These events serve as platforms for sharing knowledge, fostering collaboration, and addressing pertinent issues such as diversity and the future trajectory of XR within specific regions, exemplified by the focus on XR Women in Africa and Africa's role in the Metaverse (see Meijers, 2021). Such initiatives underscore the expectations and hope for the democratisation of XR education and a recognition that there need to be diverse perspectives within the field, potentially leading to more inclusive and innovative applications of XR technologies worldwide. Despite originating primarily at the micro-level within specific nations (i.e., Europe and the US), the impacts of 'virtual sphere' developments are expected to reverberate on a global scale. Even individuals not directly engaged with virtual technologies are inevitably affected by their proliferation in today's interconnected world. For example, as the Metaverse transforms the job landscape, new roles and demands will be created impacting the types of jobs that are available in communities and the focus of educational programs, and this shapes the direction of local economies. That is, businesses moving into these digital spaces will need people to design virtual worlds, script avatar behaviours, and develop digital properties. This shift opens doors to entirely new career paths, but it also makes some traditional skills less important. This interconnectedness suggests that the effects of virtual sphere advancements extend beyond geographical boundaries, influencing societies and individuals worldwide, albeit sometimes indirectly. Consequently, understanding and addressing the implications of these developments become imperative for stakeholders across diverse sectors, given their far-reaching societal, economic, and cultural ramifications.

The following section examines emerging media interfaces and immersive technologies, assessing their influence on shaping diverse educational practices and pedagogies, while also delving into the philosophical implications of their role and nature within our societies. It is important to acknowledge that, despite commitments evident in plans such as those outlined above aimed at advancing VR/AR/MR technologies, several gaps persist and key issues remain unresolved. For instance, coordinating efforts across multiple governmental departments can be challenging. Ensuring consistent implementation at both national and local levels is essential for enhancing user access and participation. Additionally, securing the necessary resources and funding to support these ambitious goals is crucial. There is also a critical need for further clarification on how VR/AR/MR interface technologies will be integrated and leveraged within the emerging media and Metaverse ecosystem. Furthermore, moves to bolster supply chains and infrastructure should not overlook potential barriers related to intellectual property rights, cybersecurity, and data privacy, which are crucial for fostering innovation and ensuring consumer trust. Crucial for the success of initiatives is widespread acceptance and adoption across various sectors, which may require addressing challenges related to education and training, in tandem with developing appropriate regulatory frameworks.

Augmenting Education in Immersive Spheres

Newly emerging interfaces offer unique opportunities for engaging with complex concepts and environments in a manner that traditional educational media, as an important example, might not match. For instance, the use of 360-degree immersive videos in education immerses students in virtual spheres enabling them to observe a virtual environment in any direction such as where historical events or systems can be experienced, rather than merely observed, fostering a transformative understanding of the subject matter. Similarly, the application of AR and VR in teaching complex scientific principles or facilitating virtual simulations exemplifies how these interfaces create micro-sphere-like learning environments. These immersive spheres enable students to visualise, interact with, and understand difficult concepts in a hands-on manner, thereby bridging the gap between theoretical knowledge and practical application. Consider the impact of observing a three-dimensional heart pulsating rhythmically in AR or VR as opposed to a static image in a textbook. AR/VR allows students to visualise and engage with complex arrangements in a way that transcends traditional two-dimensional learning materials. They can rotate, zoom in, and explore every chamber and valve in a dynamically beating heart, or examine the structural integrity of a building by virtual walkthrough, gaining a comprehensive understanding of the respective mechanisms.

The works of Akçayir and Akçayir (2017) on the benefits of AR in education and Jensen and Konradsen (2018) on the use of VR head-mounted displays in education and training further substantiate the pedagogical potential of these immersive interfaces. The immersive qualities of these 360-degree videos transport students into the core of the learning environment, vividly illustrating abstract concepts that might be challenging to convey through conventional teaching methods. The heightened level of engagement and immersion offered by 360-degree videos is one of their most salient advantages (Cannavò, Castiello, Prattico, Mazali, & Lamberti, 2023). Leveraging 360-degree videos as a teaching–learning medium brings a multitude of benefits, including multi-perspective viewing that allows learners to observe movements from various angles for a comprehensive understanding of the subject matter (Rosendah, Müller, & Wagner, 2023). These videos provide a realistic and authentic experience, enhancing engagement and immersion while offering high reflective potential for analyses, aiding cognitive learning processes and decision-making in diverse contexts. They represent a resource-saving application design, requiring less effort in recording and editing compared to conventional training videos, thereby serving as an efficient training tool. Additionally, 360-degree videos support individualised learning by allowing learners to control their learning processes and speed, enabling personalised experiences. They are particularly motivating and activating, increasing learner engagement and interest. The differentiated view of movements provided by the multi-perspective, all-round view enhances understanding and skill acquisition. Educators can thus create dynamic and engaging learning experiences that cater to diverse learning styles, enhancing knowledge retention and skill acquisition (Rosendah, Müller, & Wagner, 2023).

Developing collaborative learning within a Cave Automatic Virtual Environment (CAVE)—normally a cube-shaped display that the user stands inside that surrounds them in an immersive projection—has demonstrated numerous advantages over traditional textbook-based education according to de Back, Tinga, Nguyen, and Louwerse (2020). The authors found that this immersive VR setup, which projects environments onto the walls of a room to engage one or multiple participants, leads to significantly higher learning gains due to its ability to foster collaboration among learners. The rich spatial information and interactive elements of a CAVE not only enhance student engagement and motivation but also provide strong spatial cues that are particularly beneficial for learners with low spatial abilities, helping to elevate their performance to match those of peers with higher spatial skills. Furthermore, the unique, collaborative, and interactive nature of learning in a CAVE offers an unparalleled and engaging experience that traditional textbooks cannot always match, making it a powerful tool in modern educational strategies.

Nyaal: A Purpose-Built Theatre for Teaching and Learning

The integration of cutting-edge technologies has become a pivotal focal point in pedagogical practice for enhancing learning experiences. My academic institution created such an immersive physical space for teaching and research, and I was keen to critically investigate its capacity in the higher education context. Called 'the Nyaal', it is part of a learning precinct, using an Australian First Nation's Wadawurrung word for 'to open your eyes', and it is a learning environment that enables students to engage with a variety of dynamic conditions and scenarios during their studies. Its centrepiece, a 75-sqm circular 'Theatre', features ceiling-mounted projectors for 360-degree visual simulations of high quality. Post-presentation, students can explore concepts

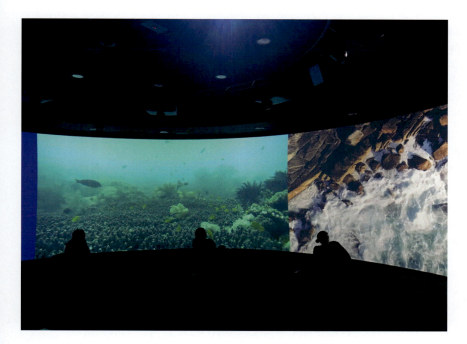

FIGURE 7.1 Nyaal Theatre Immersive Learning Space.
Source: Photographed by the author ©Toija Cinque.

146 Emerging Digital Media Ecologies

further with learning facilitators in the 'Think Tank', a 75-sqm space designed for interactive collaboration, equipped with writable surfaces and mobile video conferencing technology. Nyaal integrates creativity, digital innovation, and leading teaching practices to offer immersive experiences aimed at captivating and motivating students. Upon entering the theatre, the audience is instantly enveloped in new environments via high-quality visual and audio simulations. For instance, trainee teachers can gain experience in virtual classroom settings before entering professional environments. Similarly, firefighters can use such spaces to simulate the experience of combating bushfires and address a myriad of associated hazards before confronting actual emergencies.

The following section explores the transformative potential of immersive technologies, particularly focusing on AR, VR, and 360-degree video as innovative teaching tools in education. Situated in the Nyaal, I sought to evaluate the effectiveness of immersive 360-degree video specifically, within tertiary learning environments. I created an immersive 360-degree video that when shown in the purpose-built space (a micro-sphere) fostered a heightened sense of presence, offering learners a multi-dimensional perspective and facilitating learned experience and a deeper comprehension of abstract concepts (from the macro-sphere) (Figure 7.1).

From my field of media and communications, disciplines grappling with complex issues such as digitalisation to datafication, surveillance, and privacy, I sought to examine the affordances of the immersive and visual demonstrations provided by these technologies. By engaging learners with diverse viewpoints and reinforcing understanding through interactive components, my sense was that immersive learning experiences do hold promise as pedagogical tools in tertiary learning in elucidating threshold concepts in a manner that traditional teaching methods often struggle to achieve.

Digital Realm: A Case Study of Teaching Threshold Concepts in 360 Degree

The rising application of AR, VR, and 360-degree video in education environments signals an exciting development in pedagogical practices, particularly in teaching subject-specific threshold concepts. In addition, the immersive environment encourages learners to engage with multiple perspectives, thereby enhancing learning through active participation in social scenarios (Savickaite & Simmons, 2022). This interaction facilitates the comprehension of complex and abstract (or threshold) concepts. Threshold concepts transform the learner's thinking about a subject or experience once understood, opening new conceptual spaces that foster innovative ways of thinking (Meyer & Land, 2006, p. 3). Employing immersive learning experiences to teach threshold concepts enables learners to engage with these concepts in a powerful, affective manner, resulting in lasting impact (Lock &

MacDowell, 2023). The use of immersive digital platforms and interfaces to teach students, interweaving new and emerging technologies with conventional pedagogical practices is a powerful and effective path. Research shows that teaching Threshold Concepts by using 360-degree video to immerse students in their learning experiences can deeply demonstrate subject-specific threshold concepts such as 'datafication' in/of digital life (Hodge, 2019). Students get to explore virtually the socio-cultural/environmental implications of contemporary media ecologies such as the creation, circulation, use, and storage of data and information, in a context where data and information are increasingly vital. By simulating real-world scenarios in a teaching space, students learn in a controlled environment, receiving instant feedback from their instructor and peers. In disciplines involving complex concepts that are challenging to visualise—such as surveillance, privacy, industrial convergence, and environmental sustainability—360-degree video offers invaluable visual demonstrations that make often abstract concepts tangible. In fields such as anthropology, sociology, or communications, the immersive qualities of these videos can foster empathy, immersing learners in the experiences of others and leading to a more nuanced understanding of complex social concepts. Furthermore, the potential for collaborative learning through 360-degree video experiences is a significant benefit. With the integration of advanced technologies, learners can jointly navigate these immersive environments, fostering teamwork, collaborative problem-solving, and shared learning experiences. The immersive experience can consequently enhance understanding and retention of these critical concepts. In addition, the detailed contextual representation afforded by these videos offers a richer learning experience. As students observe concepts unfolding in real-time within a realistic environment, they develop a more profound understanding of the intricate interconnections between different aspects of a concept. Adding to the immersive experience, 360-degree video can include interactive elements, providing students with the ability to control their perspective and explore the material from various angles. This sense of agency can amplify engagement with the material and afford students diverse viewpoints on a concept, thereby enriching their understanding of a threshold concept. The compatibility of 360-degree video with a variety of devices, such as headsets or streamed video on mobile screens, renders them a flexible tool capable of delivering immersive experiences to students in remote or unconventional learning environments. The immersion and interactivity inherent in 360-degree video contribute to creating vivid, memorable learning experiences. These memories can enhance the retention and recall of the material, thereby improving the learning outcome. Importantly, while the immersive and interactive nature of 360-degree video and AR–VR are positioned here as potentially effective tools for teaching threshold concepts, it is crucial to acknowledge that these digital technologies are not a universal solution. They should be deployed

148 Emerging Digital Media Ecologies

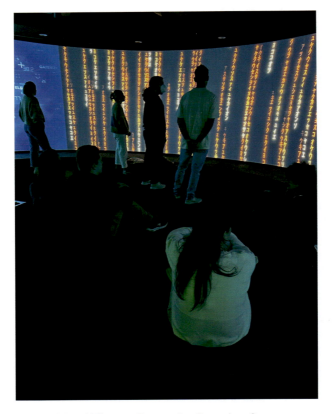

FIGURE 7.2 Nyaal Theatre Immersive Learning Space.
Source: Photographed by the author ©Toija Cinque.

in tandem with other teaching methods to provide a comprehensive, well-rounded learning experience for students (Figure 7.2).

To empirically test the wider field of research for a local context, I developed a creative treatment for an immersive audio-visual experience using mixed AR and VR that explored the socio-cultural and environmental implications of contemporary media ecology and the ways that data and information are vital. This research project received low-risk ethics clearance (ID: HAE-23-018). The research objectives were twofold. First, the creation and implementation of an immersive learning experience using 360-degree video that highlights the socio-cultural/environmental implications of contemporary media ecologies, given the increasing importance of data and information in today's digital age. Second, to evaluate students' perceptions and learning outcomes associated with the immersive 360-degree learning experiences. The provocation through the video was that digital technologies and data-driven intelligence are reshaping not only our cultural, social, and economic spheres but also the natural environment. This evolution compels us to re-examine the foundations of our interaction with both the natural and digital realms, particularly concerning our use of natural resources. The video exploration was aimed at addressing ecological challenges (e-waste and resources management) and ethical considerations in our increasingly digital lives. The notion of 'ecosophy'—the philosophy of ecological harmony and balance (Naess, 1990; see also Guattari, 2000)—was integrated as a guiding principle, emphasising sustainable and ethical use of technology in a range of media practices. Participants themselves regularly engage in a range of media practices in their lives. By looking at specific concepts that are connected to the subject such as privacy, surveillance, connectivity, and environmental concern, a spotlight is turned on the need for appropriate policies, use, and regulation that fit in with contemporary media use.

I wrote and produced a script for the 10-minute 360-degree video. The mixed reality (MR) experience comprised surround sound audio and the 360-degree video simultaneously displayed and distributed around Nyaal's circular 'Theatre' screen. I drew on empirical methods (qualitative and quantitative analysis) to test key themes and outcomes as they link to the era of digital communications technologies as critical communication tools for socio-environmental impact. My video endeavoured to encourage listener-viewers to interrogate the nexus between media evolution and environmental sustainability, examining the critical implications of increased datafication on ecological systems. It posited the essential question: 'How does the progressive datafication inherent in media's evolution affect the environmental footprint, and what are the broader consequences for sustainable development?'. This enquiry is imperative as it seeks to illuminate the balance between technological advancement and environmental stewardship, providing a vital discourse on the responsible shaping of our digital future in alignment with ecological imperatives (Figure 7.3).

This type of experiential threshold concept learning opens up new conceptual spaces for learners, transforming their thinking. Because of comprehending a threshold concept, 'there may thus be a transformed internal view of subject matter, subject landscape, or even world view' (Meyer & Land, 2006, p. 3). With this in mind, I anticipated that these technologies would open up new ways of understanding emerging communications technologies over time. My approach speculated that a novel and well-designed immersive experience would make learning inside such systems more effective, natural, and engaging to inspire learning in an experiential way. Eighty students in the subject were

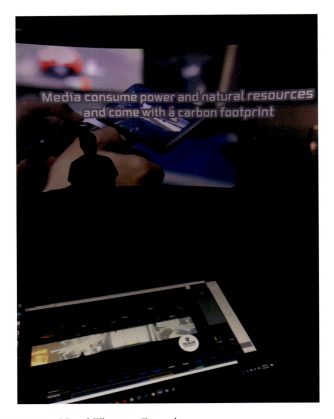

FIGURE 7.3   Nyaal Theatre Console.
Source: Photographed by the author ©Toija Cinque.

shown the video. Prior to entering the Nyaal facility, students were briefed about possible sensory or other related risks as a result of the immersive experience with a safety plan verbally outlined in regard to exiting the facility should this be necessary. This is standard procedure in the theatre facility with written warnings in place. Students engaged with post-screening deliberations and reflective discussions held in the 'Think Tank'. No covert research was undertaken for the purposes of the project.

Student's comments suggested that the experience indeed had an impact. Following are the representative feedback from participants:

'I found that having the theories/concepts/ideas in the immersive video helps visualise these and get immersed' (participant A);
'I think it could be longer, I really enjoyed watching it' (participant B);
'it makes us pay attention more than usual presentations' (participant C);

'Visually very impressive and immersive experience' (participant D);
'It was a truly unique and fun experience' (participant E),

Finally, with regard to the environmental footprint of media usage:

'I am at university—why have I never heard this before?!' (participant F).

While immersive technologies like AR, VR, and 360-degree video hold promise for enhancing educational experiences, they also present several challenges and limitations. Accessibility is a significant concern, as not all might have access to the necessary hardware or stable internet connections required to fully participate in immersive learning experiences. Moreover, the learning curve associated with mastering these technologies may pose obstacles for both students and educators, potentially widening existing disparities in digital literacy. There are also concerns about the potential for immersive technologies to distract or disengage students, particularly if not integrated thoughtfully into the curriculum. Additionally, there are ethical considerations surrounding data privacy and safety, especially when using immersive technologies that collect and analyse user data (which was not the case in the study undertaken, but private companies may). Furthermore, the high costs associated with developing and implementing immersive experiences may be prohibitive for many educational institutions, limiting access for students from low socio-economic status backgrounds. Addressing these challenges requires careful consideration of accessibility, pedagogical integration, ethical guidelines, and cost-effectiveness to ensure that immersive technologies contribute positively to education without exacerbating existing inequalities.

Digital Realm

Transitioning from this domain of 360-degree video production, wherein students alone were enveloped within immersive virtual environments and narratives, I subsequently moved into curating an exhibition as part of Melbourne Design Week 2024, an initiative of the Victorian Government in Australia in collaboration with the National Gallery of Victoria. This shift in

FIGURE 7.4 Digital Realm 2024, an Exhibit for Melbourne Design Week.
Source: Creative work and photographed by the author © Toija Cinque.

152 Emerging Digital Media Ecologies

focus moves to a broader examination of the confluence between art, ecology, and the forefront of technological innovation. Taking inspiration from the principles of 'ecosophy', the heart of this exhibition *EcoDigital Futures* lies in the artists' innovative use of technology, not merely as tools but as infrastructures and interfaces that foster sustainable and ethical design practices (Figure 7.4). My creative contribution was 'Digital Realm':

> In an era where Augmented Reality (AR), Virtual Reality (VR), and 360-degree videos are impacting our engagement with the digital realm, this work explores the potential of these technologies beyond the classroom, reaching out to a broader public audience. Digital Realm delves into how immersive media can introduce complex concepts related to privacy, surveillance, data security, and the ethical use of data, offering a rich, multi-perspective understanding of these critical issues. The work focuses on leveraging the immersive and interactive qualities of 360-degree video to foster a deeper comprehension of the socio-technological and environmental implications inherent in contemporary digital landscapes. By presenting these themes through engaging, experiential formats, Digital Realm provokes us to critically consider the ethical and ecological dimensions of our increasingly connected world. The goal is not merely to afford educational outcomes, but to inspire a collective reflection on how we can navigate and shape the digital age in harmony with ecological principles, thus contributing to a more sustainable and just society.

These practices are not ends in themselves but means to a more profound understanding and rethinking of our interaction with the digital systems that permeate our lives. By illuminating the omnipresence of data and its potential for creative appropriation, the exhibition revealed the untapped possibilities of digital realms to reflect and enhance our ecological sensibilities. By exploring how digital infrastructures and interfaces can serve as conduits for critical and creative practices that honour and advance ecological harmony, the exhibition invited visitors to contemplate the role of technology in forging a sustainable future. It was a call to action—a reminder that in the quest for ecological balance, creativity and innovation can lead the way in transforming our collective consciousness and societal structures.

Conclusion

In conclusion, the synthesis of Floridi and Sloterdijk's spheres with Scolari's conception of interfaces offers a way for understanding digital media environments as intricate, immersive spaces that significantly influence user experience and knowledge acquisition. This chapter emphasises the critical importance of engaging thoughtfully with both our digital and physical surroundings, recognising the profound implications of our coexistence within

Extended Reality's Critical Interfaces and Applications **153**

these interwoven spheres. As we navigate the complexities of the infosphere, philosophical reflection remains indispensable in comprehending and shaping our collective destinies. The integration of these perspectives, alongside the practical application of interfaces in education—particularly in conveying threshold concepts through immersive technologies—presents a valuable approach to learning and understanding in the digital era. The explorations, converging within the realm of medialogy, provide a framework for developing deeply engaging and transformative educational experiences through interfaces, with the potential to redefine teaching and learning paradigms in profound ways. Looking ahead, emerging technology trends suggest a future where machines can comprehend human emotions and thoughts, potentially enabling personalised learning experiences tailored to learners' emotional states and cognitive capacities, as discussed by McStay (2018). However, echoing Postman's (1998) cautionary note, we must approach technological innovation with vigilance, noting its vast, unpredictable, and largely irreversible consequences.

The empirical research employed immersive 360-degree video to explore the socio-cultural, environmental, and ethical dimensions of contemporary media ecologies, underscored by the growing predominance of data in the digital era. Through the evaluation of students' perceptions and learning outcomes regarding immersive learning experiences, the study highlights the potential of such approaches to deepen engagement and understanding among participants. Student feedback indicates the efficacy of 360-degree video in enhancing comprehension and interest, suggesting its value as a tool for immersive education and consciousness-raising concerning ecological challenges and ethical considerations in the digital milieu. Beyond its immediate implications for academia, this research holds broader societal significance. As we bravely enter virtual worlds, it offers insights into innovative pedagogical strategies that leverage immersive technologies to simultaneously deepen understanding and engagement with complex topics, fostering interdisciplinary collaboration and critical reflection.

Adopting 'ecosophy' as a foundational principle, the study highlights the need for a critical reassessment of human interactions within both the natural and digital environments, emphasising ecological harmony and sustainable technology (Naess, 1990). This discussion sets the stage for Chapter 8, which delves into First Nations' media, showcasing the long-standing indigenous practices centred around ecosophy. These practices have championed ecological balance and sustainability well before these concepts became part of the global conversation. First Peoples offers vital perspectives for contemporary media analysis. By integrating ethical and ecological considerations into media practices and education, the study contributes to the cultivation of a more sustainable and ethically informed digital future, encouraging responsible technology use and societal dialogue.

8

INDIGENOUS NARRATIVES AND THE DYNAMICS OF MEDIALOGY

First Nations

The discourse surrounding Indigenous media emerges as a critical juncture in our understanding of the complexities of media consumption, production, and the layered undercurrents of power that infuse these processes. This is particularly significant in conceptually framing medialogy, a task that involves charting the important and evolving techno-media tendencies and critically considering the subsequent impacts of media interaction and consumption. This chapter is a multifaceted exploration of how First Nations communities, leveraging the affordances of digital media, are redefining the narrative space, fostering cultural preservation, and engaging in a dialogic process that both transcends and challenges traditional media paradigms. The significance of Indigenous media for First Nations cannot be overstated.

The term 'First Nations' refers to the diverse and distinct Indigenous groups, each with their own unique cultures, languages, histories, and governance structures, who continue to advocate for their rights and sovereignty in the legal and political landscapes of the respective countries in which they live. 'First Nations' is also a term of respect that recognises First Peoples' status as original inhabitants with an ongoing custodial relationship with their ancestral lands and waters, cultures, and communities. In the Australian context, 'First Nations' serves as an inclusive term that acknowledges the sovereignty and prior ownership of the land by Aboriginal and Torres Strait Islander peoples before British colonisation, though the acknowledgement has evolved, it continues to be a matter of significant debate and development. This use of 'First Nations' in Australia reflects a growing movement towards recognising the rights, histories, and cultures of Indigenous peoples and a step towards

DOI: 10.4324/9781003178149-10

reconciliation between Indigenous and non-Indigenous Australians. Indeed, the issue of sovereignty remains contentious. Many Indigenous Australians assert that their sovereignty was never ceded and argue for a treaty or treaties between Indigenous peoples and the Australian government. The call for a treaty is about recognising Indigenous sovereignty and negotiating the terms of coexistence between sovereign entities. In Canada, 'First Nations' is a 'designated group' under Charter jurisprudence (*Canadian Charter of Rights and Freedoms, 1982*) and refers to the Indigenous peoples who are neither Inuit nor Métis (Canada, Government of Canada, 2011). The Māori concept of Kaitiakitanga, denoting guardianship and environmental stewardship, emerges from a philosophy that perceives humans and the natural world as kin. This concept, now resurgent in New Zealand's conservation efforts, exemplifies the symbiotic relationship between culture, nature, and revitalisation. Furthermore, within the fabric of Māori ontology, humans are integrally woven into the natural order, not as dominators but as constituents. The tangata whenua—people of the land—embody the principle through their ancestral ties and custodianship, highlighting a dialogical relationship with the environment.

When discussing the relationship between Indigenous cultures and the land, it is imperative to understand that this connection is rooted in a profound and complexly textured consideration of place. Aboriginal cultural knowledge, for instance, is intricately linked to specific locations within the local geographic landscape. These places serve not as backdrops but as active repositories of cultural narratives, often ritually embedded in the landscape in ways that may remain unseen to those outside these cultural traditions. Caution is, however, necessary in this discourse. The profound bond many First Nations have with the land—often referred to as 'country' and an entity that transcends mere geographical or physical dimensions to encompass living beings, culture, spirituality, language, law, family, and identity; and, thus serving as a fundamental locus of belonging, being, and belief (Terare & Rawsthorne, 2020)—should not be simplistically equated with a mere closeness to nature. Such an equation can be a subtle form of denigration, that diminishes Indigenous sovereignties and complexities.

One might recognise the construct of 'nature', as being a separate entity from the vibrancy of life, as a Western abstraction. The concept of 'animism', deeply rooted in various cultures and epitomised in the Latin *anima* for 'breath, spirit, life', suggests a 'premodern' intrinsic vitality within all elements of our world, whether they be sentient beings, geological structures, or botanical entities (Latour, 1993, pp. 12, 39; Descola, 2005). In other words, animism embodies a worldview wherein a spiritual essence is attributed to entities within the natural world, such as animals, plants, and often inanimate objects, highlighting a rich tradition of interconnectedness and respect within various Indigenous cultures. This notion transcends the confines of organised

156 Emerging Digital Media Ecologies

religions and persists robustly in the secular modern sphere, thereby embodying a persistent and inclusive cosmological view. Drawing parallels with Lovelock's Gaia hypothesis that 'the total ensemble of living organisms which constitute the biosphere can act as a single entity to regulate chemical composition, surface pH and possibly also climate … as an active adaptive control system able to maintain the Earth in homeostasis' (Lovelock & Margulis, 1974, p. 3; Lovelock, 1972), animism posits an organising principle of the universe, an interplay of matter and spirit.

Indigenous knowledge systems, such as those of the Māori, offer valuable insights into this worldview. Birds, within this cosmology, are not mere fauna but are conduits for navigation, oratory, and musical inspiration, a testament to the intricate interspecies dialogues that have historically informed Māori culture and which continue to resonate (Flintoff, 2004). For the First Nations peoples, birds such as the koekoeā in New Zealand or the brolga in Australia embody their advanced understanding of the environment. For instance, the annual return of the long-tailed cuckoo to Aotearoa (New Zealand) and the migration of the Eastern koel each spring from Papua New Guinea and Indonesia to Queensland and New South Wales in Australia are significant. These migrations mark the change of seasons and align with the natural cycles of the world. Such ecological attuning reflects an intimate knowledge system where birds, as just one example, are integral to understanding and interacting with the land and sea. In the realm of oratory, the sonorous calls of the tui are not simply nature's background music but were once integral to the formal ceremonies of the Māori (Flintoff, 2004). The bird's diverse calls resonate with the enriched cultural communication, enhancing ceremonial occasions with a soundscape that bridges the human and the avian (Taylor, 2017). Furthermore, the Māori crafted their sonic world with instruments inspired by the bird chorus around them. Taonga Pūoro, designed to emulate the calls of birds, goes beyond musical expression; they serve as conduits to the ancestral plane, reinforcing the interconnectedness of all life and the Māori belief in the unity of the cosmos (Flintoff, 2004). Birds have long been venerated through cultural practices, not simply for their beauty or song but as co-creators in a shared existential symphony. However, colonisation has frayed this auditory thread, leaving behind echoes of a tradition where the tui's voice might be said to parallel that of the orators of the land.

The essence of this chapter lies in perspective, that is, who narrates the story significantly shapes its substance and authenticity. Indigenous media emerges as pivotal in this context. It encompasses various forms of expression that are conceptualised, produced, and disseminated by Indigenous peoples themselves. These media forms act as vital conduits for cultural preservation, artistic expression, political self-determination, and the assertion of cultural sovereignty.

Indigenous Media: Agency, Narrative Sovereignty, and Cultural Identity in a Global Context

Across Networked Infrastructures

Understanding Indigenous media requires appreciating its role as a platform for Indigenous agency and narrative sovereignty. The broad and interdisciplinary scope of Indigenous media and communication studies thus reveals the rich layers of how First Nations communities use media to navigate the complex interplay between cultural identity and the global media landscape—which is fraught. For example, early work by Vidmar and Rokeach (1974) on bigotry as presented in the television show 'All in the Family' came to the important conclusion that racial and ethnic prejudice is reinforced through deliberate construction and repetition. Along the same lines, Weston (1996) has argued with regard to media that some practices, traditions, and forms of journalism, rather than challenging the stereotypes in popular culture, have repeated, exacerbated, and reinforced them. Scholars like Faye Ginsburg have emphasised the 'cultural activism' aspect of Indigenous Media, illustrating how these platforms can, however, become spaces for cultural resilience and political advocacy (Ginsburg, 2002). According to Ginsberg (2002, p. 53):

> Rather than destroying Inuit cultures as some predicted would happen, these technologies of representation—beginning with the satellite television transmission to Inuit communities of their own small-scale video productions—have played a dynamic and even revitalizing role for Inuit and other First Nations people, as a self-conscious means of cultural preservation and production and a form of political mobilization.

Aboriginal Australians, an exemplifying case in point, represent just a fraction of the global Indigenous populations that have turned to media not only as tools of engagement but also as formidable instruments of cultural preservation and autonomy. In Australia during the early 1980s, when television was not readily accessible to most remote Australian communities, residents of some remote Indigenous communities engaged in video production. For First Peoples, this (then) innovative medium provided an exciting opportunity to create local content and became a powerful means to preserve and share stories that resonated with their community:

> A decade after the Inuit post-war encounter with televisual media, Indigenous Australians faced a similar crossroads. In part because of their early consultation with Inuit producers and activists, they too decided to 'invent' their own Aboriginal television … by making video images and narratives about and for themselves, shown locally via illegal low-power

158 Emerging Digital Media Ecologies

outback television similar to the Inuit projects described above. By the late 1990s, Aboriginal media production had expanded from very local television in remote settlements to feature films made by urban filmmakers that have premiered at the Cannes Film Festival.

(Ginsberg, 2002, p. 55)

The development of Indigenous media initiatives in Australia and elsewhere is emblematic of the resistance and adaptation of marginalised communities. In Australia, the establishment of basic production and broadcasting units under the Remote Indigenous Media Sector (RIBS) signified a strategic appropriation of new technological infrastructures to preserve cultural autonomy. The endeavours of Ernabella Video and Television (now known as Pitjantjatjara Yankunytjatjara Media 'PY' Media) and the Warlpiri Media Association (now PAW Media and Communications), catalysed by the Broadcasting for Remote Aboriginal Communities Scheme (BRACS) and influenced by the *Out of the Silent Land* report (Willmot, 1984), embodied a critical response to the potential homogenisation of culture and language posed by mainstream satellite broadcasting. Despite subsequent criticisms of insufficient funding, training, wages, and support (Turner, 1998), such grassroots movements in media production became pivotal in documenting and transmitting Indigenous cultural narratives. The 1984 report noted that 'The fact that local programmes are still broadcast regularly at all in more than 70 remote communities is testament to the dedication of community operators' (Willmot, 1984, p. 8), thereby enacting a form of technological self-determination that integrated traditional knowledge into the wider fabric of the media networks of the time, reinforcing the cultural resilience and identity of Indigenous communities.

For visual anthropologist, Eric Micheals, the context for the above may be clarified by thinking of visual media such as video and television by analogy to books and print with questions towards understanding and interpretation highlighted by literacy models. That is: '[h]ow are people with minimal experience of European language and culture making sense of the more unfamiliar Hollywood genres?' (Michaels, 1990, p. 5). The study focused on the Warlpiri-speaking people of the Yuendumu community in Australia's Northern Territory. Michaels found that video's success in Aboriginal Australia and people's rapidly coming to video literacy was contrasted to literacies associated with books and print not only because of inherent properties of these media themselves (needing to be able to read and understand English in the first instance for example) but importantly where they were free to explore and trial the use and creation of video on their terms because there was little interest and intervention from Europeans. Michaels found that 'people's readings of media are based as much on their lived experience, historical circumstances and cultural perspectives than any inherent instructions in the text itself on how something ought to be interpreted' (Michaels, 1990, p. 21). Further:

> Aboriginal responses ... have been to intercept the technology and engineer sub-networks of production and transmission attempting to link their own local interpretative circles to the national [broadcasting] system, as well as to maintain filters for alien media. Aboriginal media organizations' bids for TV licenses both locally and in competition with regional suppliers, seek to create 'Aboriginal Media for Aboriginal People' connected to, but textually independent of European media systems.
>
> *(Michaels, 1990, pp. 28–9)*

Decades hence, the National Indigenous Television (NITV), an Australian free-to-air television channel, was launched via satellite in 2007 to broadcast programming produced and presented largely by Aboriginal and Torres Strait Islander people (later on the Special Broadcasting Service from 2010). The channel is dedicated to showcasing content that highlights the lives, culture, and stories of Aboriginal and Torres Strait Islander peoples. Its programming aims to showcase communities by featuring their narratives, documentaries, and other forms of media that emphasise their rich heritage and contemporary experiences. Additionally, NITV seeks to bridge cultural gaps by engaging non-Indigenous Australians, offering them a window into First Nations storytelling. Through its diverse content, NITV serves as a platform for Indigenous voices, promoting understanding, respect, and appreciation among the broader Australian population (see www.beyondthreepercent. com.au/nitv), empowering communities to produce and broadcast their own material, tailored specifically for their local audiences.

On Television

The 12-episode drama television series across two seasons *Cleverman* (2016/ 2017, dir. Blair and Purcell) with its innovative integration of Indigenous Australian narratives (Cleverman serves as a conduit between the present and the Dreaming—a spiritual realm) and contemporary sci-fi/superhero genres represents a transformative moment in the media landscape, both as a cultural artefact and as a mechanism of socio-economic intervention. The series features an 80% Indigenous cast which not only broke ground in terms of on-screen representation but also addressed structural employment disparities within the media industries. *Cleverman* therefore extends beyond entertainment, acting as a cultural prism that refracts critical social issues such as racism, asylum seeking, and border protection through the lens of Aboriginal Dreamtime stories re-contextualised in a futuristic setting. This reimagining not only challenges stereotypical perceptions of animism as regressive but also positions

160 Emerging Digital Media Ecologies

Indigenous cosmologies as a source of speculative and futuristic visions. For Indigenous communities, the impact of *Cleverman* has been multifaceted. It has provided a platform for cultural expression, facilitated engagement with globally relevant themes from an Indigenous perspective, and contributed to a showcasing of Indigenous storytelling that aligns traditional knowledge with contemporary media narratives, fostering a deeper understanding and appreciation of Indigenous cultures in the broader public sphere. The series gained notable awards and nominations such as the 'John Hinde Award for Excellence in Science-Fiction Writing' at the Australian Writers' Guild Awards for its screenplay—the prize was given for episode five of the series, which aired on ABC TV in June 2016 (Glyer, 2016); and, *Cleverman* was a finalist in the Entertainment section of the US Peabody Awards, which were conceived by the National Association of Broadcasters in 1938 as the radio industry's equivalent of the Pulitzer Prizes and now honour compelling and empowering stories in wider electronic media. Here, *Cleverman* was nominated alongside works like Beyoncé's visual album *Lemonade*, the Netflix series *Stranger Things*, and Donald Glover's Golden Globe Award-winning series *Atlanta* (Blanco, 2017).

Other television programs that—like *Cleverman*—incorporate Indigenous perspectives, themes, or production involvement and have made significant contributions to the representation of Indigenous cultures on screen include *Mystery Road* (from 2018), an Australian television crime drama series notable for its Indigenous lead characters and its exploration of social and racial issues in Australia), and *Redfern Now* (2012–2013), an Australian drama series about the lives of Indigenous Australians living in the Sydney suburb of Redfern, produced by Indigenous Australians and significant for its authentic representation of urban Indigenous life. From the US is *Reservation Dogs* (2021–2023) an American comedy-drama series that follows four Indigenous teenagers in rural Oklahoma. The show is notable for an almost entirely Indigenous cast and crew and presenting a contemporary view of Indigenous American life; *Spirit Rangers* (from 2022) is an American children's animated series created by a Native American 'showrunner' (this is a significant role in the television industry and the individual is responsible for overseeing the production and creative aspects of a television series), featuring Indigenous characters and incorporating Native American folklore and storytelling. From Canada is *Mohawk Girls* (2010–2017), a comedic drama series set in the Mohawk community of Kahnawake, Quebec, focusing on the lives of four young women navigating their personal and cultural identities. *Shortland Street* (from 1992) is a long-running New Zealand soap opera that has been commended for integrating Māori characters and storylines, reflecting New Zealand's cultural diversity (Horrocks & Perry, 2004, p. 212).

Thus we can appreciate the considered use of media to serve not only as a repository of cultural memory but also as a dynamic form of engagement that is both deeply personal and broadly communal. Critical to this discussion is the understanding of power dynamics inherent in media production and access. The ability of Indigenous communities to tell their own stories, in their own ways as Michaels (1990) has suggested, represents a reclaiming of narrative authority that has been historically marginalised. Other studies by Meadows have further illustrated how Indigenous radio in Australia serves as a vital tool for community cohesion and cultural preservation (Meadows, 2021). This aligns with the broader global process of 'mediatisation', where media becomes embedded in every facet of societal interaction, further underscoring the importance of Indigenous control over their media narratives. Moreover, the transfer from 'legacy' media forms to digital media has amplified the potential for hyper-personalised media also offering Indigenous communities unprecedented access to global audiences while maintaining the local specificity of their cultural narratives. The work of scholars like Wilson and Stewart (2008) on the Indigenous use of digital media highlights the transformative potential of these platforms in fostering global Indigenous networks that are rooted in shared struggles and cultural affirmation. This represents a vital area of academic enquiry that speaks to broader themes of cultural resilience, narrative authority, and the dynamic interplay between local identities and global media ecologies. As Indigenous communities continue to navigate and reshape the media landscape, their efforts not only contribute a rich complexity to global media but also offer critical insights into the power of media as a tool that is anything but neutral and able to enact cultural preservation and social change. The critical examination of these evolving media practices remains essential for understanding the multifaceted aspects of globalised media environments and the pivotal role of First Nations media within them.

While there are notable examples of Indigenous representation in media, the broader landscape often reveals a pattern of 'surface-level inclusion', necessitating a more profound and systemic integration of Indigenous perspectives across mainstream media networks to truly honour and reflect the depth of Indigenous cultures and experiences (see All Together Now, 2021). According to Thomas and Paradies (2021, np), surface-level inclusion is the 'absence of negative stereotypes, but excluding Indigenous authors, perspectives, historical and cultural contexts, and voices'. The report entitled *When Inclusion Means Exclusion: Social Commentary and Indigenous Agency* (2021) that these authors contributed to outlines a series of transformative recommendations for the wider Australian media sector that might be similarly directed towards international media industries. The report called for mainstream media agencies to embrace a diverse range of Indigenous voices at every tier, empowering and entrusting these voices to take the helm in crafting their narratives. It emphasises the necessity for non-Indigenous media and commentators to proactively seek and heed Indigenous perspectives, especially on topics that are pivotal to Indigenous communities. A collaborative rapport

162 Emerging Digital Media Ecologies

between non-Indigenous media and Indigenous-controlled media is advocated for, with the intent to refine how Indigenous stories are received and engaged with. According to the 2021 report, there remains a pressing need for mainstream media to confront and reconcile its historical contribution to the propagation of racist ideologies and deficit-based discourses about Indigenous people. The report also urges the media to commit to the consistent integration of Indigenous people and their viewpoints in reporting on Indigenous issues and in the broader spectrum of news coverage, fostering a media space that is both inclusive and representative. This call for a reformed media landscape underscores the crucial role the media play not only in shaping public perceptions but also in serving as platforms for expressing Indigenous identity, reinforcing self-determination, and forming cultural narratives.

Media as a Platform for Defining Indigeneity: Asserting Sovereignty and Constructing Identity

Indigenous Media

Indigenous media is a central term that refers to the myriad forms of media expression that are conceptualised, produced, and circulated by First Nations peoples across the globe. These media manifestations serve as critical vehicles for multifaceted communication, embodying essential roles in cultural preservation, the expression of cultural and artistic identity, the pursuit of political self-determination, and the assertion of cultural sovereignty. To delineate further, Indigenous media is not an isolated phenomenon but exists within a continuum that intersects with other forms of minority-produced media. This intersectionality is not merely coincidental. It is underpinned by shared philosophical and political motivations, illuminating kinships that transcend mere media production. These motivations are deeply rooted in the historical and ongoing struggle for recognition, voice, and agency, positioning Indigenous media as an instrumental force in the reclamation and revitalisation of Indigenous cultures, languages, and identities (Wilson & Stewart, 2008). Moreover, the concept of Indigenous media cannot be fully appreciated without acknowledging its critical relationship with the broader media ecosystem. On the stage of global interconnectivity now, media serves as 'neural networks' of society, platforms for the construction of identity, and battlegrounds for the negotiation of power (Salazar, 2007). In this chapter, we are exploring the transformative role of Indigenous media in shaping the contours of power through communication flows, situating the concept of Indigeneity—with both its imposed definitions and self-determined expressions—at a critical juncture of cultural sovereignty and representation (see Merlan, 2009). We might approach the dialogue on Indigenous media by first unpacking the layered complexity of Indigeneity itself. The term Indigeneity has been historically

Indigenous Narratives and the Dynamics of Medialogy **163**

fraught, encumbered by a legacy of essentialism and constructed through a binary lens that positions Indigenous cultures as the perpetual 'other' in contrast to a supposed norm, primarily defined by the dominant narratives of the Anglo-Western discourse (Hokowhitu & Devadas, 2013). This dichotomy not only simplifies but also marginalises literally casting Indigenous peoples as actors outside the mainstream historical narrative, often overlooking their rich connections of cultural traditions, languages, and systems of knowledge (Glynn & Tyson, 2007).

Important is to illuminate the transformative capacity of Indigenous peoples to reclaim and articulate their own narratives (Carlson, 2023). Often this is through the strategic use of media. Here, Indigenous media emerges as a pivotal force in the process of cultural self-definition and political self-determination, enabling people of First Nations around the globe to forge spaces of expression within the global media ecologies that are often dominated by hegemonic cultural codes. These media practices, far from being mere tools of communication, become sites of resistance, preservation, and innovation, facilitating the transmission of cultural knowledge across generations and borders. They embody the dynamic interplay between tradition and modernity, challenging reductive notions of Indigeneity while highlighting the diverse realities of Indigenous communities. Moreover, Indigeneity transcends racial or biological categorisations, proposing instead that it is a discursive field shaped by relational dynamics. This perspective resonates with the constructivist views of identity (Butler, 1990; Hall, 1990) which posits that identities are formed and reformed through interactions within networks of social relations and cultural exchanges. In the context of this book, the role of media is emphasised for its part as spaces for the articulation, negotiation, and affirmation of Indigenous identities within the global cultural landscape. Here Indigenous media, in this context, is not simply a medium of artistic expression or cultural preservation alone but a complex matrix of social interactions that contribute to the ongoing process of decolonisation and cultural renewal and are a means for Indigenous peoples to articulate their own identities and histories in the face of dominant media narratives (Ginsberg, 2002). Fisher's work on Indigenous publics and media practices in northern Australia also highlights how Indigenous communities use media to assert their sovereignty and challenge the imposed narratives of the state or dominant cultures. Fisher's analysis suggests that through media, Indigenous groups engage in a dynamic process of identity construction that is both reflective of and constitutive of their social relations and cultural exchanges. For example, in several remote Indigenous communities in northern Australia, local radio stations are operated by and for Indigenous people. These stations broadcast in local Indigenous languages and cover content that is relevant to the community's cultural and daily life, such as local news, stories, music, and educational programs. This use of radio as a media form allows these

164 Emerging Digital Media Ecologies

communities to maintain and strengthen their linguistic and cultural heritage, asserting their sovereignty by controlling the narrative that is disseminated within their community. It challenges the state or dominant cultures' narratives by providing a platform for Indigenous voices and perspectives, which are often marginalised in mainstream media. The formal legitimisation of palawa kani through the Tasmanian (Australia) government's Aboriginal and Dual Naming Policy of 2013, which endorsed the concurrent use of Aboriginal and also introduced names for official landmarks, illustrates a further and significant step in recognising and preserving Australian First Nations Dual Languages, as evidenced by the dual naming of places like kanamaluka/Tamar River, kunanyi/Mount Wellington, lutruwita (Tasmania), Meanjin (Brisbane), Naarm (Melbourne) or Gadigal (Sydney) (see Traditional Place names in Australia https://auspost.com.au/community-hub/traditional-place-names/meanjin-exploring-traditional-place-name-of-brisbane).

Indigenous media, by virtue of its existence and resilience, challenges the dominant narratives and offers an alternative paradigm reflective of First Nations' perspectives and realities and a way for Indigenous peoples to assert their presence and articulate their narratives within the global media landscape. By doing so, Indigenous media not only contributes to the diversity of cultural expression but also plays a crucial role in the ongoing struggle for social justice, equity, and the right to self-determination. In the opening scene of the Australian film *Ten Canoes* (2006, dirs. de Heer and Peter Djigirr) a voice narrates:

> 'Once upon a time, in a land far, far away' ... (deep laughter) ... 'nah, not like that!! I'm only jokin'! But I am going to tell you a story. It's not your story, it's my story. A story like you never *seen* before. (author's emphasis)

This opening sequence is narrated by Australian actor David Gulpilil Ridjimiraril Dalaithngu, a man of the Mandjalpingu (Djilba) clan of the Yolngu people, Arnhem Land in the Northern Territory of Australia (*My Name is Gulpilil*, 2021, dir., Reynolds). Dalaithngu's 'yarning' welcomes the listener-viewer and offers us a way to 'see', or deeply 'know', the people and their land. The film relies heavily on oral storytelling traditions, mirroring the way stories are passed down through generations in Indigenous communities. The narrative is guided by Dalaithngu's voice as a storyteller, providing a continuous link to the oral tradition and drawing listener-viewers into the storytelling culture of the Yolŋu people. The 2006 film *Ten Canoes,* made in close collaboration with the Indigenous community of Arnhem Land, demonstrates Indigenous storytelling and oral history in an experimental, multimedia way. It also stages a decolonial strategy within media—one of imagining a past, a thousand years ago in Arnhem Land, Northern Australia, that is also part of the present—thus creating a complex narrative that blends time frames and stories. The use of black-and-white photography for the historical timeline and colour for the stories within stories adds a multimedia dimension that helps to distinguish the different layers of the narrative. The film engages in a decolonial strategy by centring the Indigenous perspective and reclaiming historical narratives from an Indigenous viewpoint. By imagining a past that is intrinsically connected to the present, *Ten Canoes* challenges the colonial notion of linear history and emphasises the continuity of Indigenous culture and knowledge. It presents a vision of history that is not detached from the present but is a living, breathing part of the community's identity. Moreover, this co-collaborative approach ensured cultural authenticity and allowed the community to have a voice in how their stories and culture were represented on their terms.

In the same vein, Indigenous filmmakers in northern Australia have been producing films and documentaries that tell stories from their own perspectives, highlighting issues of land rights, cultural heritage, and the impacts of colonisation. These visual media productions serve as a powerful tool for expressing Indigenous identity and history, as well as for educating wider audiences about the complexities of Indigenous experiences in Australia. Warwick Thornton, for example, a film director, screenwriter, and cinematographer from Kaititya in the Northern Territory saw his debut feature film *Samson and Delilah* win the Caméra d'Or at the 2009 Cannes Film Festival and the award for Best Film at the Asia Pacific Screen Awards. He also won the Asia Pacific Screen Award for Best Film in 2017 for *Sweet Country*. Thornton's most recent film *The New Boy* (2023) premiered at the 76th Cannes Film Festival; and he directed a video that was used to advocate for the 'Yes' campaign in the 2023 Australian Indigenous Voice referendum (14 October) intended to, but unsuccessful in making, change to the Australian Constitution and enshrining a Voice to Parliament for Indigenous Australians. By creating and distributing their own media content, Indigenous communities assert their sovereignty and challenge the often stereotypical portrayals of Indigenous peoples in mainstream Australian media. These films and documentaries become a dynamic medium through which Indigenous identity is constructed and communicated, reflecting and constituting the community's social relations and cultural exchanges.

The Australian 15-minute virtual reality film *Collisions* (2015, dir. Wallworth) represents a significant leap forward in the media field for presenting Indigenous knowledge and the representation of First Nations. The film, which explores the impact of a nuclear bomb test on the Indigenous community of the Western Desert of Australia, transcends traditional storytelling by using 360-degree video, drone aerial footage, animation, and virtual reality to immerse the viewer in a narrative that is both historical and deeply personal. *Collisions* goes further in the Indigenous media field by employing immersive technology to grant the audience not

166 Emerging Digital Media Ecologies

just a window into Indigenous experiences but a doorway. It allows viewers to stand alongside Nyarri Nyarri Morgan, a Martu man, and hear and 'feel' the warm breeze that stirs the fragrant dry grass and also witness his firsthand account of the dramatic and life-changing event. This is not merely storytelling, but an act of sharing lived experience in a way that is intimate and that traditional media cannot replicate. By leveraging VR, *Collisions* provides a visceral understanding of Indigenous perspectives, placing the viewer within the narrative space of the Martu people. This innovative use of technology as a storytelling medium allows for a profound engagement with Indigenous knowledge, one that respects and prioritises the voice and agency of First Nations. It challenges conventional media paradigms by offering a form of narrative sovereignty, allowing Indigenous stories to be told according to cultural protocols and from an authentically Indigenous viewpoint. Circling back to Coyne's (2018) notion of *Network Nature* in Chapter 1, we find an example in this film that clearly demonstrates the critical role of technology in preserving Indigenous narratives and fostering a dialogue that bridges traditional wisdom with digital advancements. It respects the cultural significance of the story it tells while using the latest in media technology. *Collisions* not only showcases Indigenous knowledge but also invites a global audience to understand and appreciate the complexities of Indigenous histories and identities in the digital age.

By situating Indigenous media within the broader concept of medialogy, it is clear how these media forms represent more than just alternative narratives; they are integral to the reconfiguration of power relations within global, media/data/information-based societies. They offer pathways for First Nations to navigate the challenges of visibility and voice in a world where the digital divide and cultural homogenisation pose constant threats to diversity. Indigenous media stands as a testament to the resilience and agency of Indigenous peoples, asserting their right to participate fully in the global conversation on their own terms, thereby enriching the collective human experience with their unique perspectives and wisdom.

Indigenous Media Practices: Bridging Oral Traditions and User-Generated Digital Content

The profound relationship many Indigenous peoples maintain with the land emerges as a fundamental cornerstone of Indigeneity. This connection, deeply rooted in the knowledge of and through the land, transcends the superficial categorisations often imposed by colonial narratives. Such a perspective is essential in understanding the distinct difference between the Indigenous relation to place and the generalised concept of 'nature' often construed by dominant cultures. This distinction is vividly illustrated in the colonial misinterpretation of Australian landscapes, where the unique flora of the continent was often misrepresented to resemble European vegetation, erasing the specificity and significance of Indigenous lands. Through the lens of Albert Namatjira's art, as discussed by Burn and Stephen (1992), we witness a clear example of how Indigenous artists use their craft to assert cultural sovereignty and articulate their enduring connection to the country. Namatjira's paintings, rooted in the landscapes of the Arrernte people, defy colonial interpretations of the land, offering instead a vibrant testament to Indigenous presence and rights: 'Namatjira's paintings in their conveyance of totemic landscapes are not only understood as ideological but also as political communiques with intention to challenge the prohibitions enforced in the mission environment' (Hall, 1994, pp. 21–22). Moreover, the dialogue around Indigenous media underscores its role not just in cultural preservation but in the broader struggle for political self-determination and decolonisation. Indigenous media is distinguished by its origin and purpose—a form of expression that is conceptualised, produced, and circulated by Indigenous peoples themselves. It stands in stark contrast to the representations of Indigenous cultures crafted by dominant groups, which often veer into cultural appropriation or misrepresentation.

Tyson Yunkaporta uses the concept of 'yarning' with a deep understanding of Indigenous epistemologies and a critical stance towards Western conceptions of knowledge transmission (Yunkaporta, 2019; see also Robertson, Demosthenous, & Demosthenous, 2005). By fostering a dialogue or 'conversation' that is inclusive and multivocal, yarning breaks down the barriers of hierarchical knowledge systems and democratises the process of learning—an emergent decolonising methodology that has long been used by Indigenous cultures (Cajete & Williams, 2020) and noted in the example of *Ten Canoes* (2006) above. In Indigenous cultures, oral language and storytelling are the oldest traditions. Yarning, as Yunkaporta explains, is not just casual conversation but a sophisticated and structured cultural practice integral to Indigenous communities. It embodies a holistic approach to knowledge, encompassing story, humour, gesture, and mimicry, all of which are essential for consensus-building, meaning-making, and innovation (Yunkaporta, 2019, p. 131). For Yunkaporta, yarning is a dynamic process where knowledge is not simply transmitted but emerges through interaction. This process is underpinned by protocols of active listening and mutual respect, ensuring that everyone's voice is heard and valued, and knowledge is built collectively. Through this lens, yarning is not just a method of communication but a profound way of engaging with the world, a process that is inherently participatory, reflective, and deeply connected to the Indigenous ways of knowing and being. Furthermore, Christensen (2022) has highlighted the transformative power of yarning as decolonising practice in navigating history from multiple perspectives, allowing a richer, more nuanced understanding of the past and its impact on the present and future. It challenges the conventional

168 Emerging Digital Media Ecologies

notions of knowledge acquisition and stands as a testament to the innovative and complex knowledge systems of Indigenous peoples.

Through various forms, including storytelling, language preservation, and artistic expression, Indigenous media acts as a bulwark against cultural erasure, fostering a space for self-definition and recognition. The critical distinction between Indigenous connections to land and the simplistic notion of being 'closer to nature' lies in the narrative agency. It is not merely about geographical or physical proximity but about a profound understanding and relationship with the environment that is encoded in cultural practices, knowledge systems, and languages. This perspective, mediated through Indigenous voices and channels, challenges colonial discourses and advocates for a re-evaluation of Indigenous roles in global ecological conversations and cultural narratives. Thus, Indigenous media becomes a vital tool for resistance, offering pathways towards decolonisation and reasserting Indigenous sovereignty.

With increased digitalisation and access to communications infrastructures— comprised of routers, switches, and servers interconnected by various transmission media like fibre optics and 5G; where data travels in packets using protocols like TCP/IP, with routing algorithms determining the most efficient paths; and services like the Domain Name System (DNS) translate user-friendly domain names to machine-readable IP addresses—mobile media emerges as a powerful instrument for amplifying the voices of marginalised communities. Mobile media is a phenomenon that reflects the transformative potential of technology in reshaping communication landscapes. It extends beyond mere technological innovation to embody a form of empowerment for those often relegated to the periphery of societal discourse. Burum (2013) defines 'Mojo' as a new mobile journalism project that empowers Indigenous people in isolated communities by providing them with skills and mobile technologies to create locally produced user-generated stories from their own perspective (see www.youtube.com/watch?v=jRmGACFJdJo&context= C4a3aeb0ADvjVQa1PpcFP3zJtsQPO7OzQrxteq7r4u8nP9ig_QXUw=). This initiative aims to enable Indigenous individuals to share their stories and perspectives through digital media, thereby contributing to a more diverse cultural voice in remote Indigenous environments (Burum, 2013). Concrete examples of the impact of Mojo are the Australian Northern Territory Mojo project that involved training Indigenous individuals in remote communities in basic journalism, filming, and editing skills using iPhones which resulted in nine mojos (mobile journalists) being able to produce high-quality content, with two of them winning major awards at a film festival in Darwin, Australia, and the project led to opportunities for the trained mojos to work with mainstream news agencies like ABC TV news and NITV on a freelance basis. Additionally, some mojos secured video commissions for the government, while others obtained ongoing media work within their communities (Burum, 2013, p. 20). For Burum (2023, p. 20):

With Indigenous communities now able to create and publish their own local stories, bypassing even the more mainstream indigenous media organisations, this negotiation becomes an ongoing internal cultural process, which mainstream media will need to buy into, or risk missing out on the real news. With MSM [mainstream media] now showcasing mojos work, schools beginning to introduce mojo practices across the curriculum, NT Mojo can be seen as a first important step to democratizing the heavily mediated Indigenous media sphere.

According to Burum and Quinn (2015), empowerment through mobile media is not just about providing the tools and training for content creation; it is fundamentally about reshaping the narrative power structures. By enabling individuals to convey their own stories, experiences, and perspectives, mobile media democratises the media landscape, challenging traditional hierarchies and fostering a more inclusive representation. This shift is crucial for enhancing visibility and affirming the identities of marginalised groups within the global media ecosystem. Moreover, the essence of direct communication facilitated by mobile media dismantles the barriers erected by conventional media gatekeepers. This directness is not merely a logistical advantage but a radical alteration of the communicative process, allowing for unmediated storytelling that can resonate more authentically with a global audience. The immediacy and personalisation of this communication underscore a significant change in how narratives are constructed and disseminated. The contribution of diverse content by marginalised communities through mobile journalism is another critical aspect, enriching the media landscape with varied cultural expressions and experiences. This diversity is not additive but transformative (see Postman, 1998) with the capacity for fostering a more comprehensive and precisely differentiated public sphere where multiple voices and narratives coexist and interact (Burum, 2016). Such a pluralistic media environment is essential for the development of a resilient and dynamic civil society, as it reflects the warp and weft of human experiences and identities. Community engagement and the participatory nature of mobile media creation are pivotal in cultivating a sense of ownership and agency among marginalised groups. This participatory process is indicative of a broader trend towards more networked and horizontal structures of media production. The role of skill development in empowering individuals within marginalised communities cannot be overstated (Burum, 2016). By acquiring digital and media production skills, individuals not only enhance their capacity for storytelling but also improve their employability and economic prospects in the digital economy. This aspect of mobile media underscores the interplay between technological empowerment and socio-economic advancement, reflecting broader shifts towards more inclusive and participatory models of economic and cultural production.

170 Emerging Digital Media Ecologies

Now in the present TikTok-dominated digital era, Mojo initiatives and their like remain crucial, and their relevance is underscored by emphasising quality, credibility, and ethical storytelling. Mojo for its part counters the superficial breadth of social media trends with depth, fostering diverse representation and amplifying underrepresented voices. It offers comprehensive training in journalism, video production, and digital storytelling, thus equipping individuals with skills to produce impactful content across various media channels. Moreover, Mojo nurtures community engagement and collective narrative ownership, distinguishing itself from the largely individual-centric nature of platforms like TikTok (but also used strategically as discussed further below), 'X', and Instagram. Importantly, it promotes media literacy and critical thinking, empowering individuals to navigate and shape the digital landscape thoughtfully, making Mojo an indispensable element in cultivating a more informed, diverse, and responsible media ecosystem.

Also using mobile technologies, Tyson Mowarin's innovative application of technology through the 'Welcome to Country' app represents a pivotal shift in how Indigenous cultural narratives may be conveyed and preserved, underpinning the broader societal movement towards acknowledging and integrating Indigenous knowledge and First Nations heritage into digitally networked societies. By harnessing digital tools to map and share the profound depth of Indigenous Australian cultures, Mowarin's app, featuring cultural protocols and languages of the different territories, affords a new space where traditional knowledge intersects with contemporary digital media. For some areas, a traditional owner delivers the introduction. For Mowarin: 'I'd like to see one day that every kid in Australia, black, white or otherwise, can name the local tribes in the place they live or they're travelling to' (Mowarin, cited in Booth, 2015, n.p.).

This confluence of Indigenous and minority media, particularly in community-based projects, represents a powerful counter-narrative to dominant discourses, emphasising the enduring vitality and contemporary relevance of Indigenous cultures in shaping a more inclusive and diverse media landscape. Indigenous methodologies, like conversation and yarning, embody more than just the transmission of knowledge; they are an integral part of a broader cultural fabric that includes storytelling, language preservation, and artistic expression. These elements are fundamental to Indigenous media, which serves as a bulwark against cultural erasure, actively fostering spaces for self-definition and recognition. Storytelling, as a central aspect of yarning, is not merely about recounting events but is a way of understanding the world, encoding ethics, and connecting to the past, present, and future. Similarly, language preservation is not just about maintaining words but about nurturing the worldview and cultural wisdom that the language carries. Artistic expression, too, is a potent form of media, encapsulating the essence of Indigenous identity, history, and spirituality in a manner that transcends linguistic boundaries.

These forms of Indigenous media act collectively to counteract cultural erasure. They provide platforms for Indigenous peoples to define themselves on their own terms, showcasing the richness of their cultures and the complexities of their histories to broader audiences. One might, therefore, articulate the transformation of anthropology into digital auto-ethnography through the lens of contemporary Indigenous media practices. This transition is markedly visible when Indigenous groups seize media for storytelling, effectively weaving their narratives through the fabric of modern technology while staying deeply rooted in oral traditions. The relationship between Indigenous communities and various forms of media, including radio, film, TV, the internet, and mobile technologies, mirrors a return to oral forms of communication, which are inherently more aligned with Indigenous epistemologies than the static nature of print media. The historical presence and recent resurgence of Indigenous newspapers (the *National Indigenous Times* is Australia's leading news media organisation for Indigenous affairs), or the establishment of the Native American Journalists Association, or Whakaata Māori (Māori Television) cannot be overlooked, particularly for their respective roles in the revitalisation of Indigenous languages and cultures. In Aotearoa New Zealand, for instance, the renaissance of Te Reo Māori is manifested in cinema, with films like *Utu* (dir. Murphy, 1983) spoken entirely in Māori, marking a pivotal moment in the preservation and celebration of Indigenous language and identity.

The evolution of Indigenous media into a burgeoning sector in the digital age exemplifies the dynamic interplay between cultural preservation and modern communication. Recognised formally in 2007 through Article 16 of the United Nations Declaration on the Rights of Indigenous Peoples (UNDRIP), Indigenous media's trajectory underscores not merely a quest for self-expression but a profound exercise in sovereignty and identity assertion. These media outlets have transcended traditional formats, adopting digital technologies to extend their reach and influence, thereby facilitating broader engagement and understanding of Indigenous perspectives globally. As noted above, such expansion has been instrumental in preserving languages, cultures, and traditions, while simultaneously propelling Indigenous issues into the global discourse. This progress has fostered civic participation and inclusivity, contributing to the enrichment of democratic societies through a diversified media landscape. However, the digital era poses unique challenges, with dominant business models and algorithms often sidelining Indigenous content. Therefore, a concerted effort towards enhancing journalistic practices, technical acumen, and operational standards is imperative. The United Nations Educational, Scientific and Cultural Organization's (UNESCO) initiative (UNESCO, 2023b), following the United Nations Permanent Forum on Indigenous Issues's (UNPFII) recommendations, aims to fortify Indigenous media, ensuring they not only survive but thrive, thus enabling them to fulfil a pivotal role in shaping a pluralistic, democratic, and ethically attuned

172 Emerging Digital Media Ecologies

media environment. The findings from the study on Indigenous media are to be presented at the annual session of the UNPFII in 2025. There might, however, be apprehensions regarding the technological and infrastructural focus. One fear is that it could overshadow the substantive content and cultural significance of Indigenous media. While improving technical capabilities and access is important, equal attention must be given to supporting the content that is culturally and linguistically relevant to Indigenous communities, ensuring it remains grounded in their traditions, knowledge, and perspectives. Representation of Indigenous people in senior positions as decision-makers within 'big' media organisations is also a key component. Latimore puts it simply: 'we need more black producers and editors' (Latimore, 2016, np.).

Indigenous Digital Sovereignty: Navigating Cultural Preservation and Identity on Social Media

The digital realm emerges not as a foreign imposition but as a landscape skilfully navigated by Indigenous communities, within Australia and in other nations, to extend their narratives and cultural fibres across the globe. The depth of this phenomenon transcends simple technological uptake and is a testament to the enduring vibrancy of storytelling and the communal fabric inherent in Indigenous culture. The youth, stepping into the vanguard of this movement, have not only embraced social media as a canvas for personal and collective identity but also as an instrumental force in the arenas of cultural safeguarding, knowledge dissemination, and socio-political engagement. IndigiTUBE exemplifies this profound connection—an initiative launched in 2018 as a cultural conduit, dedicated to Indigenous Australian communities (https://firstnationsmedia.org.au/projects/indigitube). It stands as a digital repository that is vibrant with stories, music, and visuals that resonate with ancestral echoes and present-day experiences. This platform does not merely archive but is a living, breathing forum that fosters cultural dialogue, intergenerational linkages, and geographical interconnectivity. Through IndigiTUBE, the youth actively chart their own narratives, spotlighting their traditions, dialects, and creative vignettes. The platform deftly marries the ancient art of oral storytelling with the new-age digital canvas, dissolving barriers and democratising access to Indigenous lore and expression. Technology, thereby, is not simply an accessory in communication but a holistic extension of Indigenous praxis, weaving together the threads of community unity, cultural perpetuity, and the reassertion of Indigenous identities in the post-digital age.

The ability of these platforms to support visual and oral traditions aligns closely with Indigenous epistemologies, offering a natural extension of Indigenous oral and visual cultures into the digital age. This alignment underscores a critical aspect of digital culture being harnessed by Australian First Nations communities for the preservation and continuation of cultural

Indigenous Narratives and the Dynamics of Medialogy **173**

narratives and languages in a medium that resonates with traditional forms of knowledge transmission. Indeed, Australian First Nations communities are engaging with digital culture through a variety of social media in ways that are deeply enmeshed with their social and cultural fabric. This engagement demonstrates a dynamic utilisation of social media for intergenerational connectivity, allowing the communities to bring into conversation traditional and contemporary experiences, thus fostering a continuum of cultural identity and heritage:

> These new black voices are located in diverse places and participate in the news sphere in diverse forms. Many have been assisted in no small part by the @IndigenousX Twitter account. Many others have emerged from Facebook community or group pages. There are also many new new media outlets to write for, such as Guardian Australia, Buzzfeed, New Matilda and Junkee. There's also the persistent audience interest in Indigenous-relevant blogs and much more recently, Indigenous-focused Medium pages.
>
> *(Latimore, 2016)*

Indigenous use of TikTok draws attention to the potential to reflect and nurture specific cultural or subcultural identities, across a digital space where Indigenous creators and communities can express, explore, and celebrate their heritage and contemporary experiences. Through the creative adaptation of TikTok's features—like its sound library, visual effects, and short-form video format—Indigenous users engage in a form of digital storytelling that resonates with their cultural frameworks of understanding and aesthetic sensibilities. These digital expressions range from playful engagements with popular memes to profound acts of cultural and political assertion, such as addressing issues of racism, land rights, and the visibility of murdered and missing Indigenous women, girls, and 'Two-Spirit' individuals. According to Loyer (2020), Indigenous TikTokers not only navigate the platform's algorithmic terrain to reach like-minded individuals but also craft content that speaks directly to their communities, embodying a distinct form of insider communication rich with in-jokes, cultural references, and languages that might elude non-Indigenous listener-viewers. This self-referential humour and cultural specificity underscore a digital autonomy and resilience, challenging the pervasive surveillance and commodification in online spaces (Loyer, 2020). Moreover, the Indigenous presence on TikTok disrupts conventional narratives and representations, crafting a dynamic space where Indigenous voices and visions can flourish, free from the constraints of traditional media and cultural institutions. This dynamic illustrates how Indigenous TikTokers are not just participants in digital culture but active creators of a digital landscape where Indigenous life is celebrated in its fullness—joyous, complex, and enduring. Thus, TikTok becomes more than a platform for content sharing; it can be a site of cultural preservation,

174 Emerging Digital Media Ecologies

innovation, and identity affirmation for Indigenous communities, highlighting the platform's capacity to embody and amplify specific cultural and subcultural expressions in the digital age. But it is not without concerns.

As highlighted above, social media has long served as a critical platform for the expression and revitalisation of Indigenous cultures, including language preservation and the strengthening of communal bonds (Carlson, 2017). It transcends geographic limitations, enabling Indigenous Australians to form a global network of solidarity, sharing experiences of colonisation and supporting each other's struggles and resistances. However, this positive integration of digital culture is marred by persistent challenges. Indigenous users frequently confront racism and discrimination, leading to a sometimes cautious engagement with these platforms (Carlson, 2017). Additionally, the pervasive flow of traumatic content relating to Indigenous experiences of violence and dispossession exacerbates the collective trauma rooted in historical colonial oppression according to Carlson (2017). The capacity for social media impact—acting as a space for empowered cultural expression and at times a source of potential harm—highlights the complex interplay between technology and Indigenous realities in Australia and beyond. This differentiated engagement underscores the need for a deeper understanding and supportive framework that recognises the potential of digital spaces to heal and harm, thus shaping the ongoing discourse around Indigenous presence in digital culture.

For example, the use of social media in Indigenous communities, while facilitating broad and instant connectivity, has brought about critical shifts in traditional modes of interaction and authority structures, leading to several socio-cultural challenges. First, the transition to digital communication platforms like social media can disrupt established norms of face-to-face engagement, which are often rich in non-verbal cues such as gesture, sign, and gaze (Channarong, 2018). These traditional forms of interaction are not just about conveying information but also about maintaining social harmony and resolving conflicts within the framework of community customs and elder oversight (Haines, Du, Geursen, Gao, & Trevorrow, 2017). Understanding Elders' knowledge creation is crucial to strengthen Indigenous ethical knowledge sharing. Social media's text-based or digital nature can, however, strip away these layers of communication, rich in their complexity, potentially leading to misunderstandings and conflicts that might have been resolved more amicably in person (Channarong, 2018).

The concerns raised by senior women in Aboriginal communities about Facebook undermining traditional authority relations highlight this broader issue of how social media can alter power dynamics within Indigenous societies (Staal, 2014). Feuds and conflicts that once might have been contained and resolved through established hierarchical and respectful processes can now escalate quickly and publicly, with the potential to cause widespread discord

Indigenous Narratives and the Dynamics of Medialogy **175**

before elders have the opportunity to intervene (Staal, 2014). Importantly, the role of elders in Indigenous communities as custodians of cultural knowledge and as arbitrators in conflict resolution is challenged by the instantaneous and sometimes anarchic nature of social media interactions (Emery, 2000). Elders, who traditionally exercised social control and provided guidance, may find their authority diminished when community members, particularly the younger generation, turn to social media for communication and conflict resolution. The speed at which information—and mis/dis/malinformation—can spread on these platforms often outpaces the ability of elders to mediate and manage disputes effectively. Additionally, the anonymity or physical separation provided by social media can lead to unchecked cyber-abuse, contributing to mental health crises and even suicide among community members, particularly when such abuse goes unnoticed or unaddressed by community leaders and elders who traditionally would have played a role in conflict resolution and social support.

While technologies will change, their relevance will also remain significant, albeit with intricately detailed shifts in context and application. The core insight—that TikTok and social media more generally serve as a vibrant platform for Indigenous expression and cultural continuity—reflects wider trends in digital media use and reception that are likely to persist and expand over time. As digital platforms evolve, so too do the ways in which cultural and subcultural groups use these spaces to represent and communicate their identities. The dynamism of TikTok and the like, characterised by its rapid content turnover and algorithm-driven engagement, illustrates the fluidity of digital culture. Indigenous creators' use of the platform to affirm identity, challenge stereotypes, and foster community speaks to enduring aspects of cultural resilience and adaptability. These phenomena are not fleeting but are indicative of broader movements towards inclusivity and representation in digital spaces—as both promising and controversial. Furthermore, the issues of digital sovereignty, cultural appropriation, and the politics of representation will remain relevant as technology advances. The ways in which First Peoples navigate these challenges, using social media platforms to assert control over their narratives, offer valuable insights into the interplay between technology, identity, and power.

Conclusion

The contemporary discourse around the place and site-specificity within the post-humanities (Braidotti, 2013) underscores the intrinsic connection between Indigenous knowledges and the broader understanding of media ecologies. This intersectionality emphasises the importance of recognising and integrating Indigenous perspectives into ecological dialogues, not as a form of exploitation but as a collaborative engagement that honours the

176 Emerging Digital Media Ecologies

origins of these epistemologies. Indigenous media use does not merely articulate cultural understandings of country and environment; it serves as a dynamic interface through which the essence of Indigenous ecologies is communicated and understood. This integration of Indigenous knowledge into the fabric of medialogy studies challenges us to reconceptualise our approach to the environment, advocating for a more inclusive, respectful, and holistic understanding of ecology that appreciates the deep-seated wisdom and contributions of Indigenous peoples.

In contemporary societies, where the flow of information shapes our reality, the principle of animism represents a pre-digital, yet profoundly intricate networked ecology of relationships. It is a cultural system where every natural entity—be it animal, plant, or even the seemingly inanimate—carries a spiritual significance, binding all elements in a shared cosmic connectivity. This is not mere superstition but a complex tradition of symbiosis and respect, integral to the social structures of Indigenous cultures around the world. It is a way of decoding the world's complexity, embodying a harmonious dialogue between humans and the environment, which echoes in social practices and collective beliefs. When applied to media, various forms like books, television, the internet, and other communication technologies can be seen as having their own 'spiritual essence' or intrinsic effects and personalities that interact with human society.

Circling back to the beginning of this book, and taking inspiration from deep ecology (Naess, 1990; Guattari, 2000), the heart of this chapter—and indeed of medialogy—lies in critically understanding the innovative use of technology, not merely as tools but as infrastructures and interfaces that can foster sustainable and ethical media practices. These practices are not ends in themselves but are means to a more profound understanding and rethinking of our interaction with the digital systems that permeate our lives. By exploring how digital media interfaces can serve as conduits for critical and creative practices that honour and advance ecological harmony, we might contemplate the role of technology in forging a sustainable future at a critical time of climate change. The question of whether the media forms discussed in this chapter will retain relevance in the future opens a broader enquiry into the evolving dynamics of Indigenous engagement with digital technologies. Given the rapid pace of digital innovation and the increasing centrality of social media in global communications, these trends have likely not only persisted but intensified. The advent of platforms like TikTok, Meta, and 'X' has further demonstrated the potential of social media to reflect and amplify specific cultural and subcultural expressions. Indigenous peoples' use of TikTok, for instance, extends the tradition of storytelling into a format that is accessible and engaging to younger generations, enabling the transmission of cultural knowledge in ways that are novel yet deeply connected to traditional practices. However, these opportunities also bring to the fore concerns over privacy and the potential for cultural misappropriation, emphasising the need for Indigenous communities' ongoing vigilance and innovation in how they choose to navigate, negotiate, and ultimately redefine their digital footprints.

The Indigenous use of social media affords strategic assertions of sovereignty, identity, and resilience. Concerns over privacy and the challenges of maintaining cultural integrity online speak to the larger struggles faced by Indigenous peoples in safeguarding their traditions and stories against external misinterpretations and appropriations. Yet, the strategic use of these platforms for cultural preservation, education, and political activism reveals a highly refined understanding that is core to medialogy; it is distinct yet interconnected with broader media practices. By illuminating the omnipresence of media in the datafication of our everyday lives, the untapped possibilities of digital realms to reflect and enhance our ecological sensibilities might be revealed. Exploring how digital infrastructures and interfaces can serve as conduits for critical and creative practices that honour and advance ecological harmony, we are encouraged to more deeply contemplate the role of technology in forging a sustainable future.

CONCLUSION

Media, Humanity, and Non-human Others in a Post-Digital Future

In envisioning the horizon of a post-digital society, we discern a world where media transcends its role as an 'overlay' to reality, to become an indelible part of human sensory experience. The initial proliferation of handheld devices that signalled the dawn of digital omnipresence has gradually yielded to more intimate, yet sophisticated, forms of media consumption. Wearable devices like smartwatches, 'smart friends', fitness trackers, and 'smart glasses' to innovative technology such as contact lens eye-trackers and recorders which capture our visual field signify the impending integration of media into our very essence. This 'confluence', a concept for medialogy studies, is reshaping our interaction with the environment, merging the physical with the digital in unprecedented ways. Here the notion of 'confluence' speaks to the point where two or more elements, such as ideas, theories, or phenomena, come together and intersect. It implies a merging into a unified whole where the individual components interact and potentially create something new or more complex. Confluence suggests an integrative approach that acknowledges the interplay and mutual influence of diverse elements, leading to emergent properties or insights that were not present in the isolated components. This concept is critical in various fields, including interdisciplinary studies, where it can represent the blending of methodologies, the cross-pollination of academic disciplines, or the synergistic effects of combined technologies. The socialising agents of our time—media, schools, peers, cultures—are now inextricably linked with this integrated datafied landscape, modelling cognition in a manner that can weave together traditional lore with digital insight. Cultural rites and peer exchanges, augmented by layers of digital enhancement, imbue the social landscape with a richness that can both foster deeper community bonds and simultaneously sow discord within and between them. Within this post-digital

DOI: 10.4324/9781003178149-11

society, the pervasiveness of computing hardware and software, coupled with a constellation of satellites and wireless communication protocols, including undersea cables forms the bedrock of a telecommunications infrastructure that is as unobtrusive as it is ubiquitous. Ubiquitous computing, also known as pervasive computing, is the concept where computing is made to appear anytime and everywhere. In such a scenario, the internet serves as the mainstay.

Ubiquitous computing epitomises technology as invisibly woven into the fabric of everyday life, enabling 'frictionless' interactions through a myriad of interconnected components. It is underpinned by wireless communication protocols such as Wi-Fi, Bluetooth, and cellular networks that knit devices together, allowing them to exchange data effortlessly. Embedded sensors and actuators constantly gather and respond to environmental data, while microprocessors and microcontrollers provide on-the-spot processing capabilities. The Internet of Things (IoT) extends this connectivity to a vast array of devices from air-conditioning, thermostats, security systems, refrigerators, televisions, cars, pollution, and traffic monitoring thus creating 'smart' homes, 'smart' vehicles, and 'smart' cities, to healthcare and personal devices (hearing aids and watches), virtual assistants and immersive entertainment/learning experiences to interactive public displays (digital signage) that respond to the presence of people, providing information or entertainment tailored to the audience. These devices are collectively facilitate an integrated 'lived' network. Cloud computing offers expansive storage and sophisticated data processing power, complemented by edge computing that localises data handling to improve efficiency. Sophisticated data analytics and machine learning algorithms are essential for interpreting the vast streams of information, leading to 'intelligent' decision-making processes. In parallel, robust cybersecurity measures are indispensable to protect the integrity and privacy of data. The software platforms that form the operating systems and middleware are developed with the goal to ensure smooth interoperability between a diverse range of devices and user interfaces, which adapt to touch, gesture, and voice, making interaction intuitive. Energy-harvesting technologies further empower devices by enabling self-sufficiency by having the capacity to power devices autonomously through solar, thermal, or kinetic energy.

Underpinning this ecosystem are the undersea telecommunications cables which act as vital conduits for the high-speed transfer of data across continents, bridging the gap between localised, personalised computing and the vast resources of the global network for many (but not all due to cost and capacity to engage with the technologies). For those with access, the advancement of ubiquitous computing heralds a transformative era for emerging interface devices, making interactions seem more intuitive, responsive, and integrated within our daily environments. These devices capitalise on the vast and seemingly unified infrastructure provided by technologies, such as wireless

180 Emerging Digital Media Ecologies

communications, sensors, and cloud computing, to offer user experiences that are increasingly context-aware and tailored to individual needs. With computing power becoming more widespread and less visible, interface devices are evolving to become more anticipatory of user intentions, employing natural user interfaces that facilitate interactions through gestures, voice, and movement, often harnessing machine learning to personalise the user experience. The undersea telecommunications cables, integral to this ecosystem, ensure that these devices can function with high-speed connectivity, accessing global networks and cloud services. This enables a fluid exchange of data, making it possible for interface devices not only to react to immediate commands but also to proactively offer services and information pertinent to the user's context, enhancing everyday tasks with a layer of digital intelligence. As devices become more adept at interpreting a multitude of contextual cues and reacting to them in a sophisticated yet unobtrusive manner, they contribute to a media landscape that is less about consuming content on a screen and more about engaging with a digitally enhanced reality. The post-digital future envisions a world where the boundaries between media and humanity blur, with technology serving not as a tool for information and entertainment but as a dynamic partner in shaping human experience, cognition, and social interaction. Yet such a society is poised before the significant task of ensuring that ethical frameworks and privacy protections evolve in tandem with these technological strides. Inhabitants of this emergent world must navigate an intricate ethical and moral landscape, where issues of surveillance, data ownership, and cognitive autonomy are of paramount importance. Accordingly, new pedagogies of digital literacy emerge, wherein understanding the ramifications of embedded media is as essential as learning to read and write.

This book is an attempt to critically overview and evaluate the expansive mediascapes that form the backbone of contemporary digital culture, drawing attention to the considerable media-metamorphosis that characterises the present day. This overview spans a wide array of concepts and frameworks related to media and communications studies, offering a deep dive into the evolution of media technologies, their societal implications, and the emerging challenges posed by digital cultures. The changes, incremental at times and seismic at others, have been the subject of this book's critical examination. We might observe the digitalisation of broadcast infrastructures not as an end but as the beginning of a cascade of interconnected innovations that are still unfolding. Streaming platforms, advanced broadband, and cloud platforms are catalysing a transformative shift from dedicated infrastructures towards more fluid, networked forms of media distribution. Time shifting, place shifting, and the vast global networks facilitating the distribution of content are but mere indicators of a deeper, more profound change—a transformation in the fundamental ways we engage with media and each other. The implications of these shifts are staggering, from the disruption of traditional media distribution

Conclusion **181**

forms to the profound changes in the markets for content and communications, to the music and creative industries. In addressing the historical and cultural dimensions of media technologies through media archaeology and the concept of medialogy, it was underscored that media technologies are not only shaped by cultural and technological developments but are also profoundly influenced by economic conditions and market forces.

For example, expanding critically upon this are the ambitious initiatives from corporations like Meta (formerly Facebook), Google's 'X' (the Moonshot Factory, e.g., Codey, X's moonshot to create code that writes and rewrites itself revealed at Google I/O in 2023), and pioneers in VR and mixed reality technologies, including Apple's forays into the sector. Meta's commitment to the metaverse bespeaks an aspiration to construct virtual spaces as tangible and social as our physical reality. Here, the media is woven not only around the individual but also within the fabric of a collective, virtual experience. Industry hopes are for social VR whereby entire communities inhabit virtual environments as layered and intricate as our physical towns and cities, with each person navigating digital landscapes assisted by Meta's advanced VR headsets (for one example) or AR glasses, and perhaps in the envisioned future, through the contact lenses and retinal implants. Apple, while often reticent about its explorations in emerging technologies, launched in February 2024 its 'Apple Vision Pro' headset affording the company's interpretation of mixed reality and goal to replace the television and/or computer monitor (only available in the US at the time of writing, see www.apple.com/apple-vision-pro/). With Apple's powerful design ethos, the devices might not only embody technological innovation but also cultural acceptability, and even desirability. Their entry could mark a watershed moment when these technologies transition from niche to mainstream.

Yet, with such technological leaps come critical considerations of privacy, data security, and ethical use. There are profound implications for the nature of work, social interaction, and human identity itself—rendered spectres of our real selves, or mere avatars. Entities like Meta and Apple wield substantial influence in shaping these futures, as custodians of extensive personal data reserves. The balancing act between personalised media experiences and the potential for surveillance and data exploitation requires careful, critical examination. Such a speculative future promises the genesis of new art forms, novel educational methods, and revolutionary reality experiences. However, it also necessitates rigorous dialogues about the governance of such technologies, the safeguarding of individual rights, and the maintenance of human agency. I envisage a future where these technologies are harnessed to advance humanity positively, steering clear of a dystopian slide towards privacy erosion and diminished individuality. This obligation rests not solely with the creators of these technologies but with the societies that adopt them. It is a shared responsibility to ensure that our digital enhancements reflect our core

182 Emerging Digital Media Ecologies

values of fairness, consent, and collective welfare. This monograph has aimed to unravel many tangled threads, critically engaging with the driving forces behind such shifts and examining the repercussions for markets, industry, users, and technological progress itself.

The initial foray to unpack an umbrella concept of medialogy aimed to focus through a comprehensive lens by which to understand the interconnectedness of media, societal transformation, and holistic integration. It is within this framework that we can appreciate the extent to which media now shapes societal structures and the perceptions of individuals. Through the exploration of media evolution, akin to biological processes, I have endeavoured to parallel the transformation of communication, societal norms, and political landscapes. This examination of media and communication systems as interconnected environments influenced by and also influencing societal and individual behaviours has led us to an impasse where we must reconsider the ontological status of media artefacts, systems, and practices through the excavation of media archaeology. We have challenged the conventional narratives that constrain media to a purely anthropocentric perspective. Instead, conceptually, medialogy is positioned to reveal the entangled existence of technology, culture, and biology—with revelations made lucid by the metaphors of cyborgs, insect media, and the posthuman condition. This analysis aimed to broaden understanding of media's role and impact within the fabric of contemporary society through nuanced discussion including the ethical dilemmas they present, such as data privacy, surveillance, and the potential for exacerbating social inequalities. The intention of this study of medialogy was also to grapple with how media and communication practices impact the environment and contribute to ecological issues by discussing the environmental footprint of digital technologies, from reliance on natural resources and data centres to device production and waste management.

Media Archaeology emerged as a special and crucial interdisciplinary approach in Chapter 2, where we delved into the historical dimensions of media technologies and their evolution. This method provided a counter-narrative to the linear progression of media development, asserting the significance of seemingly obsolete technologies within our modern media ecology. Theoretical constructs like 'zombie media' and 'imaginary media' enriched the discussion of the temporal dynamics of media, revealing its recursive nature. By sifting through the strata of communication's past, this chapter sought to embed a holistic understanding of media's historical and future trajectories. We integrated this perspective into the broader discourse of medialogy, promoting an understanding that captures the essence of media's multifaceted history and its consequential impacts on culture, technology, and environmental concerns. In the third chapter, the discourse on Next Nature and techno-media ecologies took us on a journey from post-war technological landscapes to contemporary media

Conclusion **183**

forms, which have become intrinsically woven into the social and natural orders. This exploration highlighted the emergence of new forms of media that reshape human interaction and communication paradigms. We contemplated the future impact of quantum computing and blockchain technology as not merely technological advancements but as foundational shifts in our infrastructural realities. This recognition brought to light the imperative to reimagine governance and ethical frameworks to navigate the nascent techno-media ecologies. This chapter served as a clarion call for a comprehensive re-evaluation of the intertwinements of technology, society, and nature and presented an urgent need to address these entanglements within the context of rapid technological progress.

Chapter 4 brought us to the intersection of the biological and the technical through the concept of 'biomedia'. This analysis explored the ramifications of biomedia on our conceptions of the human–technology interface and the ensuing challenges to traditional boundaries. Eugene Thacker's (2004) perception of life understood as data, and flesh rendered programmable, laid the foundation for this investigation. The chapter thus spanned across disciplines and highlighted the ubiquity of biomedia in everyday life through wearable technologies, biometric systems, and their implications in fields such as psychology, gaming, and vision science. We grappled with the ethical and philosophical enquiries precipitated by these integrations, engaging with the concepts of transhumanism and posthumanism. This chapter also ventured into the realm of digital entities endowed with potential autonomy and agency, spurred by advancements in artificial intelligence and robotics. It underscored the need for a rigorous ethical examination of emerging media entities, questioning the essence of life and the status of media in our world. The culmination of this analysis called for a re-conceptualisation of the ontological status of new media forms, recognising the post-digital age as a reality where media may be interpreted anew as an active, integral part of the human experience.

The transformative impact of advanced AI systems and large language models on societal dynamics, personal behaviour, and media infrastructures was the focus of Chapter 5. Here, we explored the core roles of these technologies as facilitators of complex social interactions and disruptors of socio-economic norms. The narrative highlighted the historical progression from image recognition breakthroughs to contemporary applications of AI in content generation. We scrutinised the role of AI-driven agents for their part in shaping the 'digital self', consequently redefining media consumption anew and subsequently the parameters of our interactions. As we explore the role of media in shaping collective memories and narratives, we see that media not only reflects but also constructs social realities. In an environment where news can be faked and opinions and perceptions algorithmically manipulated, there are significant implications for democracy and cultures. The chapter

184 Emerging Digital Media Ecologies

stressed the need for a balanced perspective that considers the innovation potential against the ethical dilemmas posed by AI, concluding with reflections on the necessity of evolving media literacy frameworks to contend with the complexities of modern media ecologies.

Chapter 6 provided a critical analysis of online extremism and the challenges it poses, focusing on the digital media ecosystem's exploitation for propagating extreme views and ideologies. We examined the adaptability of internet frameworks, the capacity of Large Language Model-based co-pilot tools and the essential role of content moderation and digital literacy in counteracting radical or biased narratives. This chapter emphasised the need for a multifaceted counter-extremism strategy that blends technological practicality with social science. It concluded with a call for balanced use of AI in digital literacy initiatives, advocating for a transparent and culturally sensitive application to ensure they serve as constructive tools in the fight against online extremism. In Chapter 7, we considered the transformative influence of emerging media interfaces and immersive technologies on education and critical skill development. We looked at strategic efforts to integrate immersive technologies, such as VR, AR, and MR, across various sectors, and I argued for their practical application in educational settings. This chapter underscored the potential of these technologies to create engaging and transformative learning experiences, positioning them as pivotal pedagogical tools. Finally, Chapter 8 examined the critical role of Indigenous media in shaping contemporary media consumption, production, and power dynamics. This chapter emphasised the importance of recognising and integrating Indigenous perspectives into media dialogues, advocating for sustainable and ethical media practices that reflect Indigenous wisdom and contributions. The chapter concluded with a call for a deeper contemplation of technology's role in crafting a sustainable future that merges Indigenous knowledge with digital innovation.

Taken together, these chapters map a landscape in which media is both a reflection and an agent of important change, an intrinsic part of our post-digital society. This monograph has served as a guide through the complex interplay of media, technology, and culture, offering a multifaceted perspective on the significant forces shaping our world and urging us to engage with their impacts thoughtfully and critically. Media technologies can either bridge or widen gaps in global inequalities, including issues related to internet access, digital literacy, and cultural representation. As we look to the future, we do so with a deeper understanding of the role of media in our lives and the myriad ways it will continue to evolve and influence societies. This concluding chapter, thus, presents a narrative that intertwines the potential of a future enriched by technology with a note of prudence. It portrays a world where the harmonious fusion of technology with human experience is pursued, all the while conscious of the responsibilities that such fusion incurs.

Next Steps: Data Provenance and Protections

In contemplating the future steps for a field that is perpetually on the precipice of the next technological advancement, it is essential to engage with the forces of data abundance and the ever-growing sophistication of analytical tools. The deluge of digital information presents challenges and opportunities for media and communications studies. On one hand, there is the daunting task of curation and the necessary cultivation of technical acumen required to navigate this landscape. On the other with varying degrees, there lies the potential for ground-breaking cross-disciplinary scholarship, where data becomes the shared link between disparate fields of study, leading to a richer understanding of media and communications ecosystems refined with precision. In between these two points are discussions regarding continuous growth in the pool of technical skills and the scholarship in the field which must be harnessed to foster environments that not only allow for but encourage the sharing of data and methodologies. This willingness to engage in a sharing economy of data, and the 'best' ways to do so, must become the backbone of research moving forward, with sustainable platforms serving as the public squares for intellectual exchange. Furthermore, enabling greater access to these data 'lakes' must be done with an eye towards sustainability, ensuring that platforms evolve alongside the data they host and the communities they serve. Engaging with existing infrastructures and considering data sovereignty from the vast repositories of the web archives to the collaborative niches of community science platforms presents a viable strategy. These platforms should not only be used but also be enhanced, creating networks that are more than the sum of their parts. The integration of systems, such as the Centre for Urban Science and Progress (CUSP, www.kcl.ac.uk/research/cusp), a collaboration between King's College London and New York University; and a multi-disciplinary research centre that brings together researchers, businesses, and government agencies to apply data science and visual analytics to challenges in and for London; to The Amsterdam Institute for Advanced Metropolitan Solutions (AMS Institute, www.ams-institute.org) in the Netherlands which focuses on urban challenges such as mobility, water, waste, energy, data science, and digital technology through research and projects in collaboration with MIT and Wageningen University and Research (WUR); or Singapore-ETH Centre, the Swiss Federal Institute of Technology's collaboration with Singapore's National Research Foundation (NRF) (Singapore-ETH Centre, n.d.), which aims to enhance sustainable solutions that address global challenges affecting Switzerland, Singapore, and nearby regions (see also https://sec.ethz.ch) are a few examples of the types of research being undertaken. There is an increased need now for local initiatives with programs aimed at being robust, dynamic, and reflective of the complex interplay between data, information, technology, and context awareness for the society in which it operates.

186 Emerging Digital Media Ecologies

The term 'Non-Human Others' refers to entities that are not human but are also considered in relation to humans, often in the context of ethics, law, and society. This can include animals, artificial intelligences, digital entities, and ecological systems. The future for Non-Human Others is poised to be complex and multifaceted. As artificial intelligence and robotics advance, we are likely to see an increased presence of autonomous non-human entities in everyday life, leading to new ethical considerations and potential legal rights for these entities. The ongoing environmental crisis is also prompting a re-evaluation of how non-human life forms and ecosystems are valued and protected. Furthermore, the intersection of technology with biology, as seen in the growth of biotech and synthetic biology, is blurring the lines between what is considered natural and artificial. The future may hold a redefined legal and moral status for Non-Human Others, recognising their roles and rights within a shared ecosystem. Additionally, as we progress into a more interconnected world, there is a growing philosophical movement that advocates for a broader recognition of the sentience and rights of Non-Human Others, possibly leading to more inclusive societies that value all forms of consciousness and life.

Central to future steps is the imperative to navigate the policy maze that often encumbers data access and usage. Policies must be reimagined to uphold the principles of accessibility, accountability, and privacy in equal measure, striking a balance between protection and utility. In the arena of technical aspects, the proliferation of tools such as multi-modal AI analysis holds promise. They can also be leveraged to parse through the vastness of data, enabling users to uncover patterns that can enlighten and inform research and development, as well as industry. These tools could provide a lens through which the 'noise' of media communications can be deciphered, leading to insights that are both profound and practical. Community and collaboration should, however, remain at the heart of all future endeavours. Overall, the next steps will require not just technological adeptness but a commitment to collaborative innovation, ensuring that studies in medialogy remain at the forefront of enquiry and social development.

Medialogy in Global Context

In this discourse, I propose a four-pillar model of key existential risks that presently confront the human condition: ecological disequilibrium, technological disruption, geopolitical instability, and the erosion of social cohesion. Each pillar embodies a critical vector of risk that, together, demand an integrative and philosophically robust response—a response that recognises the interdependent nature of these threats and the imperative for a coherent and ethically informed infosphere capable of underpinning a sustainable and equitable human/non-human project. The ongoing anthropogenic detriment to Earth's biosphere presents not merely an environmental crisis but a philosophical conundrum, questioning the ethical framework within which we have so long operated. It necessitates a re-conceptualisation of our constitutive categorisation of 'natural resources' and compels the transition towards a more bio-centric form of stewardship, one that is informed by an informational worldview that appreciates the intrinsic value of biotic and abiotic entities alike. Here, the role of emerging media forms may be paramount in facilitating a global epistemic community, one that is knowledgeable and sensitive to the symbiotic relationships inherent in our ecological systems.

The rapid evolution of artificial intelligence, with its potential to restructure economies, cultural norms, and political institutions, demands rigorous philosophical engagement. The emergence of AI presents a fundamental metaphysical challenge to the distinction between agents and artefacts. In the narrative of a post-digital existence, the evolution of AI represents an acceleration of informational patterns that may outpace our current ethical, legal, and societal frameworks. We need to ensure that the media we consume simultaneously affords a platform for the critical discourse on these developments, promoting a global intellectual solidarity that underpins regulatory and ethical consensus.

In the complexity of current global affairs, Ukraine continues to endure the repercussions of Russian military aggression, an event that has significantly destabilised the region since 2022. Concurrently, the Middle East is witnessing severe conflicts, particularly in Gaza, where the hostilities between Israeli forces and Hamas have escalated to one of the most violent years for the region in decades. The situation has led to a severe humanitarian crisis, with significant destruction in Gaza and a high number of civilian casualties. Both Israeli military operations and actions by Palestinian militant groups, including rocket fire into Israeli territory, have contributed to the ongoing violence. Civilians on both sides have suffered, with children in Gaza facing malnutrition and dehydration, while Israeli communities live under the threat of continued rocket attacks. Despite international calls for a ceasefire, the conflict remains unresolved, exacerbating tensions in the West Bank and leading to further instability in the region. The conflict has severe implications beyond the immediate humanitarian toll, as it could destabilise the entire region, disrupt global trade, and undermine international diplomatic relations (United Nations (UN News, 2024)). Sudan is ravaged by one of the most severe conflicts in recent memory, with catastrophic levels of human displacement and fatalities. To the northeast, Ethiopia has been entrenched in a brutal civil conflict within the Tigray region, though recent developments suggest a movement towards a ceasefire. Myanmar remains unsettled by the military coup of 2021, with the resultant strife showing little sign of abatement. Africa, Nigeria, Somalia, and Burkina Faso grapple with devastating terrorist insurgencies that continue to claim lives. Mexico's long-standing war on drug cartels shows no signs of resolution, continuing to inflict widespread societal

188 Emerging Digital Media Ecologies

and economic damage. Yemen, despite a nominal truce, remains embroiled in conflict, as intermittent violations exacerbate the suffering and instability (see for regular updates <www.crisisgroup.org/global/watch-list-2024>). Global war is not just a destructive force in its own right but also a hindrance to addressing the two above-mentioned risks. If we take the premise that the unification of humanity is critical to effectively tackle ecological and AI-related challenges, then global unity is currently compromised by ongoing conflicts and rising geopolitical tensions, which could be precursors to a broader war, akin to historical precedents (e.g., the Second World War was not immediately recognised as a global war). That is, there is the potential for a truly global conflict to divert resources and attention away from solving critical issues like ecological collapse and the safe development of AI. This suggests that cooperation, as observed in natural ecosystems, is a viable and essential path for human societies.

The fourth key existential risk is for social cohesion and inequality. A forthright examination of contemporary social dynamics reveals that escalating social inequality and the erosion of social cohesion represent an existential risk in their own right. This threat is multifaceted, encapsulating not only economic disparity but also informational inequality—access to, and control of, information. It is within the crucible of this informational inequality that society's capacity to respond to ecological, technological, and militaristic challenges is forged. Here lies the intricate relationship between information policy, societal structures, and the ethical imperatives of digital citizenship.

This demands that we look beyond traditional compartmentalisation and adopt a holistic worldview. The global information and communication community is called upon not only to disseminate knowledge but also to actively participate in the shaping of a resilient infosphere. This infosphere should be designed to sustain human flourishing, preserve the integrity of our ecological position, ensure the beneficence of artificial agents, and maintain the cohesion of the social fabric. These considerations necessitate a proactive, philosophically informed engagement with the axiology of technology, the ethics of information, and the governance of global systems. Here we stand at a pivotal juncture in the evolution of our information-based and algorithmically driven societies, where the choices we make today will indelibly shape the 'infosphere' and the physical world that young people now and those to come will inhabit. It is incumbent upon us to ensure that these decisions are guided by wisdom, foresight, and an unwavering commitment to the common good of humanity and the broader environment within which we coexist.

REFERENCES

Abbeel, P. (Host) and Obradovic, B. (Producer). (2023, May 11). 'Geoff Hinton, the "Godfather of AI", quits Google to warn of AI risks' [Video]. YouTube. www.yout ube.com/watch?v=rLG68k2blOc

Agar, N. (2010). *Humanity's End: Why We Should Reject Radical Enhancement.* MIT Press.

Agarwal, S., Krueger, G., Clark, J., Radford, A., Kim, J. W. and Brundage, M. (2021). 'Evaluating clip: towards characterization of broader capabilities and downstream implications'. arXiv preprint arXiv:2108.02818.

Agnihotri, A. and Bhattacharya, S. (2023). *Neuralink: Invasive Neurotechnology for Human Welfare.* Sage. https://doi.org/10.4135/9781529611762

Aitchison, M. (2023, June 19). 'Stunning moment Aussie China watcher is questioned by police over vile false threats to "rape and kill" a young Chinese woman – as it's revealed China's spies were really behind the email', *Daily Mail* online. www.dailym ail.co.uk/news/article-12207833/Chinese-secret-police-Australian-Andrew-Phe lan-grilled-cops-fake-email-threats.html

Akçayır, M. and Akçayır, G. (2017). Advantages and challenges associated with augmented reality for education: A systematic review of the literature. *Educational Research Review*, 20, 1–11.

Al-Emran, M. (2023). 'Beyond technology acceptance: Development and evaluation of technology-environmental, economic, and social sustainability theory'. *Technology in Society*, 75, 102383.

Alizadeh, M., Kubli, M., Samei, Z., Dehghani, S., Bermeo, J. D., Korobeynikova, M. and Gilardi, F. (2023). 'Open-source large language models outperform crowd workers and approach ChatGPT in text-annotation tasks'. arXiv preprint arXiv:2307.02179.

All Together Now. (2021). *When inclusion mean exclusion: Social commentary and indigenous agency*, a joint report from All Together Now, University of Technology Sydney, Deakin University and Cultural and Indigenous Research Australia.

Allcott, H. and Gentzkow, M. (2017). 'Social media and fake news in the 2016 election'. *Journal of Economic Perspectives*, 31(2), 211–236.

Altheide, D. L. and Snow, R. P. (1979). *Media Logic.* Sage.

190 References

Anderton, J. (2024). 'OpenAI May Design Their Own Chips'. www.engineering.com/openai-may-design-their-own-chips/

Ang, I. (1991). *Desperately Seeking the Audience,* Routledge: London.

Ang, I. (1996). *Living Room Wars: Rethinking Media Audiences for a Postmodern World*. London: Routledge. DOI: https://doi.org/10.4324/9780203129432

Aouragh, M. and Chakravartty, P. (2016). 'Infrastructures of empire: Towards a critical geopolitics of media and information studies'. *Media, Culture & Society*, *38*(4), 559–575.

Asimov, I. (1942). 'Runaround'. In *Astounding Science Fiction* magazine, March. Street & Smith.

Azuma, R. T. (1997). 'A survey of augmented reality'. *Presence: Teleoperators and Virtual Environments*, 6(4): 355–385. DOI: https://doi.org/10.1162/pres.1997.6.4.355

Bajaj, H., Sharma, A., Arora, D., Yadav, M., Sharma, D., and Bajwa, P. S. (2024). 'Challenges in e-waste management. Sustainable management of electronic waste'. In Abhishek Kumar, Pramod Singh Rathore, Ashutosh Kumar Dubey, Arun Lal Srivastav, T. Ananth Kumar and Vishal Dutt (eds.) *Sustainable Management of Electronic Waste* (pp. 201–220). Wiley Online Library. DOI:10.1002/9781394166923

Barr, T. (2000). *Newmedia. com. au: The Changing Face of Australia's Media and Communications*. Allen & Unwin.

Basalla, G. (1988). *The Evolution of Technology*. Cambridge University Press.

Bateson, G. (1940). *Steps to an Ecology of Mind: Collected Essays in Anthropology, Psychiatry, Evolution, and Epistemology* (pp 73–87). University of Chicago Press.

Baudrillard, J. (1981, 2010). 'Simulacra and simulations'. In Chris Greer (ed.), *Crime and Media* (pp. 69–85). Routledge.

Belk, R. and Tumbat, G. (2005). 'The cult of Macintosh'. *Consumption Markets & Culture*, 8(3), 205–217.

Beniger, J. (1986). *The Control Revolution: Technological and Economic Origins of the Information Society*. Harvard University Press.

Benjamin, W. (1969). 'Theses on the philosophy of History'. In Hannah Arendt (ed. and trans.), Harry Zohn (trans.). *Illuminations*. Schocken.

Benjamin, W. (1983). *Das Passagen-Werk* (First Volume). Suhrkamp-Verlag.

Benkler, Y. and Nissenbaum, H. (2006). 'Commons-based peer production and virtue'. *Journal of Political Philosophy*, 14(4), 394–419.

Bennett, C. H. and Brassard, G. (2014). 'Quantum cryptography: Public key distribution and coin tossing'. *Theoretical Computer Science*, 560, 7–11.

Bennett, J. (2010). *Vibrant Matter: A Political Ecology of Things*. Duke University Press.

Bennett, W. L. and Kneuer, M. (2023). 'Communication and democratic erosion: The rise of illiberal public spheres'. *European Journal of Communication*, 1–20. DOI: 10.1177/02673231231217378

Berg, C., Davidson, S. and Potts, J. (2019). *Understanding the Blockchain Economy: An Introduction to Institutional Cryptoeconomics*. Edward Elgar. https://doi.org/10.4337/9781788975001.00006

Berger, A. A. (1995). *Essentials of Mass Communication Theory*. Sage.

Berry, D. M. and Dieter, M. (2015). 'Thinking postdigital aesthetics: Art, computation and design'. In David M. Berry and Michael Dieter (eds.) *Postdigital Aesthetics: Art, Computation and Design* (pp. 1–11). Palgrave Macmillan.

Blanco, C. (2017, 7 April). 'Cleverman cast and crew over the moon for Peabody Award nomination'. SBS/NITV. Retrieved from www.sbs.com.au/nitv/article/cleverman-cast-and-crew-over-the-moon-for-peabody-award-nomination/ptfxlbeb9

Blumler, J. G. and Katz, E. (Eds.) (1974). *The Uses of Mass Communications: Current Perspectives on Gratifications Research*. Sage Publications.

Boido, C. and Aliano, M. (2023). 'Digital art and non-fungible-token: Bubble or revolution?'. *Finance Research Letters*, 52, 103380.

Bolter, J. D. and Grusin, R. (2000). *Remediation: Understanding New Media*. MIT Press.

Booth, A. (2015, 27 August). 'Welcome to Country app can "instil" cultural pride'. NITV/SBS. Retrieved from www.sbs.com.au/nitv/article/welcome-to-country-app-can-instil-cultural-pride/oclw8kt7w

Bostrom, N. (2005, April). 'A history of transhumanist thought'. *Journal of Evolution and Technology*,14(1), 1–25.

Bostrom, N. (2014). *Superintelligence: Paths, Dangers, Strategies*. Oxford University Press.

Bounfour, A. (2016). *Digital Futures, Digital Transformation: From Lean Production to Acceluction*. Springer.

Bouwmeester, D., Pan, J.W., Mattle, K., Eibl, M., Weinfurter, H. and Zeilinger, A. (1997). 'Experimental quantum teleportation'. *Nature*, 390(6660), 575–579.

Bowles, N. (2017, 6 May). 'The world's most valuable resource is no longer oil, but data'. *The Economist*. www.economist.com/leaders/2017/05/06/the-worlds-most-valuable-resource-is-no-longer-oil-but-data

boyd, d. (2017). 'Did media literacy backfire?'. *Data & Society: Points*. Retrieved from https://points.datasociety.net/did-media-literacy-backfire-7418c084d88d

Boykoff, M. T. and Roberts, J. T. (2007). 'Media coverage of climate change: Current trends, strengths, weaknesses'. *Human Development Report*, (3), 1–53.

Braidotti, R. (2013). *The posthuman*. Polity Press

Braidotti, R. (2017). *Posthuman, All too Human: The Memoirs and Aspirations of a Posthumanist*. Tanner Lectures, Yale University, 1–2.

Braidotti, R. (2019). *Posthuman Knowledge*. Polity Press.

Bratton, B. (2015). *The Stack: On Software and Sovereignty*. MIT Press.

British Broadcasting Corporation (BBC)/Independent Broadcasting Authority (IBA). (1985). *Public Service Idea in British Broadcasting: Main Principles*, July, Broadcasting Research Unit (BRU).

Brooker, C. (Creator). (2011). *Black Mirror* [TV series]. Zeppotron/House of Tomorrow.

Brundage, M., Avin, S., Wang, J., Belfield, H., Krueger, G., Hadfield, G., Khlaaf, H., Yang, J., Toner, H., Fong, R. and Maharaj, T. (2020). 'Toward trustworthy AI development: mechanisms for supporting verifiable claims'. *arXiv preprint arXiv*:2004.07213.

Bruns, A. (2008). *Blogs, Wikipedia, Second Life, and Beyond: From Production to Produsage* (Vol. 45). Peter Lang.

Brynjolfsson, E. and McAfee, A. (2014). *The Second Machine Age: Work, Progress, and Prosperity in a Time of Brilliant Technologies*. WW Norton & Company.

Bubeck, S., Chandrasekaran, V., Eldan, R., Gehrke, J., Horvitz, E., Kamar, E., Lee, P., Lee, Y. T., Li, Y., Lundberg, S., Nori, H., Palangi, H., Ribeiro, M. T. and Zhang, Y. (2023). Sparks of Artificial General Intelligence: Early experiments with GPT-4. *arXiv*. https://doi.org/10.48550/arXiv.2303.12712

192 References

Bucher, T. (2012). 'Want to be on the top? Algorithmic power and the threat of invisibility on Facebook'. *New Media & Society*, 14(7), 1164–1180.

Buckingham, D. (1998). 'Media education in the UK: Moving beyond protectionism'. *Journal of Communication*, 48(1) Winter, 33–43.

Burn, I. and Stephen, A. (1992). 'Namatjira's White Mask: a partial interpretation'. In J. Hardy, J. V. S. Megaw and M. Ruth Megaw (eds.) *The Heritage of Namatjira – The Watercolourists of Central Australia* (pp. 249–282). William Heinemann Australia.

Burum, I. (2013). 'Using mobile media to create a more diverse public sphere in marginalised communities: How to mojo'. *The International Journal of Community Diversity*, 12(1), 1–11.

Burum, I. (2016). *Democratizing Journalism through Mobile Media: The Mojo Revolution*. Routledge.

Burum, I. and Quinn, S. (2016). *MOJO: The Mobile Journalism Handbook: How to Make Broadcast Videos with an iPhone or iPad*. Focal Press.

Bush, V. (1945, July). 'As we may think'. *Atlantic Monthly*, 101–108.

Butler, J. (1990). *Gender Trouble: Feminism and the Subversion of Identity*. Routledge.

Cajete, G. A. and Williams, D. R. (2020). 'Eco-aesthetics, metaphor, story, and symbolism: An Indigenous perspective: A conversation'. In Amy Cutter-Mackenzie-Knowles, Karen Malone and Elisabeth Barratt Hacking (eds.) *Research Handbook on Childhoodnature* (pp. 1707–1733). Springer International Handbooks of Education. https://doi.org/10.1007/978-3-319-67286-1_96

Canada, Government of Canada (2011). Crown-Indigenous Relations and Northern Affairs (7 June 2011), 'First Nations in Canada'. www.rcaanc-cirnac.gc.ca.

Cannavò, A., Castiello, A., Pratticò, F. G., Mazali, T. and Lamberti, F. (2023). 'Immersive movies: the effect of point of view on narrative engagement'. *AI & Society*, 1, 1–15. doi.org/10.1007/s00146-022-01622-9

Caprica. (2009–2010). [TV series]. Syfy. Universal Cable Productions.

Carlson, B. (2017, 27 April). 'Why are Indigenous people such avid users of social media?', *The Guardian*. Retrieved from www.theguardian.com/commentisfree/2017/apr/27/why-are-indigenous-people-such-avid-users-of-social-media

Carlson, B. (2023). 'Global perspectives on Indigeneity: Indigenous perspectives on global Indigeneity'. In Bronwyn Carlson, Tristan Kennedy and Madi Day (eds.) *Global Networks of Indigeneity* (pp. 9–26). Manchester University Press.

Carr, N. (2010). *The Shallows: What the Internet Is Doing to Our Brains*. W. W. Norton & Company.

Castells, M. (2000a). 'Materials for an exploratory theory of the network society', *British Journal of Sociology*, 51(1), 5–24.

Castells, M. (2000b). *The Rise of the Network Society: The Information Age–Economy, Society and Culture*, vol. 1, 2nd edn. Blackwell.

Castells M. (2010) *The Rise of the Network Society*, 2nd edn. Wiley-Blackwell.

Castillo, D. R. and Egginton, W. (2017). *Mediaologies: Reading Reality in the Age of Inflationary Media*. Bloomsbury Academic.

Catts, O. and Zurr, I. (2008). 'The ethics of experiential engagement with the manipulation of life'. In Beatriz da Costa and Kavita Philp (eds.) *Tactical Biopolitics- Art, Activism, and Technoscience* (pp. 125–142). MIT Press.

Chadwick, A. (2017). *The Hybrid Media System: Politics and Power*. Oxford University Press.

Channarong, I. (2018). 'Indigenous peoples, social media, and the digital divide: A systematic literature review', *American Indian Culture and Research Journal*, 42(4), 85–111. DOI: 10.17953/aicrj.42.4.intahchomphoo

Chawla, L. (1998). 'Significant life experiences revisited: A review of research on sources of environmental sensitivity'. *The Journal of Environmental Education*, 29(3), 11–21.

Chen, C., Murphey, T. D. and MacIver, M. A. (2020). 'Tuning movement for sensing in an uncertain world'. *eLife*, 9. DOI: https://doi.org/10.7554/eLife.52371

Cherp, A., Vinichenko, V., Jewell, J., Brutschin, E. and Sovacool, B. (2018). Integrating techno-economic, socio-technical and political perspectives on national energy transitions: A meta-theoretical framework. *Energy Research & Social Science*, 37, 175–190.

Christensen, K. (2022). 'Yarning as decolonising practice'. *International Journal of Narrative Therapy & Community Work*, 2, 1–8.

Chun. W. (2012). *Programmed Visions: Software and Memory*. MIT Press.

Cinque, T. (2015). *Changing Media Landscapes: Visual Networking*. Oxford University Press.

Cinque, T. (2022a). 'Quantified me: curatorial lives and the pixelated spectre of self'. In T. Cinque and J. B. Vincent (eds.) *Materializing Digital Futures: Touch, Movement, Sound and Vision* (pp. 1–24). Bloomsbury Academic.

Cinque, T. (2022b). 'Protecting communities during the COVID-19 global health crisis: health data research and the international use of contact tracing technologies', *Humanities and Social Sciences Communications Journal*, 9(99), www.nature.com/articles/s41599-022-01078-8

Cinque, T. (2023). 'A study of Mastodon, Galaxy3 and 8Kun as post-social media in dark webs: the darker turn of our intimate machines'. In Toija Cinque, Alexia Maddox and Robert Gehl (eds.) *The Dark Social: Online Practices of Resistance, Motility and Power*, pp. 19–31. Routledge.

Cinque, T. (2024). 'Exploring the paradox: Perceptions of AI in higher education – a study of hype and scandal', *Explorations in Media Ecology*, Special Issue on Artificial Intelligence and Media Ecology, pp. 199–215.

Clark, A. (2003). *Natural-born Cyborgs: Minds, Technologies, and the Future of Human Intelligence*. Oxford University Press.

Cleverman. (2016/2017). Television series (52 mins). Wayne Blair and Leah Purcell (dirs.). Australian Broadcasting Commission (ABC).

Cohen, B., Shenk, J. and Guggenheim, D. (dirs.) (2006). *An Inconvenient Truth*. Produced by Participant, Paramount Pictures, Lawrence Bender, Actual Films Production, Participant Prods.

Colllisions. VR film. (2015). Lynette Wallworth (dir.). Infinite Field, with support from the World Economic Forum, the Sundance Institute, the MacArthur Foundation, the Skoll Foundation, the Ford Foundation, the Fledgling Fund, the Pritzker Foundation, the Omidyar Network, the Australia Council for the Arts, and the Adelaide Film Festival Fund, in partnership with Jaunt VR. www.collisionsvr.com

Costil, A. (2013). 'Top 10 places that have banned Google Glass', *Search Engine Journal*, 7 August. www.searchenginejournal.com/top-10-places-that-have-banned-google-glass/66585/

Couldry, N. (2012). *Media, Society, World: Social Theory and Digital Media Practice*. Polity Press.

194 References

Couldry, N. (2016) 'Life with the media manifold: Between freedom and subjection'. In L. Kramp, N. Carpentier, A. Hepp, R. Kilborn, R. Kunelius, H. Nieminen, T. Olsson, P. Pruulmann-Vengerfeldt, I. Tomanić Trivundža, and S. Tosoni (eds.) *Politics, Civil Society and Participation: Media and Communications in a Transforming Environment* (pp. 25–39). edition lumière.

Couldry, N. and Hepp, A. (2017). *The Mediated Construction of Reality*. Polity Press.

Coyne, R. (2018). *Network Nature: The Place of Nature in the Digital Age*. Bloomsbury.

Cramer, F. (2014). 'What is "post-digital?"' In David M. Berry and Michael Dieter (eds.) *Postdigital Aesthetics: Art, Computation and Design* (pp. 12–26). Palgrave Macmillan.

Crawford, K. (2016). 'Can an algorithm be agonistic? Ten scenes from life in calculated publics'. *Science, Technology, & Human Values*, 41(1), 77–92.

Crawford, K. (2021). *The Atlas of AI: Power, Politics, and the Planetary Costs of Artificial Intelligence*. Yale University Press.

Croteau, D. and Hoynes, W. (2014). *Media/Society: Industries, Images, and Audiences*. 5th edition. Sage.

Curran, J. (1998). 'Crisis of public communication: a reappraisal 1998'. In T.L. Glasser and S. Craft (eds.) *Media, Ritual and Identity* (pp. 175–202). Routledge.

Curran, J. (2005). 'Rethinking the media as a public sphere'. In *Communication and Citizenship* (pp. 27–57). Routledge.

Curran, J. (2010). *Media and Society*. Bloomsbury.

Davis, M. (2023, November 25). 'Blockchain for NFTs: How Blockchain Technology Empowers Non-Fungible Tokens'. *Doubloin*, Retrieved from www.doubloin.com/learn/blockchain-for-nfts

de Back, T. T., Tinga, A. M., Nguyen, P. and Louwerse, M. M. (2020). Benefits of immersive collaborative learning in CAVE-based virtual reality. *International Journal of Educational Technology in Higher Education*, 17, 1–18. doi.org/10.1186/s41239-020-00228-9

Deleuze, G and Guattari, F (1987). 'Introduction: rhizome'. In Brian Massimi (Trans) *A Thousand Plateaus: Capitalism and Schizophrenia* (pp. 3–25). University of Minnesota Press.

Demharter, S., Pearce, N., Beattie, K., Frost, I., Leem, J., Martin, A., et al. (2017, 25 May). 'Ten simple rules for surviving an interdisciplinary PhD', *PLoS Computational Biology* 13(5), 1–7. e1005512. https://doi.org/10.1371

Derrida, J. (1994). *Spectres of Marx*. Routledge Classics.

Derrida, J. (1995). 'Archive fever: A Freudian impression'. In Eric Prenowitz (Trans) *Diacritics*, 25(2), 9–63.

Descola, P. (2005). *Par-delà nature et culture*. Gallimard.

Descola, P. and Pálsson, G. (eds.) (1996). *Nature and Society: Anthropological Perspectives*. Routledge.

Deutsch, D. (1985). 'Quantum theory, the Church–Turing principle and the universal quantum computer'. *Proceedings of the Royal Society of London. A. Mathematical and Physical Sciences*, 400(1818), 97–117.

Deuze, M. (2006). 'Participation, remediation, bricolage: Considering principal components of a digital culture'. *The Information Society*, 22(2), 63–75.

Dignum, V. (2018). 'Responsible Artificial Intelligence: designing AI for human values'. *ITU Journal: ICT Discoveries*, 1(1), 20–27.

Dishon, G. and Ben-Porath, S. (2018). 'Don't @ me: Rethinking digital civility online and in school'. *Learning, Media and Technology*, 43(4), 434–450.

Doudna, J. A. and Charpentier, E. (2014). 'The new frontier of genome engineering with CRISPR-Cas9'. *Science*, 346(6213), 1258096.

Doyle, R. (1997). *On Beyond Living: Rhetorical Transformations of the Life Sciences*. Stanford University Press.

Drengson, A. and Inoue, Y. eds. (1995). *The Deep Ecology Movement: An Introductory Anthology*. North Atlantic Publishers.

Dubois, E. and Blank, G. (2018). 'The echo chamber is overstated: The moderating effect of political interest and diverse media'. *Information, Communication & Society, Online*. DOI:10.1080/1369118X.2018.1428656

Dwyer, T. (2010). *Media Convergence*. McGraw-Hill Education, UK.

eSafety Commission (NSW, Australia). (2021, July). 'Best Practice Framework for Online Safety Education (Stage 1)'. www.esafety.gov.au/sites/default/files/2020-06/Best%20Practice%20Framework%20for%20Online%20Safety%20Education_0.pdf?v=1722563657848

Edwards, R. and Ugwudike, P. (2023). *Governing Families: Problematising Technologies in Social Welfare and Criminal Justice*. Taylor & Francis.

Eilish, B. (2019). *When We All Fall Asleep, Where Do We Go?* [Album]. Darkroom/Interscope Records.

Ekert, A. and Jozsa, R. (1996). 'Quantum algorithms: Entanglement-enhanced information processing'. *Philosophical Transactions of the Royal Society of London. Series A: Mathematical, Physical and Engineering Sciences*, 354(1719), 3199–3222.

Emery, A. R. (2000). *Guidelines: Integrating Indigenous Knowledge in Project Planning and Implementation*. Canadian International Development Agency. Retrieved from www.kivu.com/wp-content/uploads/2012/01/Partnership-Guidelines.pdf (Archived by WebCite® at www.webcitation.org/6uCw2FHrf)

Ernst, W. (2013). *Digital Memory and the Archive* (Vol. 39). University of Minnesota Press.

Ernste, H. (2018). 'The geography of spheres: An introduction and critical assessment of Peter Sloterdijk's concept of spheres'. *Geographica Helvetica*, 73(4), 273–284. DOI: doi.org/10.5194/gh-73-273-2018

Escobar, A. (2020). *Pluriversal Politics. The Real and the Possible*. Duke University Press.

European Commission, Directorate-General for Communication. (2023). European Citizens' Panel on virtual worlds–Final report, Publications Office of the European Union. https://data.europa.eu/doi/10.2775/472

Eveleth, R. (2018, 12 December). 'Google Glass Wasn't a Failure. It Raised Crucial Concerns', *Wired*. www.wired.com/story/google-glass-reasonable-expectation-of-privacy/

Fernández-Caramés, T. M. (2020). 'From pre-quantum to post-quantum IoTF security: A survey on quantum-resistant cryptosystems for the Internet of Things', in *IEEE Internet of Things Journal*, 7(7), 6457–6480, July. DOI: 10.1109/JIOT.2019.2958788.

Flintoff, B. (2004). *Taonga Puoro. Singing Treasures: The Musical Instruments of the Maori*. Craig Potton Publishing.

Floridi, L. (2014). *The Fourth Revolution: How the Infosphere Is Reshaping Human Reality*. Oxford University Press.

Flusser, V. (2002). *Writings, Electronic Mediations*, Eric Eisel (trans). University of Minnesota Press.

Foucault, M. (1972). *The Archaeology of Knowledge and Discourse on Language*, A. M. Sheridan Smith (trans). Pantheon.

196 References

France 24 International News. (2024, 9 April). Broadcast on the Special Broadcasting Service (SBS) Australia (19:17–22:45).

Fraser, N. (1990). 'Rethinking the public sphere: A contribution to the critique of actually existing democracy'. *Social Text*, 25/26, 56–80. https://doi.org/10.2307/466240

Fukuyama, F. (2002a). *Our Posthuman Future: Consequences of the Biotechnology Revolution*. Profile Books.

Fukuyama, F. (2002b). Social capital and development: The coming agenda. *SAIS Review*, 22(1), 23–37.

Fuller, M. (2005). *Media Ecologies: Materialist Energies in Art and Technoculture*. MIT Press.

Gabrys, J. (2011). *Digital Rubbish: A Natural History of Electronics*. University of Michigan Press.

Galloway, A. R. (2006). *Gaming: Essays on Algorithmic Culture*. University of Minnesota Press.

Galloway, A. R. (2012). *The Interface Effect*. Polity Press.

Gartner (2022). 25% of people to spend 1 hour daily in the metaverse by 2026. https://futureiot.tech/gartner-25-of-people-to-spend-1-hour-daily-in-the-Metaverse-by-2026/

Gerbner, G., Gross, L., Morgan, M. and Signorielli, N. (1986). 'Living with television: The dynamics of the cultivation process'. In Jennnings Bryant and Dolf Zillmann (eds.) *Perspectives on Media Effects* (pp. 17–40). Lawrence Erlbaum Associates.

Gibson, W. (1984). *Neuromancer*. Ace Books.

Giddens, A. (1993). *Sociology*, 2nd edn. Polity Press.

Gillespie, T. (2010). 'The politics of "platforms"'. *New Media & Society*, 12(3), 347–364.

Ginsburg, F. (2002). 'Screen memories: Resignifying the traditional in indigenous media'. In Faye D. Ginsburg, Lila Abu-Lughod and Brian Larkin (eds.) *Media Worlds: Anthropology on New Terrain* (pp. 39–57). University of California Press.

Gitelman, L. (2006). *Always Already New: Media, History, and the Data of Culture*. MIT Press.

Gitlin, T. (1998). 'Media sphericules'. In T. Liebes and James Curran (eds.) *Media, Ritual and Identity* (pp 79–88). Routledge.

Glyer, M. (2016, December 1). 'John Hinde Award for Science Fiction'. *File 770-Mike Glyer's news of science fiction fandom*. Retrieved 6 April 2024, from https://file770.com/2016-john-hinde-award-for-science-fiction/.

Glynn, K. and Tyson, A. F. (2007). 'Indigeneity, media and cultural globalization: The case of Mataku, or the Maori X-Files'. *International Journal of Cultural Studies*, 10(2), 205–224.

Goddard, M. (2015). 'Opening up the black boxes: Media archaeology, "anarchaeology" and media materiality'. *New Media & Society*, 17(11), December, 1761–76. https://doi.org/10.1177/146144481453219

Goffman, E. (1956). *The Presentation of Self in Everyday Life*. Doubleday.

Goggin, G. (2006). *Cell Phone Culture: Mobile Technology in Everyday Life*. Routledge.

Google. (n.d.). 'Google Glasses - Official Video (HD)' [Video]. *YouTube*. Retrieved [20 July 2023], from www.youtube.com/watch?v=WhYhn_-8dMY.

Grace, H. (2014). 'Culture, aesthetics and affect in ubiquitous media: the prosaic image'. *Media, Culture and Social Change in Asia Series*. Routledge.

Grossman, M., Peucker, M., Smith, D. and Dellal, H. (2016). *Stocktake Research Report: A Systematic Literature and Selected Program Review on Social Cohesion, Community Resilience and Violent Extremism 2011–2015.* Community Resilience Unit, Dept. of Premier and Cabinet, State of Victoria.

Grover, L. K. (1996, 22–24 May). 'A fast quantum mechanical algorithm for database search'. *Proceedings of the Twenty-Eighth Annual ACM Symposium on Theory of Computing,* 212–219. doi.org/10.1145/237814.237866.

Groys, B (2009). 'Comrades of time'. *E-Flux Journal* 11. www.eflux.com/journal/11/61345/comrades-of-time/

Guattari, F. (2000). *The Three Ecologies.* I. Pindar and P. Sutton (trans.). Athlone Press.

Guggenheim, D. (Director). (2006). *An Inconvenient Truth.* Film (97mins). Paramount Classics.

Habermas, J. (1989). *The Structural Transformation of the Public Sphere: An Inquiry into a Category of Bourgeois Society,* translated by Thomas Burger with the assistance of Frederick Lawrence. MIT Press.

Haines, J., Du, J. T., Geursen, G., Gao, J. and Trevorrow, E. (2017). '"Understanding Elders" knowledge creation to strengthen Indigenous ethical knowledge sharing', *Proceedings of RAILS – Research Applications, Information and Library Studies, 2016,* 22(4), np. School of Information Management, Victoria University of Wellington, New Zealand, 6–8 December, 2016.

Hall, L. A. (1994). Aboriginal art-resistance and dialogue: The political nature and agency of Aboriginal art (Master of Art Theory, dissertation, UNSW Sydney). https://doi.org/10.26190/unsworks/4393

Hall, S. (1973, September). 'Encoding and Decoding in the Television Discourse'. A paper for the Council of Europe Colloquy on 'Training in the Critical Reading of Televisual Language', organised by the Council and the Centre for Mass Communication Research, University of Leicester. Birmingham: Centre for Contemporary Cultural Studies. https://core.ac.uk/download/pdf/81670115.pdf

Hall, S. (1990). 'Cultural identity and diaspora'. In J. Rutherford (ed.), *Identity: Community, Culture, Difference* (pp. 222–237). Lawrence & Wishart.

Hall, S. (2019). 'Encoding and decoding in the television discourse' (originally 1973; republished 2019). In D. Morley (ed.) *Essential Essays, Volume 1 Foundations of Cultural Studies* (pp. 257–276). Duke University Press.

Haraway, D. J. (1985). 'A manifesto for cyborgs: Science, technology and socialist feminism in the 1980s'. *Socialist Review,* 15(80), 190–233.

Haraway, D. J. (1991). *Simians, Cyborgs, and Women: The Reinvention of Nature.* Routledge.

Haraway, D. J. (2003). *The Companion Species Manifesto: Dogs, People, and Significant Otherness (Vol. 1).* Prickly Paradigm.

Haraway, D. J. (2008). *When Species Meet.* University of Minnesota Press.

Harvey, D. (1993). 'From space to place and back again: Reflections on the condition of postmodernity'. In J. Bird, B. Curtis, T. Putnam, and G. Robertson (eds.), *Mapping the Futures: Local Culture, Global Change* (pp. 3–29). Routledge.

Hassan, S. (2019). *The Cult of Trump: A Leading Cult Expert Explains How the President Uses Mind Control.* Free Press.

Hayles, N. K. (1999a). 'The illusion of autonomy and the fact of recursivity: Virtual ecologies, entertainment, and "infinite jest"'. *New Literary History,* 30(3), 675–697.

198 References

Hayles, N. K. (1999b). *How We Became Posthuman: Virtual Bodies in Cybernetics, Literature, and Informatics*. University of Chicago Press.

Hepp, A. (2013). *Cultures of Mediatization*, K. Tribe (trans.). Polity Press.

Herrera, M. (2017). 'Mocking Spongebob Meme'. USU Student Folklore Fieldwork. Paper 83. https://digitalcommons.usu.edu/student_folklore_all/83

Hertz, G. and Parikka, J. (2012). 'Zombie media: Circuit bending media archaeology into an art method'. *Leonardo*, 45(5), 424–430.

Heskett, J. (2005). *Design: A Very Short Introduction*. Oxford University Press.

Heskett, J. (2002). *Toothpicks and Logos: Design in Everyday Life*. Oxford University Press.

Hodge, S. (2019). 'Transformative learning for knowledge: From meaning perspectives to threshold concepts'. *Journal of Transformative Education*, 17(2), 133–153.

Hokowhitu, B. and Devadas, V. (eds.) (2013). *The Fourth Eye: Maori Media in Aotearoa New Zealand*. University of Minnesota Press.

Holevo, A. S. (1973). 'Bounds for the quantity of information transmitted by a quantum communication channel'. *Problemy Peredachi Informatsii*, 9(3), 3–11.

Hope, A. (2013). 'The politics of online risk and the discursive construction of e-safety'. In K. Facer and N. Selwyn (eds.) *The Politics of Education and Technology: Conflicts, Controversies and Connections* (pp. 83–98). Palgrave Macmillan.

Horkheimer, M. and Adorno, T.W. (1944, 1972). *Dialectic of Enlightenment*. Allen Lane.

Horrocks, R. and Perry, N. (2004). *Television in New Zealand: Programming the Nation*. Oxford University Press.

Hoskins, A. (2009). 'Digital network memory'. In Astrid Eril and Ann Rigney (eds.) *Mediation, Remediation, and the Dynamics of Cultural Memory*, (pp 91–108). Walter de Gruyter.

Howe, P. D. L., Fay, N., Saletta, M. and Hovy, E. (2023). 'ChatGPT's advice is perceived as better than that of professional advice columnists'. *Frontiers in Psychology*, 14, 1281255.

Hughes, C. (2012). 'Dialogue between Fukuyama's account of the end of history and Derrida's hauntology', *Journal of Philosophy: A Cross-Disciplinary Inquiry*, 7(18), 13–26.

Huhtamo, E. (2013). *Illusions in Motion: Media Archaeology of the Moving Panorama and Related Spectacles*. MIT Press.

Huhtamo, E. and Parikka, J. (2011). *Media Archaeology: Approaches, Applications, and Implications*. University of California Press.

Huld, A. (2022). 'Building China's virtual world – the new action plan for metaverse technology', *China Briefing*. November 14. www.china-briefing.com/news/virtual-reality-in-china-new-action-plan-for-developing-industry/#:~:text=The%20Virtual%20Reality%20and%20Industry%20Application%20Integration%20Development,development%20goals%20for%20the%20period%20up%20until%202026.

Imbrie, A., Daniels, O. and Toner. (2023, October). *Decoding Intentions: Artificial Intelligence and Costly Signals*. Center for Security and Emerging Technology. https://doi.org/10.51593/20230033

Immersive Tech Africa. (2023, April 17). *XR Innovation Summit 2023: Driving innovation and social impact with extended reality (XR) in Africa*. May 25–27. https://xrmust.com/xrmagazine/xr-innovation-summit-2023/

Innis, H. A. (1951). *The Bias of Communication*. Intro. Marshall McLuhan. University of Toronto Press, 1964.

References   **199**

International Energy Agency (IEA) (2024, January). 'Electricity 2024: analysis and forecast to 2026'. *International Energy Agency*, www.iea.org. Retrieved from https://iea.blob.core.windows.net/assets/6b2fd954-2017-408e-bf08-952fdd621 18a/Electricity2024-Analysisandforecastto2026.pdf

Isin, E. and Ruppert, E. (2015). *Being Digital Citizens*. Rowman & Littlefield.

Ito, M. (2010). 'Mobilizing the imagination in everyday play: The case of Japanese media mixes'. In S. Sonvilla-Weiss (ed.) *Mashup Cultures* (pp. 79–97). Springer.

Jenkins, H., Ford, S., and Green, J. (2013). *Spreadable Media: Creating Value and Meaning in a Networked Culture*. New York University Press.

Jenkins, H. (2006). *Convergence Culture: Where Old and New Media Collide*. New York University Press.

Jensen, L. and Konradsen, F. (2018). 'A review of the use of virtual reality head-mounted displays in education and training'. *Education and Information Technologies*, 23, 1515–1529.

Jones, P. (2020). *Bodies, Technologies, and Methods*. Routledge.

Jones, R. H. and Hafner, C. A. (2012). *Understanding Digital Literacies: A Practical Introduction*. Routledge.

Jue, M. (2020). *Wild Blue Media: Thinking through Seawater*. Duke University Press.

Kahane, A. (2017). 'Transformative scenario planning: A new way to work with the future 1'. In Katrin Muff (ed.) *The Collaboratory* (pp. 112–123). Routledge.

Khanjani, Z., Watson, G., and Janeja, V. P. (2023, 9 January). 'Audio deepfakes: A survey'. *Front Big Data*, 5, 1001063. doi: 10.3389/fdata.2022.1001063. PMID: 36700137; PMCID: PMC9869423.

Kant, T. (2020). *Making It Personal: Algorithmic Personalization, Identity, and Everyday Life*. Oxford University Press.

Kasneci, E., Sessler, K., Küchemann, S., Bannert, M., Dementieva, D., Fischer, F., Gasser, U., Groh, G., Gunnemann, S., Hullermeier, E., Krusche, S., Kutyniok, G., Michaeli, T., Nerdel, C., Pfeffer, J., Poquet, O., Sailer, M., Schmidt, A., Seidel, T., … Kasneci, G. (2023). 'ChatGPT for good? On opportunities and challenges of large language models for education'. *Learning and Individual Differences*, 103, 102274. https://doi.org/10.1016/j.lindif.2023.102274

Kimble, H. J. (2008). 'The quantum internet'. *Nature*, 453(7198), 1023–1030.

Kirby, P. (2024). 'Belgium probes Russian interference in EU election', *BBC News*. Retrieved from www.bbc.com/news/world-europe-68797624

Kittler, F.A. (1990). *Discourse Networks, 1800/1900*. Stanford University Press.

Kittler, F. A. (1995). 'There is no Software'. *Ctheory*. In: A. Arthur and M. Kroker (eds.) Available at: www.ctheory.net/articles.aspx?id=74 (accessed 6 June 2023).

Kittler, F. A. (1996). 'The history of communication media'. *Ctheory*, 7–30.

Kittler, F. A. (1999). *Gramophone, Film, Typewriter*. G. Winthrop-Young and M. Wutz (trans.). Stanford University Press.

Kluitenberg, E. (ed.) (2006). *The Book of Imaginary Media: Excavating the Dream of the Ultimate Communication Medium*. NAi Uitgevers Publishers.

Kluitenberg, E. (2011). 'On the archaeology of imaginary media'. In Erkki Huhtamo and Jussi Parikka (eds.) *Media Archaeology: Approaches, Applications, and Implications* (pp. 48–69). University of California Press.

Kochhar, A. (2022). 'Meta launches "Metaverse Academy" in France with an aim to increase employment in Europe'. *International Business Times*. June 13. www.ibti mes.com/meta-launches-metaverse-academy-france-aim-increase-employment-eur ope-3537116.

200 References

Kozinets, R. V. (1998). 'On netnography: Initial reflections on consumer research investigations of cyberculture'. In J. W. Alba and J. W. Hutchinson (eds.) *NA-Advances in Consumer Research* (Vol. 25, pp. 366–371). Association for Consumer Research.

Kozinets, R. V. (2019). *Netnography: The Essential Guide to Qualitative Social Media Research*. Sage.

Krizhevsky, A., Sutskever, I., and Hinton, G. E. (2017). 'ImageNet classification with deep convolutional neural networks'. *Communications of the ACM*, 60(6), 84–90.

Kröger, J. L., Lutz, O. H. M. and Raschke, P. (2020). 'Privacy implications of voice and speech analysis – information disclosure by inference'. In M. Friedewald, M. Önen, E. Lievens, S. Krenn and S. Fricker (eds.) *Privacy and Identity Management. Data for Better Living: AI and Privacy. Privacy and Identity 2019* (Vol. 576). Springer.

Kubrick, S. (Director). (1968). *2001: A Space Odyssey* [Film]. Metro-Goldwyn-Mayer.

Kurzweil, R. (2005). *The Singularity Is Near*. Palgrave Macmillan.

Lagerkvist, A. (2017). 'Existential media: Toward a theorization of digital thrownness'. *New Media & Society*, 19(1), 96–110.

Lasch, C. (1979). *The Culture of Narcissism: American Life in an Age of Diminishing Expectations*. W. W. Norton.

Lash, S. M. (2002). *Critique of Information*. Sage.

Lash, S.M. (2010). *Intensive Culture: Social Theory, Religion and Contemporary Capitalism*. Sage.

Latimore, J. (2016, 1 November). 'A lack of Indigenous voices is turning blackfellas off old media', *The Guardian*. Retrieved from www.theguardian.com/commentisfree/2016/nov/01/a-lack-of-indigenous-voices-is-turning-blackfellas-off-old-media

Latour, B. (1993). *We Have Never Been Modern* (Nous n'avons jamais été modernes: Essai d'anthropologie symétrique). Catherine Porter (Trans.). Harvard University Press.

Latour, B. (2005). *Reassembling the Social: An Introduction to Actor-Network-Theory*. Oxford University Press.

Laukkarinen, M. (2023). 'Social media as a place to see and be seen: Exploring factors affecting job attainment via social media'. *The Information Society*, 39(4), 199–212, DOI: 10.1080/01972243.2023.2199418

Lazarsfeld, P. F., Berelson, B. and Gaudet, H. (1944). *The People's Choice: How the Voter Makes Up His Mind in a Presidential Campaign*. Columbia University Press.

Lazzeretti, L. (2023). *The Rise of Algorithmic Society and the Strategic Role of Arts and Culture*. Cheltenham, UK: Edward Elgar.

Negroponte, N. (2015). *Being Digital*. Vintage.

Leung, C.M., De Haan, P., Ronaldson-Bouchard, K., Kim, G.A., Ko, J., Rho, H.S., Chen, Z., Habibovic, P., Jeon, N.L., Takayama, S. and Shuler, M.L. (2022). 'A guide to the organ-on-a-chip'. *Nature Reviews Methods Primers*, 2(1), 33.

Leurs, K. and Seuferling, P. (2022). 'Migration and the deep time of media infrastructures'. *Communication, Culture and Critique*, 15(2), 290–297.

Levy, S. (2024, 15 February). 'OpenAI's Sora turns AI prompts into photorealistic videos'. *Wired*. www.wired.com/story/openai-sora-generative-ai-video/

Li, T., Menegatti, S., and Crook, N. (2023). 'Breakdown of polyethylene therepthalate microplastics under saltwater conditions using engineered Vibrio natriegens'. *AIChE Journal*, 69(12): e18228. doi:10.1002/aic.18228

Liang, P. P., Wu, C., Morency, L. P. and Salakhutdinov, R. (2021). 'Towards understanding and mitigating social biases in language models'. *Proceedings of the 38th International Conference on Machine Learning*. PMLR, 139(2), 6565–6576.

Liu, S., Liu, L., Tang, J., Yu, B., Wang, Y. and Shi, W. (2019). 'Edge computing for autonomous driving: Opportunities and challenges'. *Proceedings of the IEEE*, 107(8), 1697–1716.

Livingstone, S. (2009). 'On the mediation of everything: ICA presidential address 2008'. *Journal of Communication*, 59(1), 1–18.

Livingstone, S. and Lunt, P. (1994). *Talk on Television: Audience Participation and Public Debate*. London.

Lock, J. and MacDowell, P. (2023). 'Introduction: Meaningful immersive learning in education'. In *Immersive Education: Designing for Learning* (pp. 1–12). Springer.

Lotz, A.D. (2014). *The Television Will Be Revolutionized*. NYU Press.

Lotz, A.D. (2021). *Media Disrupted: Surviving Pirates, Cannibals, and Streaming Wars*. MIT Press.

Louv, R. (2005). *Last Child in the Woods: Saving Our Children from Nature-Deficit Disorder*. Algonquin Books on Chapel Hill.

Lovelock, J. E. (1972). 'Gaia as seen through the atmosphere'. *Atmospheric Environment* 6, 579–580.

Lovelock, J. E. and Margulis, L. (1974). 'Atmospheric homeostasis by and for the biosphere: The Gaia hypothesis', *Tellus*, 26, 1–2, 2–10, DOI: 10.3402/tellusa. v26i1-2.9731

Lovink, G. (2003). *My First Recession: Critical Internet Cultures in Transition*. Nai Publishers.

Lowery, S. (1995). *Milestones in Mass Communication Research: Media Effects*. Longman Publishers.

Loyer, J. (2020, 23 April). 'Indigenous TikTok is transforming cultural knowledge'. *Canadian Art*. Retrieved from https://canadianart.ca/essays/indigenous-tiktok-is-transforming-cultural-knowledge/

Lupton, D. (2016). *The Quantified Self*. Polity Press.

Lyall, C. and Meagher, L. (2008). 'A short guide to troubleshooting some common interdisciplinary research management challenges'. University of Edinburgh. www.tinyurl.com/idwiki

Lyons, M. N. (2017). 'Ctrl-alt-delete: The origins and ideology of the alternative right'. *Political Research Associates*, 20. https://politicalresearch.org/sites/default/files/2019-05/Lyons_CtrlAltDelete_PRINT.pdf

Ma, Z., He, J., Qiu, J., Cao, H., Wang, Y., Sun, Z., Zheng, L., Wang, H., Tang, S., Zheng, T., Lin, J., Feng, G., Huang, Z., Gao, J., Zeng, A., Zhang, J., Zhong, R., Shi, T. and Liu, S. (2022). 'BaGuaLu: Targeting brain scale pretrained models with over 37 million cores'. In *Proceedings of the 2022 ACM SIGPLAN Symposium on Principles and Practice of Parallel Programming (PPoPP 2022)* (pp. 192–204). ACM. https://doi.org/10.1145/3503221.3508417

Madianou, M. and Miller, D. (2013). *Migration and New Media: Transnational Families and Polymedia*. Routledge.

Main, T. J. (2018). *The Rise of the Alt-Right*. Brookings Institution Press. www.jstor.org/stable/10.7864/j.ctt1vjqnxx.

Manovich, L. (2002). *The Language of New Media*. Cambridge, MA: MIT Press.

Manovich, L. (2020). *Cultural Analytics*. MIT Press.

Marchi, R. (2012). 'With Facebook, blogs, and fake news, teens reject journalistic "objectivity"'. *Journal of Communication Inquiry* 36(3), 246–262.

Marvin, C. (1988). *When Old Technologies Were New: Thinking about Electric Communication in the Late Nineteenth Century*. Oxford University Press.

202 References

Marwick, A.E. and Lewis, R. (2017). *Media Manipulation and Disinformation Online.* Data & Society Research Institute. https://apo.org.au/node/135936

Maslej, N., Fattorini, L., Brynjolfsson, E., Etchemendy, J., Ligett, K., Lyons, T., Manyika, J., Ngo, H., Niebles, J. C., Parli, V., Shoham, Y., Wald, R., Clark, J. and Perrault, R. (2023). The AI Index 2023 Annual Report. AI Index Steering Committee, Institute for Human-Centered AI, Stanford University. HAI_AI-Index-Report_2023.pdf (stanford.edu)

Maxwell, R. and Miller, T. (2012). *Greening the Media.* Oxford University Press.

McChesney, R. W. (2004). *The Problem of the Media: US Communication Politics in the Twenty-First Century.* NYU Press.

McDougall, J., Readman, M., and Wilkinson, P. (2018). 'The uses of (digital) literacy. Learning', *Media and Technology*, 43(3), 263–279. https://doi.org/10.1080/17439884.2018.1462206.]

McGee, M. (2013, 19 September). An interview about Google Glass, *Glass Almanac*, https://glassalmanac.com/interview-google-glass/943/

McKinsey & Company. (2022, June). *Value Creation in the Metaverse: The Real Business of the Virtual World.* www.mckinsey.com/~/media/mckinsey/business%20functions/marketing%20and%20sales/our%20insights/value%20creation%20in%20the%20metaverse/Value-creation-in-the-metaverse.pdf

McLuhan, M. (1964). *Understanding Media: The Extensions of Man.* McGraw-Hill.

McLuhan, M. (1975, January). 'McLuhan's Laws of the Media', *Technology and Culture*, 74–78.

McNeill, J. R. and Engelke, P. (2016). *The Great Acceleration: An Environmental History of the Anthropocene since 1945.* Harvard University Press.

McQuail, D. (2010). *McQuail's Mass Communication Theory.* Sage.

McStay, A. (2018). *Emotional AI: The Rise of Empathic Media.* Sage.

Meadows, M. (2021). *Voices in the Wilderness: Images of Aboriginal People in the Australian Media.* Greenwood Press.

Meijers, A. (2021). 'Global XR Conference: The largest global XR community event in the world', Microsoft tech community, December 21, https://techcommunity.microsoft.com/t5/mixed-reality-blog/global-xr-conference-the-largest-global-xr-community-event-in/ba-p/3043539

Merlan, F. (2009). 'Indigeneity: Global and local'. *Current Anthropology*, 50(3), 303–333.

Meyer, J. H. F. and Land, R. (2006). 'Threshold concepts and troublesome knowledge: An introduction'. In Jan H. F. Meyer and Ray Land (eds.) *Overcoming Barriers to Student Understanding: Threshold Concepts and Troublesome Knowledge.* Routledge.

Meyrowitz, J. (1985). *No Sense of Place: The Impact of Electronic Media on Social Behavior.* Oxford University Press.

Michaels, E. (1990). 'A model of teleported texts' (with reference to aboriginal television), *Continuum*, 3(2), 8–31, DOI: 10.1080/10304319009388164

Michel-Villarreal, R., Vilalta-Perdomo, E., Salinas-Navarro, D. E., Thierry-Aguilera, R., and Gerardou, F. S. (2023). Challenges and opportunities of generative AI for higher education as explained by ChatGPT. *Education Sciences*, 13(9), 856–874. https://doi.org/10.3390/educsci13090856

Mihailidis, P. (2018). 'Civic media literacies: Re-imagining engagement for civic intentionality'. *Learning, Media and Technology*, 43(2), 152–164.

References   203

Milgram, P. and Kishino, F. (1994). 'A taxonomy of mixed reality visual displays'. *IEEE Transactions on Information Systems*, 77(12), 1321–1329. https://cs.gmu.edu/~zduric/cs499/Readings/r76JBo-Milgram_IEICE_1994.pdf

Molka-Danielsen, J., Savin-Baden, M., Steed, A., Fominykh, M., Oyekoya, O., Hokstad, L. M., and Prasolova-Førland, E. (2013). Teaching threshold concepts in virtual reality: Exploring the conceptual requirements for systems design. Paper presented at NOKOBIT, Stavanger, Norway, 18–20 November. eprints.worc.ac.uk/3558/1/molka-danielsensavin-badensteedfominykhoyekoyahokstadprasolova-forland_nokobit2013_preprint-libre.pdf

More, M. and Vita-More, N. (eds.) (2013). *The Transhumanist Reader: Classical and Contemporary Essays on the Science, Technology, and Philosophy of the Human Future.* John Wiley & Sons.

Muller, B. (2022). 'The UN special tribunal for Lebanon (2009–2021): Who cares?', *Digest of Middle East Studies*, 31, 72–77. https://doi.org/10.1111/dome.12257

Murphy, G. (Director). (1983). *Utu* [Film]. New Zealand Film Commission.

My Name Is Gulpili. (2021). A film directed by Molly Reynolds (90 mins). Australian Broadcasting Corporation (0.16–0:57).

Naess, A. (1990). *Ecology, Community and Lifestyle: Outline of an Ecosophy.* Cambridge University Press.

Nagle, A. (2017). *Kill All Normies: Online Culture Wars from 4chan and Tumblr to Trump and the Alt-right.* John Hunt Publishing.

Nath, M. and Choudhury, C. (2020, July 30–31). 'Automatic detection of pneumonia from chest X-Rays using deep learning'. In *Machine Learning, Image Processing, Network Security and Data Sciences: Second International Conference*, MIND, Silchar, India, 2020, Proceedings, Part I 2 (pp. 175–182). Springer.

Nawaz, M. S., Khan, S. U. R., Hussain, S. and Iqbal, J. (2023). 'A study on application programming interface recommendation: state-of-the-art techniques, challenges and future directions'. *Library Hi Tech*, 41(2), 355—385.

Nielsen, M. A. and Chuang, I. L. (2010). *Quantum Computation and Quantum Information.* Cambridge University Press.

Nolan, J. and Joy, L. (Creators). (2016). *Westworld* [TV series]. HBO.

Nunes, G., and Filho, A. E. J., (2018). 'Consumer behavior regarding wearable technologies: Google Glass'. *Innovation & Management Review*, 15. 10.1108/INMR-06-2018-0034.

O'Donovan, T. (2022). 'Virtual smart cities using Metaverse, digital twins'. In *Business Transformation*, July 20. www.biznesstransform.com/virtual-smart-cities-using-metaverse-digital-twins/

O'Grady, C. and Kenyon, M. (2023, 21 February). 'How ASML became Europe's most valuable tech firm'. BBC News, *Business Daily*. www.bbc.com/news/business-64514573]

Ogone, J. O. (2020). 'Mobile phones in Africa: The politics of cultural and material integration into local economies'. *International Journal of Cultural Studies*, 23(4), 531–546.

Ohler, J. B. (2010). *Digital Community, Digital Citizen.* Corwin.

Omidyar, P. (2018). '6 ways social media has become a direct threat to democracy'. *New Perspectives Quarterly*, 35(1), 42–45.

OpenAI Community. (2023, December). 'Introducing User-Defined Bio Profiles to Enhance Contextual Interactions in ChatGPT Plus'. OpenAI. Retrieved from: https://community.openai.com/t/introducing-user-defined-bio-profiles-to-enhance-contextual-interactions-in-chatgpt-plus/538310

Oteng-Ababio, M. (2012). 'When necessity begets ingenuity: E-waste scavenging as a livelihood strategy in Accra, Ghana'. *African Studies Quarterly*, 13, 72–74.

Paraschiv, A., Ion, T. A. and Dascalu, M. (2024). 'Offensive text span detection in Romanian comments using large language models'. *Information*, 15(1), 1–21.

Parikka, J. (2010). *Insect Media: An Archaeology of Animals and Technology* (Vol. 11). University of Minnesota Press.

Parikka, J. (2012). *What Is Media Archaeology?* Polity Press.

Parikka, J. (2015). *A Geology of Media*. University of Minnesota Press.

Pariser, E. (2011). *The Filter Bubble: What the Internet Is Hiding from You*. Penguin Books.

Payne, S. L. (1999). 'Interdisciplinarity: Potentials and challenges', *Systemic Practice and Action Research*, 12(2), 173–182.

Peck, R. and Dave, P. (2024, June). 'Can the Internet's greatest authenticity machine survive Wall Street?, *Wired magazine*, 32.05, 36–49.

Penge, S. (1996). *Storia di un ipertesto: Leggere, scrivere, pensare in forma di rete* [*History of a Hypertext: Reading, Writing, Thinking in Network Form*]. La Nuova Italia.

Penley, C. (1997). *NASA/Trek: Popular Science and Sex in America*. Verso.

Peters, J. D. (2014). *The Marvelous Clouds: Toward a Philosophy of Elemental Media*. University of Chicago Press.

Peukert, C., Sen, A. and Claussen, J. (2023). 'The editor and the algorithm: Recommendation technology in online news'. *Management Science*, pp 1–16. doi.org/10.1287/mnsc.2023.4954

Phillips, W. and Milner, R. M. (2017). *The Ambivalent Internet: Mischief, Oddity, and Antagonism Online*. Polity Press.

Postman, N. (1974). Media ecology: Communication as context. Keynote address presented at the Annual Summer Conference of the Speech Communication Association (9th, Chicago, Illinois, July 12–14 1973); Also in 'Proceedings', published by Speech Communication Association, edited by R. Jeffrey and W. Work, pp. 1–10. https://files.eric.ed.gov/fulltext/ED091785.pdf

Postman, N. (1979). *Teaching as a Conserving Activity*. Delacorte Press.

Postman, N. (1985). *Amusing Ourselves to Death: Public Discourse in the Age of Show Business*. Viking.

Postman, N. (1998). Five things we need to know about technological change. Talk delivered in Denver Colorado, March 28. https://web.cs.ucdavis.edu/~rogaway/classes/188/materials/postman.pdf. Retrieved 16 February 2024.

Preskill, J. (2018). 'Quantum computing in the NISQ era and beyond'. *Quantum*, 2, 79.

Reaes Pinto, P. and Gorgel Pinto, A. (2022). 'Migrant living archive: Practice to improve cultural integration in participatory art and design projects'. In Mário Ming Kong, Maria do Rosário Monteiro, Maria João Pereira Neto (eds.) *Creating through Mind and Emotions* (pp. 313–318). CRC Press. DOI: 10.1201/9780429299070-4

Reyburn, S. (2021). 'JPG file sells for $69 million, as "NFT Mania" gathers pace'. *The New York Times*, March 25. www.nytimes.com/2021/03/11/arts/design/nft-auction-christies-beeple.html

Reynolds, L. and Scott, R. (2016). *Digital Citizens: Countering Extremism Online*. Demos. Retrieved from www.demos.co.uk/wp-content/uploads/2016/12/Digital-Citizenship-web-1.pdf

Rimol, M. (2022, 7 February). 'Gartner predicts 25% of people will spend at least one hour per day in the Metaverse by 2026'. *Gartner*.F. www.gartner.com/en/newsroom/press-releases/2022-02-07-gaFrtner-predicts-25-percent-of-people-will-spend-at-least-one-hour-per-day-in-the-metaverse-by-2026

Risius, M., Blasiak, K. M., Wibisono, S. and Louis, W. R. (2023). 'The digital augmentation of extremism: Reviewing and guiding online extremism research from a sociotechnical perspective'. *Information Systems Journal*, 1–33. https://onlinelibrary.wiley.com/doi/pdf/10.1111/isj.12454

Robertson, B., Demosthenous, H. T. and Demosthenous, C. M. (2005). 'Stories from the Aboriginal women of the yarning circle: when cultures collide'. *Hecate*, 31(2), 34–44.

Robinson, S. C. (2020). Trust, transparency, and openness: How inclusion of cultural values shapes Nordic national public policy strategies for artificial intelligence (AI). *Technology in Society*, 63, 101421. pp. 1–15. https://doi.org/10.1016/j.techsoc.2020.101421

Romero, L. E. (2023, 21 May). ' "Every Company Will Manufacture Intelligence," Says NVIDIA CEO Jensen Huang', *Forbes* online. www.forbes.com/sites/luisromero/2023/03/21/every-company-will-manufacture-intelligence-says-nvidia-ceo-jensen-huang/

Rosendahl, P., Müller, M. and Wagner, I. (2023). '360 videos as a visual training tool – a study on subjective perceptions'. *Journal of Physical Education and Sport*, 23(4), 795–801. DOI: 10.7752/jpes.2023.04100

Russell, S. J. and Norvig, P. (1995). *Artificial Intelligence: A Modern Approach*. Prentice-Hall.

Salazar, J. F. (2007). 'Indigenous people and the communication rights agenda: A global perspective'. In Virginia Nightingale and Tim Dwyer (eds.) *New Media Worlds: Challenges for Convergence*, (pp. 87–101). Oxford University Press.

Salojärvi, V., Palonen, E., Horsmanheimo, L. and Kylli, R. M. (2023). 'Protecting the future "Us": a rhetoric-performative multimodal analysis of the polarising far-right YouTube campaign videos in Finland". *Visual Studies*, 38(5), 851–866. https://doi.org/10.1080/1472586X.2023.2249430]

Sánchez, F. L., Hupont, I., Tabik, S. and Herrera, F. (2020, December). 'Revisiting crowd behaviour analysis through deep learning: Taxonomy, anomaly detection, crowd emotions, datasets, opportunities and prospects'. *Information Fusion*, 64, 318–335.

Saudi Arabia, Kingdom of. (2023). *Vision 2030*. www.vision2030.gov.sa/en/vision-2030/overview/

Saudi Press Agency (2022). Meta Partners with Ministry of Communications and Information Technology, Monsha'at to Launch 'Meta Boost' for First Time in Saudi Arabia. December 18. www.spa.gov.sa/w1827918

Savickaite, S. and Simmons, D. (2022). 'From abstract to concrete: How immersive virtual reality technology enhances teaching of complex paradigms'. In P. MacDowell and J. Lock (eds.) *Immersive Education*. Springer Nature.

Scannell, P. (1989). 'Public service broadcasting and modern public life'. *Media Culture and Society*, 11(2), 135–166.

Schäfer, M. T. and van Es, K. (eds.) (2017). *The Datafied Society: Studying Culture through Data*. Amsterdam University Press.

Schmidt, E. and Gardels, N. (interviewer). (2024, 21 May). 'Mapping AI's rapid advance', *NOEMA*. www.noemamag.com/mapping-ais-rapid-advance/

206 References

Scholte, J. A. (2005). *Globalization: A Critical Introduction*. Palgrave Macmillan.

Scolari, C. A. (2012). 'Media ecology: Exploring the metaphor to expand the theory'. *Communication Theory*, 22(2), 204–225. DOI: 10.1111/j.1468-2885. 2012.01404.x

Seay, L. (2020). What's Wrong with Dodd-Frank 1502? Conflict Minerals, Civilian Livelihoods, and the Unintended Consequences of Western Advocacy. Center for Global Development Working Paper, (284).

Selwyn, N., Nemorin, S., Bulfin, S. and Johnson, N. F. (2018). *Everyday Schooling in the Digital Age*. Routledge.

Shannon, C. E. and Weaver, W. (1949/1963). *The Mathematical Theory of Communication*. University of Illinois Press.

Shehabi, A., Smith, S., Sartor, D., Brown, R., Herrlin, M., Koomey, J., Masanet, E., Horner, N., Azevedo, I. and Lintner, W. (2016). United States data center energy usage report. Lawrence Berkeley National Laboratory.

Sheoran, M. and Das Gupta, D. (2024). 'International best practices for e-waste take back and policy interventions for India'. *Facilities*, 42(3/4), 376–404.

Shor, P. W. (1994). 'Algorithms for quantum computation: Discrete logarithms and factoring'. *Proceedings 35th Annual Symposium on Foundations of Computer Science*, IEEE, 124–134.

Shor, P. W. (1995). Scheme for reducing decoherence in quantum computer memory. *Physical Review A*, 52(4), R2493.

Silver, D., Huang, A., Maddison, C. J., Guez, A., Sifre, L., Van Den Driessche, G., Schrittwieser, J., Antonoglou, I., Panneershelvam, V., Lanctot, M. and Dieleman, S. (2016). 'Mastering the game of Go with deep neural networks and tree search'. *Nature*, 529(7587), 484–489.

Silverstone, R. (1994). 'Future imperfect: Media, information and the millennium'. In N. Miller and R. Allen (eds.), *The Post-Broadcasting Age: New Technologies, New Communities, papers from the 25th and 26th University of Manchester Broadcasting Symposia* (pp. 2–16). University of Luten Press.

Silverstone, R. (2005) `Mediation and Communication'. In C. Calhoun, C. Rojek, and B. Turner (eds), *The International Handbook of Sociology* (pp. 188–207). Sage.

Sinanan, J. (2017). 'Conclusion: social media through ethnography'. In *Social Media in Trinidad: Values and Visibility* (pp. 199–208). UCL Press.

Singapore-ETH Centre. (n.d.). *About Singapore-ETH Centre*. Retrieved August 1, 2024, https://sg-eth.create.edu.sg/about-create/research-centres/sec/

Sloterdijk, P. (2011). *Spheres, Volume I: Bubbles Microspherology*. Semio-texte.

Sloterdijk, P. (2014). *Spheres, Volume II: Globes Macrospherology*. Semiotexte.

Sloterdijk, P. (2016). *Spheres, Volume III: Foams Plural Spherology*. Semiotexte.

Sobel, D. (1996). *Beyond Ecophobia: Reclaiming the Heart in Nature Education* (Vol. 1). Orion Society.

Solon, O. (2016, 11 November). 'Facebook's failure: did fake news and polarized politics get Trump elected?', *The Guardian*. www.theguardian.com/technology/2016/nov/10/facebook-fake-news-election-conspiracy-theories

Staal, M. (2014). 'Indigenous Australians predisposed to Facebook'. *Bandt*. Retrieved from www.bandt.com.au/indigenous-australians-predisposed-facebook/

Star, S. L. and Ruhleder, K. (1996). 'Steps toward an ecology of infrastructure: design and access for large information spaces'. *Information Systems Research*, 7(1), 111–134. https://doi.org/10.1287/isre.7.1.111

Starbird, K., Arif, A. and Wilson, T. (2019). 'Disinformation as collaborative work: surfacing the participatory nature of strategic information operations'. *Proceedings of the ACM on Human-Computer Interaction*, 3(CSCW), 1–26.

Starosielski, N. (2015). *The Undersea Network*. Duke University Press.

Steffen, W., Broadgate, W., Deutsch, L., Gaffney, O. and Ludwig, C. (2015). 'The trajectory of the Anthropocene: the great acceleration'. *The Anthropocene Review*, 2(1), 81–98.

Sterling, B. and Kadrey, R. (1995). 'The Dead Media Project: A modest proposal and a public appeal'. In *International Symposium on Electronic Arts*, Montréal, September. www.deadmedia.org/modest-proposal.html.

Sterne, J. (2003). *The Audible Past: Cultural Origins of Sound Reproduction*. Duke University Press.

Sterne, J. (2006). 'The death and life of digital audio'. *Interdisciplinary Science Reviews*, 31(4), 338–348.

Stoll, C. (1996). *Silicon Snake Oil: Second Thoughts on the Information Highway*. Anchor Books.

Striphas, T. (2015). Algorithmic culture. *European Journal of Cultural Studies*, 18(4–5), 395–412. https://doi.org/10.1177/1367549415577392

Strubell, E., Ganesh, A. and McCallum, A. (2019). 'Energy and policy considerations for deep learning in NLP'. *arXiv preprint arXiv*:1906.02243.

Taffel, S. (2013). 'Scalar entanglement in digital media ecologies'. *NECSUS. European Journal of Media Studies*, 2(1), 233–254.

Tan, C. T., Leong, T. W., Shen, S., Dubravs, C. and Si, C. (2015). 'Exploring gameplay experiences on the oculus rift'. In *Proceedings of the 2015 Annual Symposium on Computer-Human Interaction in Play*, 253–263. DOI: 10.1145/2793107.2793117

Tarasov, K. (2022, 23 March). 'ASML is the only company making the $200 million machines needed to print every advanced microchip. Here's an inside look', CNBC. www.cnbc.com/2022/03/23/inside-asml-the-company-advanced-chipmakers-use-for-euv-lithography.html

Taylor, H. (2017). *Is Birdsong Music? Outback Encounters with an Australian Songbird*. Indiana University Press.

Tegmark, M. (2017). *Life 3.0: Being Human in the Age of Artificial Intelligence*. Vintage.

Terare, M. and Rawsthorne, M. (2020). 'Country is yarning to me: worldview, health and well-being amongst Australian First Nations people'. *The British Journal of Social Work*, 50(3), 944–960.

Thacker, E. (2004). 'What is biomedia?'. *Configurations*, 11(1), 47–79.

Thimsen, A. F. (2022). 'What is performative activism?'. *Philosophy & Rhetoric*, 55(1), 83–89.

Thomas, A. and Paradise, Y. (2021, np). 'Included, but still marginalised: Indigenous voices still missing in media stories on Indigenous affairs'. In Misha Ketchell (ed.) *The Conversation*, Politics, July 1. https://theconversation.com/included-but-still-marginalised-indigenous-voices-still-missing-in-media-stories-on-indigenous-affairs-163426

Tsatsou, P. (2009, July) 'Reconceptualising 'Time' and 'Space' in the Era of Electronic Media and Communications', *PLATFORM: Journal of Media and Communication*, 1, 11–32. ISSN: 1836-5132 Online.

Tucker, J. A., Theocharis, Y., Roberts, M. and Barbera, P. (2017). 'From liberation to turmoil: social media and democracy'. *Journal of Democracy*, 28(4), 46–59.

Turkle, S. (2011). *Life on the Screen*. Simon and Schuster.

Turkle, S. (2017). *Alone Together: Why We Expect More from Technology and Less from Each Other*. Hachette.

Turner, N. (1998). *National Report on the Broadcasting for Remote Aboriginal Communities Scheme*. National Indigenous Media Association of Australia (NIMAA). https://satellitedreaming.com/assets/bracsrpt.pdf

Turner, V. W. (1992). *Blazing the Trail: Way Marks in the Exploration of Symbols* (E. Turner, ed.). University of Arizona Press.

United Nations (UN) News. (2024, March). Gaza war may fuel much wider Middle East crisis, warns UN rights chief, https://news.un.org/en/story/2024/03/1147197

United Nations Educational, Scientific and Cultural Organization (UNESCO). (2016). *A Teacher's Guide on the Prevention of Violent Extremism*. UNESCO.

United Nations Educational, Scientific and Cultural Organization (UNESCO). (2017). 'Digital skills for life and work'. *Broadband Commission for Sustainable Government*. UNESCO.

United Nations Educational, Scientific and Cultural Organization (UNESCO). (2023a). *Internet for Trust: Guidelines for the Governance of Digital Platforms*. UNESCO. www.unesco.org/en/internet-trust

United Nations Educational, Scientific and Cultural Organization (UNESCO). (2023b). *The Launch of a Thematic Study on Indigenous Peoples and the Medi*. UNESCO. Catalogue no., 0000386146. https://unesdoc.unesco.org/ark:/48223/pf0000386146

United Nations Office on Drugs and Crime (UNODC.) (2021a). Defining Terrorism. www.unodc.org/e4j/en/terrorism/module-4/key-issues/defining-terrorism.html United Nations Office on Drugs and Crime.

Van Dijck, J. (2007). *Mediated Memories in the Digital Age*. Stanford University Press.

van Mensvoort, K. (2012). 'Real nature is not green'. In *Next Nature: Nature Changes along with Us*, (pp 30–34). Actar.

van Mensvoort, K. (2020). *Next Nature: Why Technology Is Our Natural Future*. MIT Press.

van Mensvoort, K. and Grievink, H.-J. (eds.). (2011). *Next Nature: Nature Changes Along with Us*. Actar.

Vaswani, A., Shazeer, N., Parmar, N., Uszkoreit, J., Jones, L., Gomez, A. N. et al. (2017). 'Attention is all you need', 31st Conference on Neural Information Processing Systems (NIPS 2017), Long Beach, CA, USA.

Vidmar, N. and Rokeach, M. (1974). 'Archie Bunker's Bigotry: A Study in Selective Perception and Exposure', *Journal of Communication*, 24(1), 36–47. https://doi.org/10.1111/j.1460-2466.1974.tb00353.x

Vinge, V. (1993). *The Coming Technological Singularity: How to Survive in the Post-Human Era*. Conference paper. NASA. Lewis Research Center, Vision 21: Interdisciplinary Science and Engineering in the Era of Cyberspace.

Waisberg, E., Ong, J., Masalkhi, M., Zaman, N., Sarker, P., Lee, A. G. and Tavakkoli, A. (2024). 'The future of ophthalmology and vision science with the Apple Vision Pro'. *Eye*, 38(2), 242–243.

Widerschein, K., N. (2016). 'The Internet of Things: A look into the social implications of Google Glass'. *Inquiries*, 8(11), 1–2.

Weston, M. A. (1996). *Native Americans in the News: Images of Indians in the Twentieth Century Press.* Greenwood Press.

Weyler, J., Läbe, T., Magistri, F., Behley, J. and Stachniss, C. (2023). 'Towards domain generalization in crop and weed segmentation for precision farming robots'. *IEEE Robotics and Automation Letters*, 8(6), 3310–3317.

Whatmore, S. (2002). *Hybrid Geographies: Natures Cultures Spaces.* Sage.

Wigley, S. (2014). 'Did Stanley Kubrick invent the iPad?', British Film Institute <www.bfi.org.uk/features/did-stanley-kubrick-invent-ipad>

Williams, R. (1974). *Television: Technology and Cultural Form.* Schocken Books.

Willmot, E. (1984). *Out of the Silent Land.* Report of the Task Force on Aboriginal and Islander Broadcasting and Communications. Australia. Department of Aboriginal Affairs, Commonwealth of Australia. Australian Government Publishing Service.

Wilson, P. and Stewart, M. (2008). 'Introduction: indigeneity and indigenous media on the global stage'. In Pamela Wilson and Michelle Stewart (eds.) *Global Indigenous Media: Cultures, Poetics and Politics,* (pp 1–35). Duke University Press. DOI: 10.1215/9780822388692-001

Winner, L. (1980). 'Do artifacts have politics?', *Daedalus,* 109(1), 121–136.

Winston, B. (1990). 'How are media born and developed?'. In John Downing, Ali Mohammadi, Annabelle Sreberny-Mohammadi (eds.) *Questioning the Media: A Critical Introduction.* Sage, 54–74.

World Economic Forum (2022). How to build an economically viable, inclusive and safe metaverse. May. www.weforum.org/agenda/2022/05/how-to-build-an-economically-viable-inclusive-and-safe-metaverse/

Xia, K., Fan, H., Huang, J., Wang, H., Ren, J., Jian, Q. and Wei, D. (2021). 'An intelligent self-service vending system for smart retail'. *Sensors,* 21(10), 3560. https://doi.org/10.3390/s21103560

Yanes, J. (2019). 'Biohybrid robots, the next step in the robotic revolution', *Openmind*, www.bbvaopenmind.com/en/technology/robotics/biohybrid-robots-the-robotic-revolution/#:~:text=Shoji%20Takeuchi%20and%20his%20team%20create%20biohybrid%20robots,move%20the%20robots%2C%20replacing%20motors%2C%20gears%20and%20cables.

Yang, A., Xiao, B., Wang, B., Zhang, B., Bian, C., Yin, et al. (2023). 'Baichuan 2: Open large-scale language models'. arXiv preprint arXiv:2309.10305.

Yaqoob, I., Salah, K., Jayaraman, R. and Omar, M. (2023). 'Metaverse applications in smart cities: enabling technologies, opportunities, challenges, and future directions'. *Internet of Things*, 23,100884, October, 1–19.

You, H., Zhou, L., Xiao, B., Codella, N., Cheng, Y., Xu, R., Chang, S.-F. and Yuan, L. (2022). 'Learning Visual Representation from Modality-Shared Contrastive Language-Image Pre-training'. https://doi.org/10.48550/ARXIV.2207.12661

Yu, Z. (2021). 'A meta-analysis of the effect of virtual reality technology use in education'. *Interactive Learning Environments*, 31(8), 4956–4976, DOI:10.1080/10494820.2021.1989466

Yunkaporta, T. (2019). *Sand Talk: How Indigenous Thinking Can Save the World.* Text Publishing Company.

Zhang, B. H., Lemoine, B. and Mitchell, M. (2018). 'Mitigating Unwanted Biases with Adversarial Learning', https://doi.org/10.48550/arXiv.1801.07593

Zhang, Z., Fort, J.M. and Giménez Mateu, L. (2023, Oct 11). 'Facial expression recognition in virtual reality environments: challenges and opportunities'. *Frontiers in*

Psychology, 14, 1280136. DOI: 10.3389/fpsyg.2023.1280136. PMID: 37885738; PMCID: PMC10598841.

Zielinski, S. (2006). *Deep Time of the Media: Toward an Archaeology of Hearing and Seeing by Technical Means* [originally published as Archäologie der Medien: Zur Tiefenzeit des technischen Hörens und Sehens, 2002 (G. Custance Trans)]. MIT Press.

Zielinski, S. and Wagnermaier, S. M. (2005). 'Depth of subject and diversity of method. An introduction to variantology'. In Siegfried Zielinski and Silvia M. Wagnermaier (eds.) *Variantolgy 1. On Deep Time Relations of Arts, Sciences and Technologies*, (pp. 7–12). Verlag der Buchhandlung.

INDEX

Note: Page locators in **bold** and *italics* represents tables and figures, respectively.

3D-printed skeletons 80
23andMe (genetic testing kit) 63
360-degree immersive videos, in
   education 143–4; case study of
   teaching threshold concepts in
   146–51; digital realm 151–2;
   effectiveness of 146

Aboriginal and Torres Strait Islander
   people 154, 159
Aboriginal cultural knowledge 155
Aboriginal Dreamtime stories 159
accessibility bias, in LLMs 128
active listening, protocols of 167
adaptive learning xxviii
age bias, in LLMs 129–31
album artworks 27
Alexa (digital agent) xxvii, 49, 90
AlexNet 82–3, 92; development and
   success of 83; success in the ILSVRC
   83
algorithm-driven engagement 175
Alibaba xii, 52
'All in the Family' (television show) 157
alt-right movement 116
Amazon: Alexa (digital agent) xxvii, 49,
   90; Mechanical Turk platform 82
Amsterdam Institute for Advanced
   Metropolitan Solutions (AMS
   Institute) 185

Anglo-Western discourse, narratives of
   163
animism, concept of 155
Anthropocene 13
anthropocentrism xxv
Apple 138; design ethos 181; Lisa 23–4;
   Vision Pro 35, 63, 138, 181
Application Programming Interfaces
   (APIs) xxix, 107, 108, 133; filter
   bubbles and echo chambers 112–15
artificial agents, beneficence of 188
Artificial General Intelligence (AGI) xi,
   65, 81
Artificial Intelligence (AI) x, xv, 50,
   89, 138, 186; advanced AI systems
   92; alignment and the problem of
   control 71–3; Azimov's principles 72;
   'bad actor' scenario 72; development
   of sustainability standards for 71;
   developments in 70, 78; efficiency
   in producing content 95; enactment
   of legislations specific to 67; EU
   regulatory framework on 67; evolution
   of 187; general 65, 81; generative
   65, 110, 120; governance of 70;
   impact assessment 71; impacts on
   human labour, education, and natural
   environment 95; integration into
   personal relationships 70; learning in
   school 120; Meta's LLaMA (Large

Index

Language Model Meta AI) 90; Open AI's ChatGPT service 68; regulating of 67–71; risk classifications 68; robot soldiers 72; scrutiny on privacy 68; significance of 68; use in augmentation of human intelligence 70
Artificial Life Rights 70–1
Asimov's Three Laws of Robotics 72
ASML (Dutch company) 91–2
Attenborough, David 16
audio recordings, authenticity of 109–10
audio-visual content, distribution of xxxi
Augmented Reality (AR) xxi, 11, 43, 77; application in teaching complex scientific principles 143; benefits of 144; and imaginary media 34; mediating between the inside and the outside 137–9; Rokid Max (AR Glasses) 138
Augmented Virtuality (AV) 139
augmenting education, in immersive spheres 143–5
Australian First Nations Dual Languages 164
Australian Indigenous Voice referendum (2023) 165
Australian Northern Territory Mojo project 168
'autonomy' of emotional responses 6
Azimov's principles 72

Baichuan Intelligence 91
Bangtan Boys (BTS) 11
Batch and Loop media technology 25–6
Bell, Alexander Graham 22
Benjamin, Walter xxv, 21
Bidirectional Encoder Representations from Transformers (BERT) 90, 122
big data x, 11, 96, 101; see also small data
'big' media organisations 172
bio-artists 77
biodiversity loss 11, 15–16
biodiversity monitoring 9
bio-engineering 8
biohybrid robots, development of 80
biological evolution 4
biology and technology, convergence of 62–5
biomedia xxvii, 47, 65, 68, 76; with agency 73–6; concept of 62–3, 84, 183; convergence of the biological and technological in 80; emergence of 78; emergent realities of 73–82; fusion with machine vision 82–5; interpretations of 64; ramifications of 183; redefinition of 'self', life, and consciousness 78–82
biometric identification systems 62
bio-profiles 99, 126
biotechnologies 53–4, 63, 67
bio-village 54
blockchain technology 50, 52, 138, 183; environmental impact of 46; influence on media transactions xx; rise of 45
Blogger 45
Bluesky 24, 44, 98
Braidotti, Rosi 67, 70, 113
brain–computer interface (BCI) 35, 43
BrainGate 48
'brain-scale' AI models xiii
British Broadcasting Corporation (BBC) 54
British colonisation 154
broadcast infrastructures, digitalisation of 180
Broadcasting for Remote Aboriginal Communities Scheme (BRACS) 158
Bubeck, Sébastien 81
Bush, Vannevar 33
ByteDance 52

carbon emissions 16–17, 52
Catts, Oron 77
Cave Automatic Virtual Environment (CAVE) 144–5
Central Processing Unit (CPU) 83
Centre for Urban Science and Progress (CUSP) 185
chatbots, AI-driven 70
ChatGPT 68, 99
ChatGPT-4 89, 92–3, 99
cheating 120
Christian conservatism 116
circuit bending, act of 36, 38
Cleverman (2016/2017) 159–60
cloud-based services 17
cloud computing 14, 91, 179
cognitive capitalism x
cognitive-enhancing technologies 66
cognitive learning 144
collaborative governance, formation of 131
Collisions (Virtual Reality film) xxx, 165–6
communal bonds, strengthening of 174

Index **213**

communication: bidirectional 21;
  channels of 21; enhanced media and
  107–8; real-time 23; from telegraph
  to tweets 21–4; through electricity,
  telephony, and media archaeology
  21–4; two-step flow of 74
communication channels 21, 110
community engagement 24, 109, 119,
  169–70
companion species, notion of 8
computer-generated technologies 77
computer/human interfaces xii
computer vision xi, 82–4
Contrastive Language-Image Pretraining
  (CLIP) 93
convolutional neural networks (CNNs)
  82, 84
corporate cyber security 49
Covid-19 pandemic xi, 47
critical thinking xxix, 53–4, 104, 119,
  121, 170
cross-disciplinary scholarship 185
cryptocurrencies 45
cultural activism 157
cultural and technological developments
  181
Cultural Centrism 124
cultural knowledge 155, 163, 175–6
cultural preservation 154, 156–7, 161–3,
  167, 171, 173, 177
cultural sovereignty 156, 162, 167
culture of narcissism 98
cyber-abuse 175
cyber-attacks 45
cyberculture xxvii, 62
cyber espionage 97
cybersecurity 53, 104, 143, 179
cyborgs 3–15, 47, 62, 65; metaphors of
  182

Dalaithngu, David Gulpilil Ridjimiraril
  164
DALL·E 89, 92, 93
DALL·E 2 (deep learning model) xiv
Dark Side of the Moon, The (1973) 27
data analytics 11, 95, 109–10, 117, 119,
  179
data centres 16–17, 79, 91, 100, 182
data cultures, materialising of x–xv
data-driven intelligence 149
datafication, digitalisation to 146
data labelling 82
data lakes, phenomena of 3

data privacy and safety 143, 151
data provenance and protections 185–6
data security xxi, 21, 104, 152, 181
data sovereignty 185
data storage, environmental impact of 79
data tracking 98
'dead' media 30–1
deep ecology, tenets of 9, 176
'deepfake' videos 35
deep learning xiii, 82, 91, 122;
  algorithms 92; power of 83
deep time, concept of 20
deliberative democracy 113
democratic societies 118; enrichment of
  171
'depth' in media theory, concept of 15
Derrida, Jacques 96
Descola, Philippe 7
Deutsch, David 55
developing skills and educating citizens,
  policies and initiatives for 140–3
dialogic evolution 47
digital age 8, 24, 148
digital analytics 50, 62
digital archiving, socio-technical
  dynamics of 29–30
digital augmentations 78
digital auto-ethnography 171
digital citizenship 113–14, 120, 132,
  188
digital communications xv, 91;
  communication channels xxviii;
  technologies 47
digital competencies xxviii
digital connection, study of x–xv
digital content 97, 108–9, 120, 139,
  xxix
digital culture xxvi, xxix, xxxi, 19, 62,
  102, 172–5, 180
digital divide 66, 106, 142, 166
Digital Echo Chambers and
  Radicalisation Pathways 110
digital ecology 136
digital economy 50, 52, 169
digital footprint 103, 106, 108, 177
digital identity verification 45
digital information xxi, 34, 77, 95, 102,
  117, 120, 185
digital innovation xxx–xxxi, 146, 176,
  184
digital intelligences 65–7, 72, 101, 180
digital intelligent interface agents, rise of
  101–5

214 Index

digitalisation, processes of 107
digital ledger 45
digital ledger technology 45
digital literacies xxix, 114, 119, 184;
application of LLMs in enhancing
131; framework for 120–1; pedagogies
of 180; strategic deployment of LLMs
in 134
digital literacy xxviii, xxix, 100, 114,
119–20, 122, 131, 134, 180, 184;
disparities in 151
digital media xvii; Indigenous use
of 161; as a platform for defining
indigeneity 162–75
digital media platforms, proliferation of
48
Digital Memory and the Archive (2013)
29
digital memory, dynamics of 30
digital minimalism 17
digital nature photography and
videography 8
digital personhood 71
digital repository 172
digital self 183
digital self-determination xxx
digital technologies 6, 12, 64, 76;
environmental footprint of 182
digital textbooks 3
digital transformation x
Domain Name System (DNS) 168

eavesdropping 57
echo chambers: filter bubbles and
112–15; implications of 112
ecological harmony and balance,
philosophy of 149
ecologically balanced society xxv
ecological metaphor 136
ecosophy, concept of xxiv, 9–11, 149
e-governance 11
Eilish, Billie 28
e-learning 3
electric communication technologies
21–4
electronic-mail-managing agent 101
embedded media, ramifications of 180
emerging media, topology of 135–7
emotional synchrony 54
energy-harvesting technologies 179
energy management 52
enhanced media: bad actors and online
harms 108–12; and communications
107–8; uses of 108

environmental crisis 11, 15, 17, 186
environmental degradation 12, 16–17,
79, 104
environmental ecology xxv, 10, 12, 16
environmental stewardship xxx–xxxi, 8,
149, 155
Ernabella Video and Television 158
Ernst, Wolfgang 29
e-Sports 45
European Commission 67, 140, 141
European Data Protection Board
(EDPB) 68
'ever-new' media 53, 62
e-waste 149; generation 10, 16;
proliferation 12
extended reality (XR) xxix–xxx, 77, 139
eXtreme Language understanding
NETwork (XLNet) 122
extreme ultraviolet (EUV) lithography
machines 92

Facebook 5, 96, 98, 107–8; Meta
118, 138; news feed algorithm 117;
rebranding of 138
facial tracking 63
fake news 66, 96, 110
Fear of Missing Out (FOMO) 66, 104
Fei-Fei Li 82, 92
Felbon, Christina 82
filter bubbles: and echo chambers
112–15; formation of 108–9
Final Fantasy VII (video game) 37
First Nations 170; Aboriginal and
Torres Strait Islander peoples 154;
in Australia 154; communities 154;
cultural identity 157; globalised media
environments 161; Indigenous media
for 154; perspectives and realities 164;
storytelling 159; voice and agency of
166
Floyd, Pink 27
forgery, AI-based 110
Foucault, Michel 20
freedom of expression, right to 114
'frictionless' interactions 138, 179
Fuller, Matthew xxiii, 13–14, 29

gating network xiii
gender bias, in LLMs 125–6
gender-specific pronouns 125
gene editing 70
generative AI (GenAI) model xiv
Generative Artificial Intelligence
(GenAI) 65, 110, 120

Generative Pre-trained Transformer (GPT) 90, 93, 122
Genetically Modified Organisms (GMOs) 49, 63, 80
genetic engineering 44, 49, 63
genetic modification 8, 49
geographic information systems (GIS) 12, 16
geo-location data 96
geo-satellites 58
geospatial technologies 16
Gibson, William 34
Ginsburg, Faye 157
global economy 79
global geopolitics 115
global interconnectivity 22, 162
globalised capitalism, age of 70
global media ecosystem 169
global positioning system (GPS) 42
global South 142
global village 54
Goddard, Michael 28
Google: Bard 89, 101; DeepMind AlphaGo 76; Google Glass 34
GPT-4o 82, 93
Graphical User Interface (GUI) 24
Graphics Processing Units (GPUs) xv, 83
Great Acceleration 59–60
'green' innovation 17
Groys, Boris 26
Guattari, Félix xxx; concept of 'ecosophy' 9–11
Gutenberg, Johannes 94
Gutenberg Press, The 53, 94

Habermas, Jürgen 54, 113
Hall, Stuart xvi
handheld devices, proliferation of 178
Haraway, Donna 6; notion of companion species 8
Hassan, Steven 113
hegemonic cultural codes 163
hierarchical knowledge systems 167
high-speed transfer of data 179
Hinton, Geoffrey 82, 92
human–animal relationships 8
human cognition 35, 43, 76–7, 137
human communication 22
human–computer interactions (HCI) xxi, 43, 47
human dignity 64–5
human intelligence 70, 103, 105
human–machine interface 7
human–technology interface 1, 183

hybrid geographies, concept of 7
hybridisation, concept of 47
hyper-personalised media confluence 107, 161; countering the myth of efficiency 103–5; digital spectre of self 95–101; rise of digital intelligent interface agents 101–3

Ideonella sakaiensis 63
ImageNet Large Scale Visual Recognition Challenge (ILSVRC) 82–3, 92–3
image recognition 82, 92, 183
imaginary media 19, 32–6, 182; archaeology of 32; and augmented reality 34; in Australia 158; bridging with zombie media 36–9; development of 158; Kluitenberg's exploration of 33
Immersive Tech Africa's XR Innovation Summit (2023) 142
immersive technologies, evolution of 43
iNaturalist 9
Independent Broadcasting Authority (IBA) 54
Indigenous Australian communities 172
Indigenous cosmologies 160
indigenous digital sovereignty 172–5
Indigenous ecologies 176
Indigenous epistemologies 167, 171–2
Indigenous knowledge xxx, 42, 156, 165–6, 170, 175–6, 184
Indigenous media 162–6, 171; across networked infrastructures 157–9; bridging oral traditions and user-generated digital content 166–72; concept of 162; 'cultural activism' aspect of 157; evolution of 171; representations of Indigenous cultures 167; on television 159–62; transformative power of xxx
Indigenous people, transformative capacity of 163
IndigiTUBE 172
industrial age 46
information consumption and decentralised interaction, new era of 89–90
information dissemination 14
information sharing 4, 24, 119
information technologies xvi, 41, 43, 107
informed decision-making 50, 94
infosphere 135–7, 153, 186, 188

216 Index

insect media 6, 18, 182
Instagram 8, 66, 98, 107, 170
intellectual property rights 143
Intelligent Traffic Systems 11
intensive culture, concept of 35
interactive digital media xviii, xxix
interactive public displays (digital
  signage) 179
intercultural contact 114
internet 66; browsing 42; high-speed
  47, 126; proliferation of xvii, 23;
  Quantum Internet 57
Internet of Things (IoT) 50, 58, 91,
  138, 179; proliferation of 101;
  relation with quantum computing 59
interpersonal communication xix, 23, 70
Inuit cultures 157
iron age 46
isolated entities within media systems,
  notion of xix

Japanese language models, development
  of 91

Kadrey, Richard 26
Kaitiakitanga, Māori concept of 155
kinetic energy 179
Kittler, Friedrich xxvii, 5, 28
Kluitenberg, Eric 38–40
knowledge acquisition 152, 168
knowledge production 67
knowledge transmission, Western
  conceptions of 167
K-pop, proliferation of 10
Krizhevsky, Alex 82, 92

lab-grown organs 80
Large Language Models (LLMs)
  89–91; ability to process and generate
  language in a human- like manner
  123; accessibility bias in 128; age bias
  in 129–31; BERT 122; capabilities
  for countering extremism online **130**;
  and civic engagement 131–3; for
  countering online extremism 121–3;
  cultural, social, and racial bias 123–4;
  de-biasing of 121–3; development
  of 92; gender bias in 125–6; gender-
  specific pronouns 125–6; language
  and regional bias 124–5; LLM-based
  Co-pilot tools 89, 101; OpenAI's GPT
  122; political and ideological bias in
  127–8; potential for misuse of 133;

RoBERTa 122; socio-economic bias in
  126–7; use in digital literacy initiatives
  134; XLNet 122
Large Learning Models (LLMs) xi
Latin *anima* 155
Lazarsfeld, Paul F. 74
leach mining 12
The Legend of Zelda: Link's Awakening
  (video game) 37
LGBTQI communities 113; rights of
  127
liberal democracies 113, 116
life cycle, of media 31
life-like behaviour in machines,
  emergence of 65–73
linear evolution, myth of 20
LinkedIn 108
Little Yellow Book (Nickelodeon) 35
lived experiences xi, xxviii, 9, 43, 96,
  158, 166
Livingstone, Sonia 76
loop media 25, 29–30, 41
Lovelock's Gaia hypothesis 156

machine intelligence xi
machine learning xi, xvi, 50, 90, 121,
  122, 138, 180; developments in 70
machine vision: fusion of biomedia and
  neural nets to 82–5; life-like behaviour
  of 84; in the post-digital age 83; role
  in precision farming 84
'macrospheres' of Globes 135
mainstream media (MSM) 169
Main, Thomas 116
manufacturing intelligence 90–5
map deforestation 9
marginalised communities xix, 124, 158,
  168–9
mass media, rise of 22
Mastodon 98
McLuhan, Marshall 3, 5, 53–4
media archaeology 5, 19–20, 26, 36,
  182; communication through 21–4;
  Huhtamo and Parikka's work on 21;
  and socio-technical dynamics of digital
  archiving 29–30
media–audiences–society relationship,
  theories of 74
media consumption practices xxv
media consumption, social nature of
  74
media cultural discourses xxvi, 19
media decline, discourses on 30

media ecologies: association with anthropogenic events 12, 15–18; concept of xviii, xxiv, 3–4, 18, 29; connection with Wolfgang Ernst's ideas found in *Digital Memory and the Archive* (2013) 29; formation of 3–15; non-linearity and dynamism of 18; rhizomatic 14; understanding of 9, 15
media, emergent realities of 73–82; with agency 73–6; 'hypodermic needle' model of 73; 'magic bullet' model of 73; myth of the mediated centre 75; 'self', life, and consciousness 78–82; socio-cultural impact of 73; 'vibrant' media 76–8
media innovations, cyclical nature of 21
media literacy, notions of 106
medialogy xv–xxi, xxx, 13; in the age of digital interconnectedness 44–9; concept of 166, 182; in global context 186–8
mediamorphosis 41
media systems, material properties of: archival and archaeological perspectives 31–2; 'dead' media 30; exploration of obsolescent systems 30–6; imaginary media and speculative realms 32–6; life cycle of 31
media technologies 19; ecosystem of 4; evolution of 180; interconnectedness of 29; nonlinear and cyclical evolution of 33
mediatisation, global process of 161
Memex 33
mental ecology xxv, 10, 12
Meta (Facebook) 138; LLaMA (Large Language Model Meta AI) 90; 'Meta (Facebook) Boost' initiative 141; Ray-Ban Meta smart glasses 138
metaverse 138; global trajectory towards 52; socio-technological concept map of *51*
Metaverse Academy 141
Micheals, Eric 158
microcontrollers 179
microprocessors 91, 179
Microsoft 138; Copilot 89; TEAMS xi
Midjourney (deep learning model) xiv, 89, 92–3
mind–body connection 43
Mixed Reality (MR) xxix, 77, 139, 149
Mixture-of-Experts (MoE) architecture xii

mobile technologies 170; in African countries 98
modding, act of 38
Mohawk community of Kahnawake, Quebec 160
Mohawk Girls (2010–2017) 160
Moore, Gordon 91
Moore's Law 91, 94
Morgan, Nyarri Nyarri 166
Mowarin, Tyson 170
music/video streaming 42

Naess, Arne xxiv, 9
nanotechnologies 80
National Indigenous Television (NITV) 159
National Telecommunications and Information Administration (USA) 68
natural language processing (NLP) xi, 90, 130
natural user interfaces 180
nature, concept of 166
nature–culture divide 7–8
naturecultures, concept of 7
NAVER Corporation (South Korea) 91
Negroponte, Nicholas 101
networked digital technologies, rise of 12
networked entanglement 57–9
networked nature, creation of 8, 9
Neuralink 35
neural interfaces 35
neural networks xi, 68, 81, 82–5
Neuromancer (1984) 34
neuroprosthetics 63
neurotechnology 63
'new media' technologies 41
newspapers, proliferation of 22
news services, telegraph-based 22
new technologies, adoption of 65
next nature 60, 182; concept of 49; exploration of 49–55; interplay between humanity, technology, and the environment 53; navigating 44–9; and techno-media ecologies 41–4
Nintendo Entertainment System (NES) 37
non-fungible tokens (NFTs) 45
Non-Human Others 186
non-Indigenous media 161–2
Noyce, Robert 91
Nvidia 138
Nyaal (purpose-built theatre for teaching and learning) 145–6, 150

218 Index

Oculus Rift 35
OhmyNews xvii
online communication 120
online content: production of 94–5;
  proliferation of xxviii
online extremism 115–19, 122;
  approach to address 119–20; challenge
  of countering 119; 'de-biasing'
  large language models (LLMs) for
  countering 121–3
Online News Outlets 45
OpenAI 99; ChatGPT 68, 99, 122;
  ChatGPT-4o x, 92, 101; ChatGPT
  Plus 99
opinion leaders 74; recognition of 75
organ-on-a-chip (OoC) technology 80
'original' digital works 46
originality, concept of 46
Out of the Silent Land report
  (Willmot, 1984) 158

Pálsson, Gísli 7
Pariser, Eli 112
PAW Media and Communications *see*
  Warlpiri Media Association
'Pepe the Frog' 119
performative activism, concept of 10
personal computers, proliferation of 24
personalised content delivery 112
pervasive computing *see* ubiquitous
  computing
Peters, John Durham 14
Phelan, Andrew 97
photography, black-and-white 165
photolithography 92
physical–digital interface 7
physiological synchrony 54
Pitjantjatjara Yankunytjatjara Media
  ('PY' Media) *see* Ernabella Video and
  Television
plagiarism 46, 120
plastic pollution 15
PlayStation video games 37
political activism xxx, 133, 177
political and cultural conservatism 116
political discourse, societal perception
  of 4
polyethylene terephthalate (PET) plastics
  63
popular culture, globalisation of 10
post-digital age 178; characteristic of 78;
  machine vision in 83; notion of 64
Posthuman Knowledge (2019) 67

postindustrial society 46
Postman, Neil 4, 44, 53
Preferred Networks 91
print media 171
Problem-Based Learning (PBL) xviii
'proof of stake' mechanism 45
'proof of work' mechanism 45
prosthetics, AI-integrated 65
Public Service Broadcasting 54
public sphere, theory of 54
Pūoro, Taonga 156

QSers 98
quality of life 11, 50, 52; role of smart
  cities in improving 52
Quantified Self 'movement' 98
quantum algorithms 55–6
quantum bits (qubits), properties of 56
Quantum Circuits 55
quantum communications 56–7
quantum computing xxi, 55–8, 60,
  183; dichotomy of 59; relation with
  Internet of Things (IoT) 59
quantum cryptography 56
Quantum entanglement 55, 57
Quantum error-correction codes 57
Quantum Internet 57
Quantum Key Distribution (QKD) 56–7
quantum mechanics, principles of 55
Quantum Teleportation 57
Quantum Turing Machines 55

radical pessimism 53
Rare Earth Elements 12
reality–virtuality continuum xxix, 139
real-time analytics 25, 60
real-time data analysis 50
record players 26–9
rectified linear units (ReLUs) 83
Reddit 107
Redfern Now (2012–2013) 160
remediation, theory of 36
Remote Indigenous Media Sector
  (RIBS) 158
remote sensing 9, 16
representation, politics of 175
Reservation Dogs (2021–2023) 160
resource optimisation 50
resources management 149
response to stimuli 80
retro-cultures 20
'right to repair' campaigns 17
risk mitigation 50

robotics xi; Asimov's Three Laws of Robotics 72
robots: biohybrid robots 80; muscle-actuated 80; robot soldiers 72
Robustly Optimized BERT pretraining approach (RoBERTa) 122
Rokid Max (AR Glasses) 138

satellite imaging technology 12
Saudi's *Vision 2030* 142
Schmidt, Eric xii
self-determination, right to 164
self, presentation of 96
self-repair 80
semiconductors 91
sender–receiver dynamics 25
Sgt. Pepper's Lonely Hearts Club Band (1967) 27
Shortland Street (from 1992) 160
Signal 98
simulacra and simulation, exploration of 34
single-lens reflex (SLR) cameras 30
Siri (digital agent) 90
skeuomorph, phenomenon of 30
Sloterdijk, Peter 135–7
small data 96, 101
small to medium-sized enterprises (SMEs) 142
smart cities 60, 179; evolution of 52; idea of 11; for improving the quality of life 52
smart clothing 62, 98
smart contracts 45
smart friends 178
'smart' homes 179
smartphone technologies 66
smart transportation system, rise of 11
'smart' vehicles 179
social ecology xxv, 10, 12
social inequality 17, 182, 188
social interactions x, xvii, xxi, xxxii, 15, 23–4, 43, 54, 109, 163, 180–1, 183
social media: data mining 16; dynamic utilisation for intergenerational connectivity 173; Indigenous use of 177; navigating cultural preservation and identity on 172–5; rise of 24
social metaverse 13
social networking platforms 138
social networks xix, xxviii, xxxi, 17, 24, 107–8, 117, 136, 138

social platform algorithms 107
social screen technologies xxix
social stigma 110, 117
societal polarisation xxi
societal transformation 182
socio-economic bias, in LLMs 126–7
socio-technological concept map of the metaverse *51*
Sony Walkman xxv
sound bites, phenomena of 3
sound technologies, exploration of 21
spatial computing xx–xxi, 11
spectre of self 95–101
sphere, concept of 135–7
Spinoza, Baruch xix
Stable Diffusion 93
Star Trek (American television series, 1966–1969) 33
Sterling, Bruce 26
storytelling 166, 170, 172
Strategic Digital Information Operations (SDIO) 117
Super NES (SNES) 37
superposition, principle of 56
supply chain management 45
sustainable development 149
sustainable economies xxii
Sutskever, Ilya 82, 92
synthetic biology 63, 186
synthetic media, prevalence of 35

technological determinism, theory of 33
technological development xxxii, 20
technological imaginaries 32
technological innovations 13, 23, 28, 34, 53, 56, 58–9, 181
technological self-determination 158
techno-media ecologies 44, 183; next nature and 41–4
technophilia 47
technophobia 47
telegraph networks, development of 22
telephone, invention of 22
Teleportation of Information *see* Quantum Teleportation
Ten Canoes (Australian film, 2006) 164–5, 167
textbook-based education 144
Thacker, Eugene 62, 183
Thorntonm, Warwick 165
Thunberg, Greta: speeches on climate change 13

TikTok x, xxx, 35, 74, 98, 107, 170; dynamism of 175; Indigenous use of 173, 176
time and space, concept of 22
traditional extremism 115–19
traditional flat (2D) video 139
transatlantic cable 22
transformative learning 184
transformer architectures 93
transhumanism, concept of 64–5
transnational terrorism 115
Twitter (now X) 5, 107

ubiquitous computing 179
undersea telecommunications cables 179–80
United Nations Declaration on the Rights of Indigenous Peoples (UNDRIP) 171
United Nations Educational, Scientific and Cultural Organization (UNESCO) 171; 'Internet for Trust' report (2023) 114
United Nations Office on Drugs and Crime (UNODC) 115
United Nations Permanent Forum on Indigenous Issues (UNPFII) 171
United Nations Special Tribunal for Lebanon (STL) 115
universal societal norms 116
'us *versus* them' narratives, creation of 112
Utu (dir. Murphy, 1983) 171

van Mensvoort, Koert 44, 53
'vibrant' media 76–8
Victimless Leather 77
video production 151, 157, 170
Video Streaming Services 45
viral texts, phenomena of 3
virtual classrooms 3, 146
virtual ecotourism 48
virtual realities (VR) xxii, xxix, 11, 21, 35, 43, 48, 138–9; application in teaching complex scientific principles 143; benefits of 144; emotion recognition 63; facial tracking

capabilities 63; head-mounted displays in education and training 144
visual art and music 27
visual media 158
Visual Networking xvii
voices, AI-generated 110

Wageningen University and Research (WUR) 185
Warlpiri Media Association 158
WeChat 5
'Welcome to Country' app 170
Western abstraction 155
Western societies, capitalist structures of 75
wet media, concept of 14
Whakaata Māori (Māori Television) 171
Whatmore, Sarah 7
When Inclusion Means Exclusion: Social Commentary and Indigenous Agency (2021) 161
When We All Fall Asleep, Where Do We Go? (2019) 28
white racialism, notion of 116
Wikipedia 12
wildlife photography 8
Williams, Raymond 38
wireless communications 179
WordNet 82
WordPress 45
World Wide Web 6, 33

XR education, democratisation of 142
XR technologies 142
XR Women in Africa 142

YouTube xxx, 98
Yuendumu community 158
Yunkaporta, Tyson 167

Zielinski, Siegfried 5, 20–1
zombie media 19, 182; bridging with imaginary media 36–9; concept of 36; nature of 40
Zoom xi
Zuckerberg, Mark 96
Zurr, Ionat 77